FROM ENLIGHTENMENT TO RECEPTIVITY

FROM ENLIGHTENMENT
TO RECEPTIVITY

Rethinking Our Values

Michael Slote

OXFORD
UNIVERSITY PRESS

50.00

OXFORD
UNIVERSITY PRESS

Oxford University Press is a department of the University of Oxford.
It furthers the University's objective of excellence in research, scholarship,
and education by publishing worldwide.

Oxford   New York
Auckland   Cape Town   Dar es Salaam   Hong Kong   Karachi
Kuala Lumpur   Madrid   Melbourne   Mexico City   Nairobi
New Delhi   Shanghai   Taipei   Toronto

With offices in
Argentina   Austria   Brazil   Chile   Czech Republic   France   Greece
Guatemala   Hungary   Italy   Japan   Poland   Portugal   Singapore
South Korea   Switzerland   Thailand   Turkey   Ukraine   Vietnam

Oxford is a registered trademark of Oxford University Press
in the UK and certain other countries.

Published in the United States of America by
Oxford University Press
198 Madison Avenue, New York, NY 10016

Library of Congress Cataloging-in-Publication Data
Slote, Michael A. From enlightenment to receptivity:
rethinking our values / Michael Slote.
p. cm.
ISBN 978-0-19-997070-4 (alk. paper)   1. Caring.   2. Empathy.
3. Ethics.   I. Title.
BJ1475.S595   2013
170—dc23   2012029228

ISBN 978-0-19-997070-4

3 5 7 9 8 6 4 2
Printed in the United States of America
on acid-free paper

In memory of my mother and father
Tisha Kunst Slote
and
Edwin Michael Slote

This sharp distinction of virtue and morality as co-ordinate and independent forms of goodness will explain a fact which otherwise it is difficult to account for. If we turn from books on Moral Philosophy to any vivid account of human life and action such as we find in Shakespeare, nothing strikes us more than the comparative remoteness of the discussions of Moral Philosophy from the facts of actual life.

H. A. Prichard in "Does Moral Philosophy Rest on a Mistake?"

CONTENTS

CONTENTS

PREFACE

I think this book began when the Japanese philosopher Seisuke Hayakawa came to visit me, some years back, in Miami. He said he wanted to have talks with me because I had stressed the receptivity of empathy in my book *The Ethics of Care and Empathy* and because he himself thought receptivity was a more important ingredient in human action than anyone had suspected. In a way, this already meant that receptivity was or might be more important than I myself had realized at the time I wrote the just-mentioned book, but that thought lay dormant or merely potential within me for a number of years—until I started seeing new and interesting examples of the importance of receptivity. By that time, I was engaged in criticizing Enlightenment rationalism from a care-ethical standpoint, but I then started to see ways in which Enlightenment thought—both in its ethical and in its epistemological aspects—showed a deficient respect for what I was now starting to consider to be the virtue of receptivity. And I then also saw that receptivity has been underappreciated in other ways that don't necessarily intersect with Enlightenment thinking. This book was off and running.

I am offering a picture of human values, of our values, that gives receptivity a central place, and I believe previous Western philosophy has largely ignored the significance of this concept. Activity, rationality, autonomy, control have dominated our conceptions of values. But a new emphasis on receptivity and on the related notions of caring and empathy that depend on it doesn't by any means push these traditionally favored ideals off the stage. Far from it. As I see it, receptivity, rather, is a *touchstone* for other values. Yes, let us have activity, autonomy, rationality, and control, but let's not let them get out of hand in our thinking. And that is what this book argues happens when these things push *receptivity* off the stage—which is what they surely have done throughout the course of Western intellectual/cultural history. According to the present book, therefore, we need to understand the importance of being receptive to the needs and aspirations of others, to what we can learn from those we disagree with, to the natural world around us, and to what our own lives have brought us or may bring us in the future; but we also need to fully appreciate the value of receptivity in order to understand where and how certain *other* very real values—the values of activity, rationality, and autonomy—are important. And the focus on receptivity also and more particularly enables us to see what is wrong with an overemphasis on rationality *in both ethics and epistemology.* On the account to be offered here, rationality and reason turn out not to be *all-important* in the way most previous Western philosophical thought has believed.

The present book owes a great debt to care ethics and to the work that psychologists have done in recent decades on the concept of empathy—also to David Hume, whose thought brilliantly anticipates both these more recent trends. The recent discussions of caring and empathy have moved us to some extent away from Western rationalism—or at least brought the rationalism into question. But I believe we also need to understand and use the new (to

philosophical/ethical discussion) notion of receptivity to understand
the full measure of what is wrong with Enlightenment rationalism
in its historical and contemporary versions. And I also believe and
have argued that without that notion we cannot begin to understand
what is wrong with the more general Faustian emphasis on activity,
domination, and control that has been so central in and influential
on Western thought and culture as a whole.[1] (The term *Faustian* is
often used to mean the sacrificing of higher values to power, curios-
ity, and material gain in the manner that is thought to be illustrated
in Goethe's *Faust*.) It seems to me that this further step is necessary
if we are to come up with a picture of our values that fairly, deeply,
and with adequate complexity represents what is most important in
or to our lives. But we are also helped here by new understandings of
and perspectives on human life and thought that have developed or
emerged in recent times (I say more about this in the introduction).
And it is no wonder that the map of values needs to be redrawn if the
values, the things we think of as important, have themselves tectoni-
cally shifted over the centuries and even very recently.

NOTES

1. In *Caring: A Feminine Approach to Ethics and Moral Education* (Berkeley:
   University of California Press, 1984), Nel Noddings stresses receptivity
   as an element in caring, in creativity, and in aesthetic appreciation; but the
   much more general idea that it can help us pinpoint the errors and distortions
   of Enlightenment thought and of Western Faustian thinking overall doesn't
   occur in her work. (This can also be said of Arne Johan Vetlesen's discussion
   of empathy and receptivity in *Perception, Empathy, and Judgment: An Inquiry
   into the Preconditions of Moral Performance*, University Park: Pennsylvania
   State University Press, 1994.) Similarly, the Eastern concept of yin (as complementary to yang) connotes both passivity and receptivity, but the case we
   shall be making against Western thought depends on the particular value of
   receptivity (as opposed to passivity) and cannot be made using the vaguer,
   more general, or more metaphorical idea of yin.

In *Totality and Infinity: An Essay on Exteriority* (Pittsburgh: Duquesne University Press, 1969), the French philosopher Emmanuel Levinas also emphasizes receptivity, but he does so in a metaphorical, evocative, highly abstract fashion that doesn't engage with specific philosophical ideas or problems in the way we shall be attempting to do here. In addition, in his essay "Transcendence and Height" (translated from the French and reprinted in A. Peperzak, S. Critchley, and R. Bernasconi, eds., *Emmanuel Levinas: Basic Philosophical Writings*, Bloomington: Indiana University Press, 1996, pp. 11–31) and elsewhere, Levinas criticizes the Western emphasis on reason/rationality for its ties to the idea and reality of domination and violence. But I think it makes more literal sense to see the emphasis on reason in ethics and epistemology as tied to failures of receptivity rather than to actual tendencies to dominate or do violence, and the present book will proceed in that less hyperbolic way. It would be better to be able to argue for things—for a general critique of Western philosophical thinking—in ways that don't rely on exaggeration or metaphor.

However, by contrast with what can be said about the Kantian, Intuitionist, or Enlightenment emphasis on reason, the desire to *dominate the environment* is quite visible in Western history, and so it is no exaggeration to tie Western views to Faustian domination in that one area. Again, though, the connection with domination is hard to sustain or argue for outside the area of our relations with our environment. Unlike Levinas (and certain other thinkers), I don't see that ethical or epistemological rationalism automatically or plausibly translates into a desire to dominate others (or women, in particular) or, for that matter, into a desire to dominate nature. (On these just-mentioned issues, see Dwight Furrow's article on "Postmodernism" in L. Becker and C. Becker, eds., *The Encyclopedia of Ethics*, New York: Routledge, 2001, 2nd edition, pp. 1350–53.) So, again, I think it is more helpful and insightful to emphasize receptivity rather than (non)domination as a general theme in trying to give a large-scale account of our deepest values.

ACKNOWLEDGMENTS

I would like to thank Heather Battaly, Justin Bernstein, Kristin Borgwald, Otávio Bueno Damien Caluori, Eli Chudnoff, Matthew Colarco, David Copp, Daniel Corrigan, Justin D'Arms, Raúl de Velasco, Daniel Hampikian, Eva Kittay, Harvey Siegel, Jennifer Swanson, Benjamin Yelle, Yuan Yuan, and, especially, Seisuke Hayakawa for helpful comments. In addition, Nel Noddings and a reader for OUP read the entire original manuscript, and the present version of this book owes a considerable debt to their suggestions. Finally, I would like to thank Peter Ohlin for his encouragement and support throughout this entire process. The present book is highly critical of a great deal of historical and current work in the field of philosophy, and I think many philosophers are going to have a negative reaction to what I am, in effect, saying about them. But Peter seems to agree that there is something, that there is much, worth saying here; and I am grateful to him for his help with and enthusiasm for such a highly controversial book project.

FROM ENLIGHTENMENT TO RECEPTIVITY

Introduction

Over the past seventy or so years, things have happened in our society and in our thinking that help us better understand ourselves—in ethical and philosophical terms—than we have been able to do previously. But we have to work hard if we want to bring together the disparate or far-flung elements of this new and better understanding. That is my aim or purpose in the present book, but of course, and already in this short space, I have bit off a great deal to chew. The new understanding of our values comes from a number of different directions. It comes from the women's movement, from feminism: not only from an insistence that what is properly valued must be valued for men and women equally but also from a relatively recent revaluation of traits and ideas such as feeling, emotion, and empathy that have been traditionally associated with women. But the new understanding also comes from some large-scale historical developments: from the green movement that has arisen largely in response to the fairly recent pollution and despoliation of our planet and also, as I believe, from the horrors of war and genocide that dominated the international landscape of the twentieth century. Finally, I should mention analytic philosophy's resistance to the postmodernist tides of moral and epistemological skepticism, nihilism, and literal self-doubt. The idea that we can come to see things more clearly in ethical terms implicitly denies postmodernist thinking, but in its more positive way of thinking, it also assumes that we can and should try to understand things better and can take advantage of social, cultural, philosophical trends that help us to do so.

Now the idea that emotion and feeling are important is hardly a new one. Romanticism is to a great extent about—or at least it exemplifies—this idea. But within the academy and among analytic philosophers, there is much less interest in feeling/emotion than in the nature and capacities of our reason, of human rationality understood in both practical and theoretical terms. In arguing, as I shall, that reason is less important than we have thought, I am using the analytic-philosophical *we* and am trying to convince my philosophical colleagues, other academics, and people with a general interest in philosophical or ethical questions. But for me at least this means arguing in analytically acceptable terms of a sort that aren't the usual coinage of attacks on or critiques of reason. It also means going beyond the recent work that analytic philosophers have done on the emotions, because that work has emphasized the importance or significance of the emotions much more than it has argued against the (more) central place of rationality and control in our philosophical thinking. I am going to argue that reason/rationality and activity/control are a lot *less* important than we analytic and/or Western philosophers have thought. They are important, to be sure, but they need to be strongly counterbalanced by a value and virtue of receptivity that has been almost totally neglected within our philosophical traditions.

Our previous philosophical thought has been dominated by the Enlightenment in a certain way. Reason has been regarded as a fundamental and overriding value both in our thinking (it is never a good idea to be cognitively irrational) and in our practical activities (we should never do what it is practically irrational to do, and it is always irrational in practical terms to act immorally). The first of these ideas is certainly a common and pervasive element in Enlightenment thinking, but the second owes its existence and persuasive powers and influence mainly to Kant.[1] In any event, I shall argue that the general picture of human life and human values that one gets from Enlightenment thinking is distorted and unhelpful in many different ways, and that task will occupy us in the first part of this book. The critique I shall offer of Enlightenment ideas will, I believe, be less extreme and *clearer* than what postmodernism has said against Enlightenment thought; and it will also be more philosophically pointed and specific than what Romanticism has typically had to say against the Enlightenment. Moreover, and as I have indicated, postmodernism has tended to be skeptical and/or nihilistic about values and the making of value judgments, but we humans can't live without making and being serious about value judgments, and my purpose here will be to argue for new thinking about values, for *rethinking* our values, rather than for abandoning seriously considered ethical and evaluative thought. I believe previous philosophy has been very one sided in the values it has espoused and defended, and, rather than (for that reason) give up on evaluative thinking altogether, I hope to be able to point us toward a more adequate and balanced picture of what is really valuable in our lives.

This will involve shuffling off certain (though hardly all) Enlightenment/rationalist assumptions about ethics and human knowledge (epistemology). But Enlightenment thinking about the all-powerful place of reason is an instance of a more general phenomenon that also deserves our attention. Reason is generally thought of as active, and feeling and emotion are historically regarded as passive; and our culture, our history—and not just the analytic philosophers—have placed a high value on activity or activeness and autonomous control as opposed to being passive and/or receptive. And, for reasons I explained briefly in the preface, this emphasis can be conveniently and pretty aptly described as Faustian.

Moreover, Enlightenment rationalism is *just one example*— though a central and important one—of the value Western civilization has placed on activeness. Green environmental philosophers or those committed to deep ecology think that our positive and praising attitude toward activity or activeness has been exemplified in a desire to dominate nature, and feminists have found a similar positive attitude toward activity and domination in the (offensive) sexist or patriarchal idea or thesis that females are more subject to their emotions and their bodies than males are, that males are (consequently) more rational than females, and that it (therefore) makes sense for men to dominate women. I shall therefore argue here that this ideal of activeness can be found in many places in our culture and thought and that it involves a mistaken and rather shallow notion of what is really valuable in life. Many, though far from all, of the examples of such thinking I shall discuss are already known. But their bearing on a more general philosophical perspective on human values hasn't been appreciated and will be the focus of our discussion in the second part of this book. There, my opposition to an exclusive and pervasive Faustian emphasis on activity/dominance/control/autonomy will emerge through a discussion of a notion that hasn't received enough philosophical or public attention: receptivity. The term is far from a familiar one either to philosophers or the public, but I shall argue that receptivity, understood in terms that don't really stray from what the word actually means in English, is a great virtue. Proper understanding of how and why and of the many ways in which this is so can show us what is lacking and callow and blinkered about the general Faustian vision that has come down to us across the ages, about a pervasive cultural attitude that long antedates the Enlightenment.

My thinking here has been most immediately influenced by the Japanese philosopher Seisuke Hayakawa, who argues that the notion of action contains an element of receptivity that hasn't been recognized or appreciated. But if *action* in the fullest sense contains an element of receptivity or passivity, there is every reason to look for other places where receptivity may play a more important evaluative or ethical role than we have suspected. Hayakawa initially indicated to me that he liked my way of using the notion of empathy because I placed greater emphasis on receptive forms of empathy (e.g., emotional contagion) than on the active projective empathy—of deliberately putting oneself in another's shoes—that cognitive scientists (often speaking of simulation) have recently had so much to say about. But the receptivity that is involved in important forms of empathy is also involved in practical aspects of our existence that don't immediately relate to empathy and that involve questions, for example, about how we plan or don't plan our lives. The discussion in the second part of this book will take up this theme and a number of related ideas that bear on the importance of receptivity and the undesirability of the Faustian attitude or philosophy. However, before I say more about the individual chapters of this book, I'd like to engage in a bit of historical speculation. Some of the ideas and concepts I will be drawing on have emerged only in recent decades, and it is worth considering how these new possibilities have or may have become available to us.

One of the principal tools of our discussion will be the notion of care or caring. Caring is clearly a feeling or emotion of some kind, one that involves, in particular, a certain kind of benign motivation, but although the term has long been part of our English vocabulary and is in everyday use, the idea of an ethics of care or caring is of fairly recent origin. To be sure, caring is a kind of benevolence or is at least related to benevolence, and the so-called ethics of care that emerged in the 1980s from the writings of Carol Gilligan and Nel Noddings owes a certain debt to the eighteenth-century moral sentimentalists Hume and Hutcheson and to others who have argued for the importance of benevolence (or sympathy) to the moral life and to moral thinking. (Interestingly, though, Hume never talks about caring, only about benevolence. The former notion may have

just been too "folksy" for him to pay it philosophical attention.)
Like the earlier forms of sentimentalism, the ethics of care sees
moral motivation and justification as growing out of the emotional
or sentimental side of our nature rather than as rooted in and justified by reference to reason or rationality; and in this respect, it
runs counter to the whole recent tradition of Anglophone ethical
thought. But I believe it is no accident that such an emphasis on
emotion should be emerging at this point in our intellectual and
social history. Carol Gilligan, who was the first to write about caring in the specific way in which we nowadays, in philosophy, think
of it, argued that women tend to approach moral problems in their
lives in terms of caring about and personal connection with other
people, whereas men rely more on rules, laws, or principles and on
considerations of justice, rights, and autonomy when addressing the
moral issues that concern *them*. But the correlation between gender
and modes of moral thinking has been questioned by many, and
even if almost all men tend to think in terms of justice rather than
caring, this turns out to be true of *a great many women as well*. In any
event, Gilligan thinks the distinction between caring approaches
and "justice" approaches to moral issues has a philosophical importance that is largely independent of any correlation with gender, and
I agree with her.

However, the ethics of care was in fact inaugurated by women,
and it is also a fact that this form of ethics emerged during a period
when, as a result of the women's movement, women's ideas and perspectives were generally gathering strength in society. I believe this
is no accident. Caring speaks more with the voice of present-day or
traditional women than with the voice of present-day or traditional
men. And the idea of caring has spread like wildfire since Gilligan's
book first appeared. To mention just two notable examples, many
HMOs now say things like "we are the caring folks," and Bob Dole
was quoted in the *Washington Post* as saying "I am essentially a

caring person and I care about America" during his campaign for the presidency in 1996. Such emphasis and reliance on the notion of caring didn't occur before Gilligan's book appeared (younger people may not know this), and I think the present abundance of talk about caring is in fact largely due to that book. But the book itself couldn't have had such an impact if women's thinking and attitudes hadn't become socially and culturally more influential than they had been previously. Gilligan was the first to talk about caring in the contemporary way, but her now largely unacknowledged influence on present-day ways of talking and thinking wouldn't have been possible if women and the women's movement hadn't at the same time been making *their* influence increasingly felt. The notion of caring is traditionally and even now associated more with women than with men, so when women become more powerful, we can expect the idea of caring to become more powerfully felt as well. And this is just what has happened. People talk about caring more than they ever did before Gilligan's book appeared, and a philosophy or ethic of caring that has been pioneered mainly by women is also becoming increasingly visible in the academy.

I shall be using the notion of caring and the ethics of care or caring to argue against Enlightenment thinking and in favor of a positive ethical view that treats emotion and feeling as having a central place in human life and human thought; and to that extent, the argument will benefit from the intellectual/historical developments involving the emergence into prominence of the concept and phenomenon of caring that I have just been discussing and speculating about. But I am no irrationalist, if by that term one means someone who thinks or imagines that reason has no serious or important place in our lives and thinking. I am simply saying, and shall be arguing, that Enlightenment thought overemphasizes the importance of reason and underestimates the importance of the emotions and/or feeling(s) in some very significant ways. And since the Enlightenment overemphasis on reason or rationality is part and parcel of the Faustian ideal of human control and activity in dealing with the world (and with thinking itself), arguments that call Enlightenment rationalist thinking into question also work against our Western Faustianism.

But the notion of caring/care isn't the only element in the argument against Enlightenment thought that I shall be offering here. There is another notion or term that is closely related to caring and that has also in recent decades become more central to the ways people think about society and each other: the notion or term *empathy*. As care ethics has developed since Noddings's and Gilligan's original contributions, the connection between caring and empathy has been increasingly noted and relied on by care ethicists, and I can't think of any care ethicist who would deny that *empathy is a crucial factor in making caring possible*. But, like the concept of caring, empathy hasn't always been so familiar or indispensable a part of people's or academics' thinking about the world. The word *empathy* wasn't introduced into English until early in the twentieth century, and when it was, its principal use was in the realm of aesthetics. The moral idea that it is important for people to be empathic with one another didn't really emerge until the latter part of the twentieth century, though, again, younger people will probably not know that. They will not have seen the difference between earlier times not so long ago, when the notion of empathy was rarely used, and the present day, when everyone (including Presidents Clinton and Obama) thinks about the role of empathy in ethically desirable human interactions.

What has led to this change? In Hume's day it was possible, at least for a genius of human psychology like Hume, to refer to empathic phenomena, but Hume mainly had to use the term *sympathy* in order to do that, with the result that the contemporary distinction between empathy and sympathy is never clearly articulated in Hume. We nowadays linguistically and intuitively distinguish between the empathy involved in "feeling someone's pain" and the sympathy that consists in feeling bad for another who is in pain and wishing him or her well or better. And Hume's talk of one person's feelings infusing themselves or spreading by contagion into another individual clearly refers to the empathic phenomenon we call feeling another person's pain, heartache, enthusiasm, and so on. But Hume also uses *sympathy* to refer to what we would nowadays prefer to call sympathy rather than empathy. We can make the relevant distinctions more clearly today (though some psychologists aren't, in my opinion, as clear about this as ordinary speech tends to be) precisely *because* we have the two terms and not just the one. But we may still be curious about why it took so long to recognize the importance of empathy even after we had the *word*. As I indicated above, the word was around and was used for technical discussions in aesthetics decades before it achieved the prominence, the common moral currency, it now has. What has made the difference? Again, let me speculate.

The psychologist Martin Hoffman has, in my opinion, written more and better about empathy than anyone else in the field of moral development. His major work *Empathy and Moral Development: Implications for Caring and Justice* describes the development of empathy in relation to a large body of psychological thinking about and studies of that phenomenon. Among other things, Hoffman talks about how parents or others can make a child become more empathic and caring, and he describes, in particular, a technique called inductive discipline, or just plain induction, that can be useful to that end. Induction involves (say) parents' noticing that their child has hurt another child and, rather than allowing their child to run off to other activities, calmly but firmly making their child (more) aware of the pain or harm he or she has caused. If the parent has a good relationship with the child, this will make the child feel bad, a kind of primitive guilt based in empathy, about what he or she (the child) has done to the other child, and if this process is repeated, a psychological link between empathically derived bad feeling and certain kinds of harmful behavior will be established in the child and lead to or constitute a resistance to hurting or harming again.

Now you may be wondering why I have brought in the notion of induction (in a sense clearly different from the usual philosophy of science meaning of *induction*), but I have in fact done so for a reason. I think induction, inductive discipline, may—may!—enable us to better understand how and why the term, the notion of, *empathy* has become so central to ordinary human thinking during the past few decades—and why it didn't have such prominence during the earlier decades of the twentieth century after the term had already been invented. During the twentieth century, the human race endured and lived through unprecedented mass human atrocities. I don't have to list them for you. You know what they are, and the fact of their historical occurrence is in fact emblazoned on our collective (moral) consciousness in a way that also, I believe, has no precedent in human history. In effect, we have had our collective noses rubbed in the facts of those atrocities to such an extent and on such a scale that we perhaps cannot any longer ignore the psychological mechanism that generates our sense of guilt and horror at the massive harm and destruction we as a race turn out to be capable of. (This may be a function both of the sheer enormity of the atrocities and of the better means of communication that make it possible for relevant facts to be more effectively and vividly communicated than would have been possible in earlier times.)[2] If Hoffman is correct, then, as with induction, it is our capacity for empathy that underlies our enormous collective guilt at what we as a race or species have done to our fellow humans, and the massive and strong way in which that guilt or horror is felt better acquaints us with our capacity for empathy than less strongly and widely experienced forms of guilt/horror would do. Because of what we humans have collectively done and what we now feel in response to what we have done, empathy has become too large in its effects on our collective psyche to be ignored as a phenomenon, and we are then in a position to become aware of empathy's pervasiveness in our lives, which is in effect what has now happened in our society and in our thought.

Am I sure about this? No, not at all. But it makes some sense to me, and if what I have just been saying is at all on the right track, then we are today in a position to understand certain things better than we were in a position to do previously (and the mass horrors of the twentieth century may actually have done us some good).[3] If empathy plays a role in caring about others and if, as care ethics holds, a capacity for empathic concern about others is central to the moral life, then we are perhaps in a better position to appreciate those realities than we have ever been in before. And since Enlightenment and Faustian thought ignores those realities, we are perhaps also in a better position to criticize such thinking than we have ever been in previously.

The present book seeks to take advantage of these new opportunities, and that is its main raison d'être. I don't think the relevance of certain recent social/intellectual developments—the new emphasis on caring and on empathy—to the validity of the Enlightenment project has been fully recognized, and I want to set the record straight, or start setting it straight, in these pages. But as I mentioned previously, the emphasis on caring and empathy leads us to see how much more important emotion and feeling are than Enlightenment or Faustian thinking can appreciate and therefore causes us to question the central and pervasive role that reason or rationality plays in that thinking. Faustianism also involves assumptions or views that are not specifically about the role or significance of reason. Its stress on being active with respect to the world around one and with respect to one's own life and thinking represents a further dimension of historical Western (male) thought that we may also want to call into question. But in order to do that, we need to introduce another concept, one that hasn't (yet) achieved the kind of social currency that characterizes the terms/concepts of empathy and caring. That further concept is receptivity.

Many care ethicists and psychologists of moral development believe that empathy is necessary to the development of genuinely altruistic concern about other people (or animals). But if caring entails and involves empathy, then the kind of empathy that is required for altruism and genuine morality, itself entails and involves a kind of receptiveness vis-à-vis the feelings, attitudes, thinking of others. (Nel Noddings was the first person I have seen *stress* this latter point.) To that extent, considerations of receptivity play a role in the argument against Enlightenment rationalism. But, unlike the notions of caring and empathy, the idea of receptivity contributes to that part of the argument against Faustianism that is not also an argument against Enlightenment rationalism. Faustian thought stresses activity, control, and dominance in various ways that are only indirectly or less immediately related to considerations of rationality. And the idea of receptivity or receptiveness will have uses in the present book that go beyond anything we can and will say by reference to caring and/or empathy. That is because our historic Faustian emphasis on activity and control needs to be tempered and qualified in major ways by considerations having to do with receptivity that are to a large extent independent of issues concerning empathy or caring.

It is my hope, therefore, that the idea of receptivity may become more familiar to us as a society and a culture. If that happened, we could perhaps all share in a more realistic sense of the *limits* of our historic Faustian ideals. To be sure, criticisms of our Faustianism have already surfaced in the work of green environmentalists. But, as I shall be arguing in the second part of this book, that critique needs to be generalized, if we are to appreciate just how ethically misguided those previous Faustian values or understandings have been. This more generalized approach might conceivably get people and not just fellow academics to pay more attention to receptivity and its value than more piecemeal criticism of Faustian attitudes has accomplished. I at any rate hope so.

It is also worth noting that empathy is a more general concept than caring and that receptivity has a wider philosophical application than either of these recently familiar notions. Caring may be grounded in empathy (I shall say more about that in what follows), but, as I shall argue here, empathy is also relevant to issues in epistemology that aren't directly connected to issues of caring (or morality). By the same token, and as I have just been suggesting, we shall see in part II of the present book that the relevance of receptivity to human life and to our philosophical view of things is much wider than anything relating either to caring or to empathy. In that measure, it will turn out that the fairly unfamiliar notion of receptivity—unfamiliar to almost all philosophers and to the general public—has both broader and in some sense deeper philosophical implications than anything we can attribute to caring or empathy. The latter concepts have made a difference to how philosophy has been done in recent decades, but I shall argue here that the notion of receptivity can and should make an even greater difference. At this point, however, it would probably make sense to give the reader a better sense of the overall structure of the present book. So let me outline the general argument, going chapter by chapter.

The Enlightenment as a whole—and emphasizing Kant's influence as it deserves to be emphasized—treated both epistemic (or cognitive) rationality and practical rationality as central to our lives, but chapter 1 begins with a discussion of certain aspects of epistemic rationality in particular. Under the influence perhaps of Enlightenment thinking, we regard epistemic/cognitive/

intellectual objectivity and fair-mindedness as depending on a certain freedom from the influence of the emotions, but I argue in this chapter that feeling is in fact essential to epistemic rationality and to the particular epistemic virtue or virtues of objectivity and fair-mindedness (or open-mindedness). That is because empathy plays an indispensable and central role in cognition, learning, and rational argument. Chapter 1 introduces the notion of empathy by reference to recent discussions and studies of empathy in the psychological literature, and it argues in particular that we are capable of empathizing with a lot more than feelings and emotions. We can also empathize with someone's attitudes, belief system, or point of view, and I argue that we must be willing and able to empathize with the beliefs and viewpoints of others if we are to be said to be (being) objective and fair minded—and therefore epistemically rational—in defending our own beliefs. But empathizing with another's point of view involves at least momentarily viewing that person's ideas and arguments in the favorable light in which he or she views them, and seeing things in a favorable light is pretty clearly a feeling, a (mild) emotion of liking or approving. Thus, contrary to Enlightenment thought, it turns out that emotion/feeling is essential to rational/cognitive thinking and cannot be banished from such thinking without paying a great epistemic/cognitive/rational price. This is a surprising result, to be sure, and one that gives a first indication of how vulnerable Enlightenment rationalism is as a general philosophy.[4] But chapter 1 also argues, more strongly, that feeling is conceptually essential to the sheer *having* of beliefs. There is no such thing as a purely intellectual belief or being purely intellectually committed to a certain idea or theory, and this clearly goes against Enlightenment rationalism and indeed against what many or most of us philosophers are inclined to say about the having of beliefs or of intellectual/theoretical opinions.

Chapter 2 continues the discussion of epistemic rationality by reference to childhood learning. Adult objectivity and fair-mindedness are a matter of being able to empathize with others' points of view, but the original acquisition of attitudes and beliefs in childhood also depends on empathy. As Hume noted in the *Treatise of Human Nature*, we empathically imbibe or pick up attitudes and beliefs from people in a fairly automatic fashion, and such processes don't have to depend on the child's going through subliminal inductive (in the philosophy of science sense) arguments concerning the reliability of the people who are telling them things. Nor is the acquisition or infusion of beliefs via empathy some new kind of rationality. Chapter 2 points out—something Hume somehow never specifically mentioned—that we tend to imbibe beliefs and attitudes more readily from those we love than from other people, and the fact of love's influence here should make us doubt and wonder whether we have really unearthed some new form of rationality. Rather, the fact, as chapter 2 argues, that love makes us irrational or less than fully rational in so many instances— for example, it makes us overestimate the good qualities of the people we love—gives us reason to think that the process of imbibing strong beliefs from those around us is epistemically unjustified and even to some extent irrational. But if such things happen, inevitably happen, *because* of love, then the achievement of perfect rationality with respect to our beliefs will require us to give up on love—or, more properly, one will be able to be epistemically rational in the fullest sense only if one isn't fortunate enough to love and be loved. Since, in any case, love is one of our highest values, something we find indispensable to living well, *we have to learn to live with and accept a certain amount of epistemic irrationality in ourselves and those around us.* And seeing that serves to further undermine the Enlightenment insistence that one should always be and strive to be as epistemically rational as possible and that society as a whole should be remade in this image.

Chapter 3 then proceeds to criticize Enlightenment/Kantian ideas about the importance of *practical* reason/rationality in the light of the newly developed or developing ethics of care. Care ethics sees morality as based in empathy-related emotion/feeling rather than in practical reason/rationality, and if it is at all on the right track, then, once again, the Enlightenment insistence on the importance of (practical) reason is called into question in a relatively new, but quite significant, way. But all of this depends on the viability or plausibility of care ethics, and chapter 3 is to a large extent occupied with showing or explaining the merits of such an approach to normative ethics—and also to metaethics. Both Enlightenment/Kantian philosophy and care ethics regard morality as very important, but if care ethics is correct, that importance is due to the importance in human life of empathy and of feelings, emotions, and relationships based in empathy, rather than to the importance of reason in itself or as a grounding basis of morality. So chapter 3 questions the Enlightenment view of practical reason and its importance, by denying that it is the source of morality and claiming that empathy, emotions, and feeling—as fed by relevant epistemic/cognitive abilities and the beliefs they put at our disposal—are what actually lie behind our moral values and practices. (There is also a discussion here, but more fully in chapter 9, of how all this is compatible with maintaining the objectivity or validity of moral judgments and even with spelling out the meaning of moral terms/concepts in terms of empathy.) Chapter 4 continues the discussion of what makes morality important and argues that our emotional/empathic attitudes toward moral and immoral actions and people are our strongest evidence of how important we take morality to be and how important it actually is.

Chapter 5 moves the discussion away from empathy and the emotions and criticizes Enlightenment rationalism from a new direction. Borrowing from and building on the ideas of Isaiah

Berlin, it argues that perfect virtue and perfect happiness are impossible in principle, and because Enlightenment thinking by and large assumed that reason could bring our values, virtues, and personal good together in a harmonious perfect whole sanctioned and justified by reference to reason, the argument for and from the impossibility of perfection challenges the Enlightenment belief in the harmoniousness of our values and in the possibility of human perfection somewhat independently of any critique of its rationalist tendencies.

In chapter 6, the discussion is turned in a more positive direction. Having said a number of different things by way of criticizing the Enlightenment worldview, I think we need to see what positive picture can and should replace that worldview. Clearly, given the argument of part I of the book, that positive ethical picture will, among other things, emphasize the importance and indispensability of empathy and feeling to our lives. The result, as I have said, will not be irrationalistic in tone or substance because we need reason and cognition, too, if we are to accomplish anything in the world and understand anything basic about the world. But our values, the things we most value, have as much or more to do with feeling than with reason, and that claim certainly represents a basic and large-scale rejection of the Enlightenment picture of things.

The second part of the book makes use of the various criticisms of Enlightenment thought that were offered in part I. However, it begins by taking up several ideas that are not specifically associated with or due to the Enlightenment and that, in fact, have a much lengthier historical provenance. (Of course, Enlightenment ideas have *their* provenance: largely in the rationalist traditions of classical antiquity. But the distinctively modern concern with epistemic rationality [and overcoming epistemological skepticism] that preoccupies so much of Enlightenment thought and its sequelae is not really to be found in ancient Greek and Roman thought.) The main theme of the second part of the book is the importance and value of receptivity, a notion that is unfamiliar enough to philosophers and the public to require a great deal of elaboration and justification. Chapter 7 initiates this discussion by focusing on a particular instance of the importance of receptivity. I believe that the Aristotelian/Rawlsian view that one should live one's life according to a life plan requires us to think of our lives as more in or under our rational control than any life should or really can be. And I argue, by contrast, that we shouldn't have plans for our whole future lives but rather should have or exemplify a more receptive attitude toward what our lives may or will bring us in the future. The chapter then discusses the modern-day liberal idea that we ought to subject all our feelings, assumptions, and relationships to critical rational scrutiny—in order to determine whether to continue with them. And I argue that such an attitude or disposition makes us less receptive to what life *has* brought our way than it is desirable for us to be.

Chapter 8 extends the discussion of receptivity to another area where its absence is or can be sorely felt: questions of environmental ethics. Some green thinkers and feminists regard the Faustian attitude/motive of domination/control over nature as exemplifying an equation of femininity, emotionality, passivity, and lesser value and an equation of masculinity, rationality, activity, and greater value. Those who accept the equations regard nature as like a woman and in equal need of being actively controlled by something or someone more rational. But of course the age-old male desire to dominate or control nature or women in this way has led, in the environmental case, to a highly undesirable despoliation of the resources and beauties of our planet, and most green philosophers or deep ecologists also think that there is something inherently wrong with or repellent about the overweening desire for active domination and control. This suggests that the human value of activity, or being active, has been exaggerated, but it doesn't make much sense to raise up passivity as a counterideal. That would hardly be an attractive alternative, but what is and would be attractive as a counterweight to the inordinate value that has traditionally (by men) been placed on activity and control is the idea of being receptive or open in one's dealings or relations with people and things (in the environment). This idea hasn't, to the best of my knowledge, been previously suggested, but I argue, and I think it is fairly evident, that such a notion makes a lot of human sense and can perhaps help us to figure out better ways of responding to and making use of our environment. The issue of the treatment of women is a major theme in much of my other work, and I won't specifically take it up here, but in chapter 8, we *will* talk about how a certain natural extension of care ethics can lead us toward a green or deep ecological general understanding of our ethical relations with the environment.

Having spelled out some ways in which the idea or ideal of receptivity can help us correct the excesses and distortions of historical Faustian attitudes in the West, in chapter 9 I reintroduce some of the Enlightenment ideas discussed in the first part of the book in order to show how thinking in terms of receptivity can help us to encapsulate and justify many of the critical and positive conclusions we arrived at earlier. If empathy is necessary to being open minded or objective about other people's ideas and arguments, then the receptivity that empathy involves is also a precondition of or an element in those aspects of epistemic rationality, and if, as I shall be arguing, the kind of empathy that is required here is less the active, deliberate, projective kind and more the automatic, associative, unself-conscious, unwilled, and receptive kind, then the importance of receptivity is further underscored. Moreover, if loving and friendly attitudes and relationships involve being empathically open and receptive to the ideas and attitudes of those we love or are friends with, then receptivity lies at the heart—pun every bit intended!—of what we consider (among) the most valuable things in life. Finally, and to speak now more specifically of morality, part I makes it clear that a normative ethics of care sees morality as anchored in emotion and empathy rather than in practical reason or rationality. But such an ethics also sees receptive rather than projective empathy as most essential to the development of caring attitudes and motivations, and so care ethics treats receptivity as much more important than any form of moral rationalism ever has or could.

But there is more. I earlier pointed out that the correlation that seems to exist between our moral judgments and our empathic tendencies suggests, and in fact is best explained by the hypothesis, that empathy enters into our moral concepts. But in order to further highlight the important connection between morality and receptivity, chapter 9 attempts to be more specific about the relationship between empathy and those concepts. Reviewing what was argued for at much greater length in my 2010 book, *Moral Sentimentalism*, chapter 9 says that genuine claims of right and wrong involve more basic psychological attitudes of approval and disapproval, and, varying things somewhat from what Hume said about these matters, it argues that moral approval typically or often consists of being warmed by the warmth some agent has displayed in her actions or attitudes toward some third party or parties and that moral disapproval similarly involves being correspondingly chilled by someone's cold-hearted actions or attitudes toward some third party or parties. When you think about it, this idea is a rather intuitive one, and it has the advantage, for the sentimentalist, of treating approval and disapproval as independent of moral concepts and judgments and thus as possibly capable of grounding such judgments. (There are reasons not to think of the disapproval that grounds negative moral judgments as a kind of anger.)

Now sentimentalism has historically gone on to treat moral claims or utterances as simply expressive, descriptive, or projective of actual or potential attitudes of approval/disapproval. But chapter 9 also points out the possibility, defended in *Moral Sentimentalism*, that the moral properties to which moral judgments refer are fixed by reference to attitudes of approval and disapproval but in no way take in those attitudes as part of their content. This allows or would allow moral claims to be as objective or valid as rationalists say they are, but unlike rationalism, it would treat moral thought as anchored in our ability and tendency to be warmed and chilled by the warm-heartedness and cold-heartedness (mainly) of others. That ability and tendency is not within people's deliberate control but involves our being empathically receptive to "infusions" of feeling from other people. So, what care ethics says about normative morality and what it says about explicit moral thinking or judgment both highlight the importance of human receptivity in a way that rationalist approaches to morality don't. Thus in a variety of ways what is said in the first part of this book not only points us toward a post-Enlightenment view of our lives and our values but gives us important reasons to focus on, make use of, and recognize the great importance of the relatively unfamiliar idea of receptivity. (None of this requires us to deny that the Enlightenment stood for and achieved a great deal that is valuable.)

Chapter 10 then proceeds to say more about how and why receptivity—the concept and the phenomenon—is so important. If receptivity is a virtue, it is one that previously "dared not speak its name." No one thinks or talks of it as a virtue, but I hope to persuade the reader that this is exactly what we all should do. The notion of caring was much neglected or underemphasized in the period before Gilligan and Noddings wrote about it—even Hume and the other sentimentalists relied on the detached-sounding notion of benevolence rather than appealing to anything as folksy and intimate sounding (indeed, they might have thought, as *female* sounding) as the idea of caring. So caring had to be rescued from oblivion or obscurity, and this has, in my opinion, had a very benign and (if I may be so cute) enlightening effect on our understanding of particular ethical issues and of the ethical as such.

Similarly, we had no term exclusively for empathy until early in the twentieth century, but our possession of that term, that concept, makes an enormous difference, as I have suggested, to our understanding of moral, ethical, and epistemological issues. And I want to show here that we need to rescue receptivity from similar oblivion, obscurity, or neglect and understand its central role as a virtue of and in human life. A good life cannot be led without a substantial degree of receptivity in one's attitudes toward or beliefs about things and people, and what characterizes people as inconsiderate, cold hearted, or just plain immoral (and/or psychopathic) is more a matter of psychologically lacking certain forms of receptivity than of any other factor. So the attempt to get beyond unhelpful and dubious (or worse) Faustian and Enlightenment attitudes requires us to introduce and emphasize this new concept/term in a way that hasn't been done by previous philosophers and that certainly hasn't occurred at a popular or social level in the way that has happened with caring and empathy. If the argument of this book works, then the concept and phenomenon of receptivity can, should, and will take a place alongside caring and empathy as a major theoretical/philosophical tool and a focus of attention and interest in people's everyday lives. I say alongside because receptivity is a *different* concept from caring and empathy, but I believe receptivity also underlies and is presupposed by these two other concepts. And because it is a more general and more widely explanatory concept than either caring or empathy, the notion of receptivity can be shown to have an even larger philosophical significance than either caring or empathy has. Two further points.

The epigraph to the present book speaks of the remoteness of discussions of moral philosophy from the actualities of human life both now and in the past. And in giving the book the title it bears, I have sought to distance myself, so to speak, from that previous remoteness. Our discussion will take in moral values but also virtues and human goods that transcend the usually understood bounds of the moral, and it will deal with large-scale aspects of the human condition (and the condition of any other intelligent beings there may be) that moral philosophers largely ignore.[5]

Finally, it is worth noting a common underlying theme of the present book that I haven't yet mentioned. The second part of this book will focus on the virtue of receptivity in a way that helps secure or reinforce part of the argument in part I against Enlightenment values, the part that focuses on the pervasive rationalism of Enlightenment thought. But a portion of our argument against Enlightenment in part I concerns its assumption that perfection is possible, and this assumption doesn't in itself seem to betray any sort of rationalism or any reliance, more generally, on Faustian values. So we seem to have two separate arguments against Enlightenment thinking, one based on its criticizable Faustian rationalism and the other based on its unrealistic or all-too-hopeful assumption that perfect virtue and happiness are possible in principle. But even if each of these arguments can be given and justified on its own, they have something in common. For reasons to be discussed more fully in this book's conclusion, they both assume that our human condition is a basically satisfactory one. Or let me put things this way. Enlightenment ethical rationalism and the Enlightenment assumption that perfection is possible can arguably both be seen as resting on a view of ordinary human life or of the human condition that regards it as fundamentally and essentially unsatisfactory. Reversing engines, then, our arguments against rationalism and against perfection and (somewhat independently) for the great value of receptivity all rest and can be shown to rest on an accepting attitude toward the possibilities of our lives. So the acceptability or basic satisfactoriness of human life or, at least, of many ordinary human lives will turn out to be the underlying theme or assumption that binds all the arguments of the present book into a coherent whole. To that extent, this book gets beyond the rejection of Enlightenment thinking and even beyond the rejection of Faustian thinking to an even larger sense of where our values lie, but we need at least to *begin* our discussion on a somewhat smaller terrain, and so our initial focus will be, specifically and exclusively, on Enlightenment modes of thinking.

NOTES

1. My critique of Enlightenment thinking will be somewhat less relevant to the British Enlightenment than to other historical Enlightenment traditions. The British moral sentimentalists of the eighteenth century put more emphasis on feeling and less on reason than did their counterparts, for example, in France.
2. I think what I am saying here is consistent with Steven Pinker's view that violence in the world has on average and overall tended to decrease over time. See his *The Better Angels of Our Nature: Why Violence Has Declined*, New York: Viking, 2011.
3. Another possibility, however, is that the present prevalence of talk about empathy is due to the same basic factors that have made caring such a household concept. If present-day women are more given to empathy than contemporary men are (and there is a lot of evidence that they are, though also some evidence that they actually aren't), then the increasing influence of women and of the women's movement in our society and culture might help explain why we talk so much more of empathy nowadays than we did previously. And we might not need to invoke the mass atrocities of the twentieth century in order to explain the increased prevalence of such talk. But in the case of caring, there is a particular event, the publication of Gilligan's very influential book *In a Different Voice*, that helps—together with the increasing power and influence of women—to explain the great popularity of talk about caring. And there is nothing similar with empathy. Bill Clinton's talk about "feeling your pain" seems to have made the general public more aware of empathy and to have helped us be clearer on or about the distinction between empathy and sympathy, but Clinton wasn't speaking on behalf of and as part of the women's movement in the way Gilligan clearly was. So it is easier to see

how Gilligan's particular claims and analyses could have worked together with the actual historical empowerment of women to create an environment where there would be increased talk of caring. Nothing really parallel seems to have occurred with the notion of empathy, so I think the hypothesis offered in the text above still makes considerable sense, even if the increasing empowerment of women also had some influence on our increased preoccupation with empathy. And let me just add that I believe the fact that women have tended to think more in terms of caring and to be more empathic than men doesn't entail that the moral concepts I shall claim are based in empathy are ambiguous as between male and female usages. In chapter 9, when I discuss the meaning of such terms as *right* and *wrong,* I shall also explain (in footnote) why I think men and women use each of those terms with a common meaning.

4. In *Descartes' Error: Emotion, Reason, and the Human Brain,* New York: Putnam, 1994, Antonio Damasio argues that reason involves emotional elements. But he isn't at all clear about whether his claims are meant to be conceptual or empirical, and I will be attempting here to give more persuasive *conceptual/philosophical* arguments for the place of feeling within our rationality than anything I can find in Damasio's work.

5. In speaking of other intelligent beings rather than of other rational beings, I betray my distrust of and opposition to ethical and epistemic rationalism before I have actually given my reasons for rejecting rationalism. But those reasons *will be given*, and the point of using the term *intelligent* is that there is such a thing as *emotional* intelligence. (See, e.g., Daniel Goleman's *Emotional Intelligence,* New York: Bantam Books, 1995.) To call us intelligent beings is therefore not to assume or presuppose that we are most essentially or fundamentally characterized by our capacity for reason, whereas if we speak of humans as rational beings, rationalism is implicitly accepted. And that is because there is no colloquial notion of emotional rationality that parallels what Goleman and others have said about emotional intelligence. (When Antonio Damasio, op. cit., speaks of reason as containing emotion or feeling, he is referring to something very different.)

PART I

BEYOND

ENLIGHTENMENT

Is a book arguing that we need to go beyond Enlightenment ideas and ideals kicking a dead horse? We live in a post-Romantic age, and Romanticism is supposed by many to have slain Enlightenment thinking and to have been itself transcended by postmodernism. But I would question this picture.

First, postmodernism has favored a much too easy relativism: it has been totally iconoclastic about received opinions and values (e.g., denying the reality of the individual human self or subject) without actually offering any sustained arguments for its relativism and iconoclasm. Most of us philosophers in the analytic tradition therefore reject postmodernism on the grounds that it too quickly rejects and discards what we consider to be serious ethical, epistemological, or metaphysical thinking. But most analytic philosophers also reject key elements of Romantic thought and most especially its idea that emotion and feeling are somehow more important within our lives and as guides to how to live life than reason or rationality is. To that extent, the Enlightenment is still pretty much alive and well within the field of philosophy as practiced in the English-speaking world and among those influenced by philosophical trends in that world (especially the Scandinavians). Now there are some tendencies toward skepticism and relativism even in that world, but by and large philosophers in the English-speaking tradition think we can think cogently and intelligently about our lives and values. And by and large, the Romantic revolution never really affected that kind of philosophy or its immediate intellectual forebears.

In a way, that isn't surprising. Philosophers have long used reason as their tool and have thought of rationality as our most important or essential gift (Aristotle *defined* humans as rational animals). There is therefore a strong persisting tendency among philosophers in the English-speaking world to accept some of the basic tenets of Enlightenment thought. And since the Enlightenment in many ways saw itself as carrying forward the rationalistic classical thought of ancient Greece and Rome, there has also been a tendency to accept the rationalism that the Greeks saw as grounding both science and morality or ethics.

Science won't be the main focus of the present book, though what I say about ethics will have at least *some* surprising implications for our understanding (and perhaps even the doing) of science. I shall be concentrating mainly, though far from exclusively, on ethical issues and arguing that the Enlightenment and ancient Greek (and Roman) thought have a very distorted picture of (our) ethical values. They see a harmony among such values when, in fact, our values are deeply and irrecusably conflicted. They see our ethical values as based in reason or rationality, when much can be said in favor of grounding our ethical or moral values in the emotional or feelingful—what has traditionally been known as the sentimental—side of our psychology and our lives. But English-speaking philosophers have not only sought to base our ethical values in our rational capacities but have thought our ability to know and have justified beliefs about the world is also based or grounded in our rational capacities. And this last assumption, if anything, seems to philosophers even more secure, more obviously true, than what philosophers have thought about morality or ethics.

After all, there is a well-known sentimentalist tradition in ethics/moral philosophy, but an even partially sentimentalist epistemology has never before now presented itself for philosophical consideration.[1] However, that is something I am going to attempt here. I shall argue and have previously argued that our ethical thought is less harmonious than has been supposed and that it has a sentimentalist basis. But I also want to argue, for the first time, that epistemology turns on questions about the emotions in unavoidable and central ways. And I hope and believe that the argument will be philosophically more forceful, plausible, and acceptable than the kind of thing we so often get from neuroscientists. My argument will be a priori and will be conducted in familiar (to philosophers) analytic terms, but, as I have just indicated (somewhat vaguely), it will attempt to show something quite radical. Empathy, sympathy, anger, and love turn out, I shall argue, to be absolutely essential to the process of learning things and arguing about them with others, and although I will need to examine some empirical findings about the nature of empathy in order to make the case, the case itself will be purely philosophical and a priori. Kant distinguished between knowledge that begins with experience and knowledge based on experience, and what I will be saying won't rest on experience but will draw on empirical studies and experiments that help illustrate—and allow us, with our limitations, for the first time to imagine—certain philosophical truths.

But let me add another point about what I am trying to do. Feminists have pointed out some biases and blinders in science as it has been practiced by men, and many of them, especially those who would call themselves social epistemologists, have said that the kind of Cartesian epistemology that views all issues from the stand-point of individual knowers doesn't allow us to make sense of all the things we need to know about human knowledge and epistemic justification. (Perhaps, for example, one's justification for a belief may in part or whole depend on whether others in one's community are justified in holding that belief—and not just be a matter of one's own experiences and reasonings.) There will be a sense in which the epistemology I am going to argue for is social and even feminist. But the considerations that favor the particular form of social epistemol-ogy—assuming that is a good way to partially describe what I am doing—I shall be advocating are very, very different from anything that has been used to defend social epistemology in the past. And much of what I say will favor feminism, but, again, the reasons, the arguments will be very different from anything that has appeared previously. I shall be focusing on how empathy and our emotions not only may affect what we justifiably believe or know (such a thing has been said by many others)[2] but are essential parts of the whole process of believing and knowing in general. This seems very bold, perhaps even wild. So let's see if anything interesting can be said in support of it. But one further point. The Cartesian standpoint in epistemology has, as I have just mentioned, been criticized for lim-iting epistemic justification to the perspective of the individual and ruling out any constitutive or causal influence from the individual's larger community. But even those social epistemologists who open up epistemology to such larger influences typically don't, I think, put enough emphasis on the epistemological importance of an indi-vidual's prior education. I am going to argue here, however, that the ways children learn and are taught about the world around them (I am not talking here about moral education) are a clue to something important, even essential, about human knowledge generally. But since much of what a child learns about the world is learned from parents or other adults (not to mention other children), childhood learning also helps to illustrate the *outside and nonindividualistic* influences that arguably play an essential role in individual learning and justification. Again, the arguments I shall give for the social or interpersonal character of knowing and learning in general won't be the same as those that have been offered by social epistemologists. They will rest on emotional aspects or dimensions of cognition that have been largely ignored but that aren't going to be ignored here.

In any event, I don't think we can at all rely on the postmodernist stance against Enlightenment ideas and values, and I believe the arguments to be presented here in criticism of Enlightenment thought are philosophically clearer and more forceful than anything we have been told by the postmodernists. Rather than question the very possibility of thinking cogently or insightfully about ethical or epistemological values, I shall be criticizing previous Western values and the arguments that have been given in their defense in order to arrive at a better—and, in particular, a more balanced—picture of what is morally obligatory and valuable in our lives. So let's see whether and how this can be accomplished.

Chapter 1

Empathy and Objectivity

THE GROUNDWORK OF EMPATHY

In this chapter, I want to explore the relevance of empathy and feeling/emotion to certain epistemological ideals or virtues. Although my work has previously focused in a very large way on the nature and uses of empathy, most of the emphasis has been on morality and moral theory. But in recent years I have come to believe that the phenomenon of empathy and certain related emotional/affective states have an important role to play in helping us understand the epistemological ideal and intellectual virtue of objectivity and in understanding the more commonplace, less intellectualistic, and perhaps more easily attainable virtues of open-mindedness and fair-mindedness.[3] I would like to begin by reviewing some of the ideas about empathy I and others have relied on in previous work on morality, ideas that will be helpful to us when we come to consider the nature of intellectual objectivity and open-mindedness largely in terms of empathy and certain affective/emotional states. (For brevity's sake, I will typically just mention open-mindedness and drop the reference to fair-mindedness. The two virtues come to pretty much the same thing, in my opinion.)

In my *The Ethics of Care and Empathy* (Routledge, 2007), I reviewed some of the psychological literature on empathy for its bearing on moral issues. I was there exploring and defending a care-ethical approach to morality and to moral theorizing, and the moral development literature of recent decades to some extent supports the idea that the development of empathy is necessary to becoming an altruistic or caring person. However, there are some notable dissenters from this view, and in a moment I want to respond briefly to that dissent. But first we need to say something about what empathy is.

To begin with, it is worth noting that the term *empathy* didn't exist in English until early in the twentieth century, when it entered the language as a translation of the German word *Einfühlung*. However, the *concept* of empathy seems to have existed much earlier, and Hume in *A Treatise of Human Nature* says important, ground-breaking things about what we would now call empathy. But he used the term *sympathy* to refer to it; and we nowadays talk (or chatter) a lot more about empathy than about sympathy, so perhaps I should at this point say something (more) about the distinction between empathy and sympathy as we now understand these notions. In col-loquial terms, we can perhaps do this most easily by considering the difference between (Bill Clinton's) feeling someone's pain and feeling (sorry) *for* someone who is in pain. Any present-day adult speaker of (American?) English will recognize that *empathy* refers to the former phenomenon and *sympathy* to the latter. (Shades of J. L. Austin's discussion of our intuitive understanding of the differ-ence between "by mistake" and "by accident.") Thus empathy in its most paradigmatic examples involves having the feelings of another involuntarily aroused in ourselves, as when we see another person in pain. It is as if the person's pain invades us, and Hume speaks, in this connection, of the infusion of one person's feeling or feelings into another person. However, we can also feel sorry for, bad for the person who is in pain and positively wish them well. This amounts, as we say, to sympathy for them, and it can happen even if we aren't "feeling their pain." And perhaps I should add that involuntary or "contagious" empathy can be described as involving a certain *receptivity,* whereas sympathy can be more naturally characterized as involving *reactivity* or *reaction.*

The recent psychological and neuroscientific literature contains many empirical studies of empathy and various discussions of the difference between empathy and sympathy. Some of this literature appeals to the distinction between matching (e.g., via "mirror neurons") and nonmatching mental states but is not directly relevant to what I am doing in this book, and I shall therefore leave further discussion of this topic to a footnote.[4] What I think we *do* need to focus on here are some results from the recent literature that are essential to the moral-theoretic uses I want to make of the notion of empathy and that will also help us to get our bearings on the potential relationship between empathy and intellectual/theoretical objectivity and open-mindedness. Much of the recent literature tends to support the idea that empathy is a crucial factor in the development of the kind of altruistic concern for or caring about others that leads us to help others who are in need or in distress. But there are notable dissenters (I will give references below). Some studies that have been done seem to argue in favor of the view that empathy helps to make altruism possible for us humans, while others seem to show and have been interpreted as showing that empathy has very little to do with altruism and/or that the age-old thesis of psychological egoism, the idea that all our motivation is egoistic rather than altruistic, has to be taken very seriously.

Now the truth of psychological egoism would be very unsettling to moral philosophy and to ordinary human thinking about morality. Most of us think we are motivationally capable of altruism and of moral conscientiousness, but these possibilities and, arguably, morality itself would be undercut if psychological egoism is true. I think some of the dissenters I have referred to are much too quick to reject or doubt our motivational moral capacities, and I make this both as an intellectual criticism based loosely on methodological conservatism and as a *moral* criticism as well. But beyond that, I believe there are philosophical and therefore methodological problems with the ways arguments against altruism have been conceived and empirically supported. Those who have made such arguments—and even many who have defended the reality of human altruism —typically assume, for example, that the desire to avoid guilt is a strictly egoistic motive, so that if empathy leads us to help others out of a fear of impending guilt feelings if we do not, empathy is not at all moving us toward altruistic/sympathetic motivation or behavior. But philosophers have long known that this is a conceptual mistake, that guilt is invariably and irrecusably a sign of concern for something other than oneself and one's own well-being and that, more particularly, it presupposes or involves a concern for others' welfare or for morality itself that is decidedly not egoistic. So bringing in guilt really cuts no ice against the hypothesis of human altruism.

Further, the arguments against the hypothesis often—though not always—assume that the desire for others' approval is strictly egoistic, and this also seems to me to be a conceptual mistake. If we intrinsically desire or need the approval of others or simply want to be liked, that shows how intrinsically important to us we take other people to be, and none of this seems particularly egoistic. So I think the psychology/philosophy literature questioning the reality of altruistic motivation and arguing in favor of psychological egoism is misconceived in a number of ways, and though I certainly can't be sure that one can undercut all possible objections to the hypothesis of psychological altruism, I do think we have reason to work with it, assume it, at this point: especially if, as the present book argues, there are commonsense and philosophical reasons to regard empathy-based altruism as central to morality.[5] But if I am going to assume here that empathy plays an important role in human altruism, then I need to say some more particular things about how empathy and altruism develop.

Psychologist Martin Hoffman, whose work has perhaps defined the psychology literature on empathy more than the work of any other individual, has argued that individual empathy develops through various stages and that its connection with altruistic or moral motivations is more ambiguous or inchoate in the earlier stages of that development.[6] A very young child or even a newborn baby can feel distress and start crying at the distress and crying of another child within hearing distance, and this operates via a kind of mimicry and also seems like a form of infusion or, as some like to say, contagion. But as a child develops conceptual/linguistic skills, a richer history of personal experiences, and a fuller sense of the reality of others, a more cognitively "mediated" form of "associative empathy" can be involuntarily aroused in response to situations or experiences that are not immediately present and are merely heard about, remembered, or read about. It also becomes possible for the normal child to deliberately adopt the point of view of other people and to see and feel things from their perspective. Although we sometimes speak of both these forms of later-developing empathy (and especially of the latter, *projective* type of empathy) as involving identification with the other, Hoffman and many others insist that the identification isn't a total merging with or melting into the other: Genuine and mature empathy doesn't deprive the empathic individual of her sense of being a different person from the person s/he empathizes with.

Hoffman also points out that as individuals' cognitive sophistication and general experience increase, they become capable of more and more impressive "feats" of empathy. Thus at a certain point, empathy becomes capable of penetrating behind superficial appearances, and we may, for example, feel an acute empathic sadness on seeing a person we know to have terminal cancer boisterously enjoy himself in seeming or actual ignorance of his own fatal condition. In other words, we eventually learn to empathize not just with what people are actually feeling but with what they will or would feel about their condition in other circumstances. (Perhaps we can even empathize with their actual physical condition or situation.) Similarly, adolescents and some preadolescents become aware of the existence of disadvantaged groups or peoples, and empathy with the plight, say, of the homeless or the residents of Darfur becomes possible for them in a way that would not have been possible earlier in their lives.

Finally, Hoffman holds that the development of genuine caring about or for others requires the intervention of parents and others making use of what he calls inductive discipline (more simply, induction) to arouse or engage the child's capacity for empathy. Induction involves noticing when a/one's child has hurt others and then (nonangrily but firmly) making the child aware of the harm s/he has done—most notably by getting the child to imagine how the child that has been hurt is/was actually feeling. (It can help if the child can remember how s/he felt when similar things were done to her or him.) Hoffman believes that if such training is applied consistently over time, the child will come to associate bad feelings (guilt) with situations in which the harm s/he can do is not yet done, an association that is functionally autonomous of parents' or others' actual intervention and constitutes or supports altruistic and, more generally, moral motivation.

Now in *The Ethics of Care and Empathy* (ECE) I argued that empathic caring is all that we need in order to be moral individuals. I attempted to show, for example, that empathy is the sentimental basis for the deontological distinctions (e.g., the moral difference between causing harm and merely allowing harm to occur) that commonsense morality subscribes to; but for the moment I don't need to make the case for such larger conclusions. It will be enough if the reader believes that empathy is an important factor in altruistic or caring motivation—however broad a role this latter can or should play in the overall moral life. What I want to do now is show how certain specific themes in ECE move us toward understanding the epistemic virtues of objectivity and open-mindedness as essentially empathic phenomena.

ECE contained a long discussion of what it is to respect the autonomy of other people. Although such respect is a crucial element in, and even basis for, Kantian morality, I argued that a care ethics that focuses on empathy can explain or explicate respect in its own sentimentalist terms. I pointed out earlier that empathy isn't supposed to require the merging of two souls or personalities. Someone who is overinvolved with another person may have difficulty in separating his or her own needs and desires from those of the other, and this may mean that such a person fails to respond empathically to what the other needs or wants. One familiar example of such overinvolvement can be found in the attitudes some parents have to their children. Some parents seek to live through (the successes of) their children and have a difficult time separating their own needs from those of their children. Such parents have ipso facto difficulty empathizing with the individual point of view—with the needs, wishes, ideas, fears, and aspirations—of their children. Thus, if the child says s/he wants to do something different from what the parent has planned, the parent will often say, and believe, something like "you don't really want to do that."

This sort of parental overinvolvement has been labeled substitute success syndrome (sss). And it has been recognized that sss involves an inability to recognize or understand the individuality or wishes of one's own children or others. To that extent, furthermore, it also seems plausible to say, as I said in ECE, that sss parents *fail to respect their children,* since respect for individuals(' autonomy) is naturally thought of as requiring respect for their wants, beliefs, fears, and whatever is individual or distinctive about them. I proposed the philosophical hypothesis that respect for individuals can in general be unpacked in terms of empathy and empathic concern for them, and in ECE this idea was tested in relation to a number of interesting ethical examples.

For instance, arrogantly dismissive and intolerant attitudes toward other people's ways of life or religion clearly express both a lack of empathy toward them and what we would naturally say was a lack of respect for them. But the matter is complicated (in an intellectually fruitful way) by the fact that those who are arrogant toward and intolerant of others typically hate and/or are angry with those others. Religious persecution has often been said (by those who ought to know better) to be based on a desire for the salvation and well-being of those being persecuted and even tortured; but as John Locke in the *Second Essay on Government* wittily and wisely points out, the "dry eyes" of the torturers and persecutors refute the notion that they are motivated by concern for people's well-being.[7] And, as I said, it seems as if religious intolerance and worse are typically based on a kind of hatred or anger. This connects with what I am saying about empathy, because anger and hatred drive out empathy, make empathy with those one hates or is angry with either difficult or impossible.

The above has bearing on what we have to say about the connection between empathy and intellectual, critical, theoretical, or scientific objectivity. Since anger and hatred toward those one disagrees with intuitively seem incompatible with being objective about their opinions, it would seem that a degree of empathy incompatible with great anger and hatred is a necessary condition of being objective or open-minded in regard to the viewpoints or opinions of others, and that idea gets us part of the way toward a more general thesis of this chapter: that objectivity and open-mindedness with respect to ideas, facts, and/or arguments are basically and solely a matter of being empathic in certain (as yet here unspecified) ways. But let me not anticipate too much at this point. We have a lot more to consider and argue for before we can be in a position to maintain that general thesis, so let me continue.

Sss parenting tends to create children who doubt themselves and their own ideas and aspirations, children who, to that extent, are lacking in the kind of autonomy we think is desirable and even necessary to an adult life. And, interestingly—or perhaps depressingly—enough, what sss parents do to their children of either sex is what, arguably, is done to little girls and women under patriarchy. As Carol Gilligan points out in *In a Different Voice*, patriarchy tends to deprecate women's and girls' opinions and aspirations.[8] If the nineteenth-century girl says she thinks it is unfair that she can't attend university, she may be told: "You can't really believe that (you're not the kind of ungrateful girl who thinks things like that); you know that your brother needs to go to university in order to have a profession, but that your place is in the home." Her viewpoint, her idea, and even her incipient belief in the unfairness of the system get nipped in the bud through such statements, which are practically as likely to have come from a nineteenth-century mother as from a father. But in crushing the young girl's idea, the system also crushes her aspirations, as, for example, when the young girl who says she wants to become a doctor is told not perhaps that she can't attend university but that she would *really* rather be a nurse than be a doctor, which is such an unfeminine profession for a woman.

As Gilligan puts it, women and girls under patriarchy learn to distrust or dismiss their own voices; and they consequently lack the autonomy that men more typically have in such conditions. This, too, as we shall see better in what follows, bears on the issue of how objectivity and empathy connect. People who doubt their every thought can no more be objective or virtuously open-minded about evidence, arguments, or ideas than those who are so filled with contempt, hatred, or arrogance toward the individuals they are interacting with that they cannot pay serious attention to what those others are saying or arguing.[9] However, in order to demonstrate the crucial role empathy plays in our being objective or open-minded, we need to say more about what it is to have empathy for or with another person's beliefs or general viewpoint.

EMPATHY, EMOTION, AND BELIEFS

The kind of objectivity I want to talk about here is not the objectivity *of* matters of fact or things in the world but objectivity in thinking and arguing *about* matters of fact and of speculation.[10] Such objectivity, therefore, is an epistemic virtue like, though arguably more exacting than, open-mindedness. Now we have seen that emotions like anger work against and/or undercut both empathy and objectivity/open-mindedness, and I have said that the unempathic way in which women and girls are treated under patriarchy and in which children are treated by sss parents makes them incapable, to a large extent, of objective or virtuously open-minded thinking. I want eventually to defend the idea that the notion of empathy is crucial to and, suitably supplemented, sufficient for the understanding of what it is to be intellectually or scientifically objective or open-minded about things. But this main thesis depends on a proper understanding of what is involved in being empathic with another person's beliefs or point of view. I want to claim that an objective or open-minded person, a person thinking in an objective or open-minded fashion, will be empathic with the beliefs or point of view of those whom she disagrees with and may be engaged in discussions with, and I need to say more, much more, about what this entails.

We are nowadays familiar with the idea that it is possible to feel another person's pain or joy, and it is also commonly held that psychopaths are incapable of this kind of associative/receptive/

contagious empathy. At most, they feel joy at another person's pain or sorrow, and this means they lack the common capacity to take in other people's feelings in an "osmotic" fashion. But as David Hume pointed out in *A Treatise of Human Nature*, we not only imbibe feelings from others but also attitudes and opinions/beliefs, and I believe that open-mindedness and objectivity involve more than the ability to projectively put oneself into another person's head but an ability to at least temporarily and perhaps in a milder or attenuated fashion take in another's beliefs in an associatively empathic and even emotional way.[11] And at least initially, this is far from obvious or even perhaps plausible.

Thus someone might argue that it is sufficient for intellectual/epistemic objectivity and open-mindedness that someone is willing and able to get into the heads of other people, see where they are coming from and how they would want to argue, and without any of this requiring the open-minded person to associatively empathize with that other person's beliefs by taking them in in something like the way we can osmotically take in another person's pain or sorrow. And in that case, objectivity and open-mindedness would certainly not involve any sort of feeling or emotion in relation to opinions one is being open minded about. But I think we need to be careful here. After all, the ability to get inside people's heads without feeling what they are feeling is characteristic of psychopaths, and is it plausible to suppose that ordinary open-mindedness or objectivity has so much in common with *them*? Perhaps these virtues require us to be capable of actually *feeling* something in relation to the beliefs, arguments, and viewpoints of others. Perhaps they require a certain degree of *intellectual sympathy* with what others believe or argue. And in that case, open-mindedness and objectivity will involve at least one emotional/feelingful element. But *do* these epistemic virtues require such sentimental/emotional reactions or the disposition to have such reactions?

Well, consider a person who is able to get into someone else's head but who lacks all sympathy for his or her views, a person, for example, who is simply trying to probe or explore for weakness in that other person's ideas and arguments in order to be able to give a better argument for her or his own intellectual position. Is such a person being open minded? Pretty clearly not. And what seems to be missing is any sort of genuine openness to the possibility that the other person is in some respects correct in his or her opinion, any kind of even minimal sympathy, therefore, with what the other person thinks. So I think real objectivity and open-mindedness require one to have or to be able to acquire a certain degree or amount of sympathy with what others think, and such sympathy clearly means having an at least somewhat favorable opinion of what others think. But to favor something or someone is to have at least a mildly positive attitude toward them, to feel to some degree positively about them, and there is no reason to think this is any less true of having a (mildly) favorable opinion about some view, argument, or theory. So if open-mindedness requires sympathetic reactions to what one through empathy (and I will say more about what this involves in just a moment) knows about someone's views, it requires mildly positive feeling or emotion and has at least one decidedly sentimental aspect. In the realm of morality, we distinguish between empathy with someone's suffering and sympathy for that suffering, and whatever we say about the empathy, the sympathy seems to involve positive feeling toward the *person* who suffers and negative feeling toward the suffering itself. But it is no accident that we use the same word *sympathy* in connection with beliefs, arguments, and theories as well. And that is because such sympathy also involves and requires positive feeling—only this time directed toward beliefs and arguments.

Now in the moral realm, empathy of an associative kind—and possibly of the projective kind, too—is widely thought necessary to genuine sympathy and altruism, and perhaps there is a similar relationship between empathy and sympathy in the epistemic realm. I said earlier, following Hume, that we can take in the opinions of others via empathic osmosis or contagion and thereby make them our own, but no one holds that one has to come to agree with other people in order to count as having been objective or open minded about their points of view. A mother can empathize with a child who is terrified of going to see the doctor, can feel, to some extent, the child's terror, and can feel sympathy with—and consequently be upset about—what the child feels, even while she insists on taking the child to the doctor. And something similar can happen with beliefs in the context of open-mindedness and objectivity. The open-minded person doesn't just get into the head of another person the way a psychopath might. She empathizes with the other's point of view, sees things to some extent in the favorable light in which the other person sees them, and this either involves or evokes what we have called (a certain degree of) intellectual sympathy with that other person's viewpoint. But, as with the child, the mother, and the doctor, this doesn't entail that one will ultimately go along or agree with that viewpoint or the beliefs that make it up.

In any event, it seems plausible to conclude that the epistemic virtues of open-mindedness, fair-mindedness, and objectivity require certain tendencies and actualities of favorable (and also unfavorable) feeling; and so we need to acknowledge that full epistemic or theoretical rationality contains previously unsuspected emotional/sentimental elements.[12] But the above argument also hints at the possibility that belief itself may contain emotional elements, and it is time to be more explicit about this.

As I said above in passing, empathy or sympathy with another person's point of view involves seeing certain things in something like the favorable light in which the other person sees them. But think what this means! It means that the other person has a favorable view of a certain argument or theory and that the open-minded, objective, or, as we may say, intellectually sympathetic person, regards that argument or theory, at least momentarily, in something like the same favorable light in which that other person views it. But that means that a person who holds a theory or sincerely advances/advocates an argument views those things in a favorable light, favors them over other (possible) arguments or theories or beliefs, in which case it follows that believing in theories and arguments as such involves a favorable/favoring attitude, some positive feeling, affect, or emotion. And so it turns out that there is no such thing as a purely intellectual or purely cognitive belief or opinion.[13] (Even Karl Popper, who said we should never accept any general scientific hypothesis, had a favorable view of and felt a positive emotion/affect toward his own skeptical recommendations/opinion.)[14] But let us get back now to our discussion of objectivity and open-mindedness.

OBJECTIVITY BASED IN EMPATHY

As I mentioned earlier, intellectual objectivity and open-mindedness aren't so much a matter of cognitive states generally but rather of how one acquires and, I think most particularly, of how one maintains certain beliefs. There are, as I shall now argue, more or less empathic ways of maintaining beliefs, and such distinctions are the ones that determine whether one is or is not being objective, open-minded, or fair-minded with regard to a given subject matter.

I already to some extent anticipated this idea when I earlier spoke of the ways in which anger with other people's beliefs or viewpoints (and with other people) can undercut both empathy and objectivity/open-mindedness in regard to those beliefs or viewpoints. The Spanish inquisitors obviously lacked both empathy and objectivity with respect to (the viewpoints or beliefs of) those they persecuted and tortured and tried to convert or make recant, and hatred and contempt for those who disagreed with them may have played a major role in producing or constituting that lack of empathy and objectivity. It is perhaps also worth noting that at the present historical juncture, the hatred Muslims feel toward the West (because of the situation of the Palestinians, because of American interference in Iranian political life decades ago, and for other reasons) and the hatred Westerners who are not Muslims feel toward Islam (because of 9/11, because of Muslim Holocaust denial, and for other reasons) make it nearly impossible for either side to be empathic with or objective/open minded about the other side's point of view. This fact, if it is one, is tragic.

However, there are examples of a lack or absence of objectivity that don't seem to involve emotions as strong as hatred or contempt, and these, too, I think, can be understood in terms of issues of empathy or its absence. In the field of philosophy, for example, there can be disagreements and disputes where it seems (at least to outsiders) that neither side really understands or has tried to understand what the other side is saying (or the other's intellectual point of view). Such cases, I think, are naturally and plausibly regarded as involving a lack of empathy on each side for the other side's point of view (alternatively, an empathic failure to see things from the other side's point of view). For example, neither side may ever actually state the other side's views in an accurate way, a way that the other side would acknowledge as acceptable. And neither side may be *capable* of doing this, in part, presumably, because their strong or rigid commitment to their own point of view makes them not want to see things through the eyes or intellect of someone who totally disagrees with them. Doesn't it seem plausible to say that in such cases neither side is being (completely) objective or open-minded about the issues that divide them? I assume that it *is* plausible to say this, and in that case we have another instance of how a failure or lack of empathy undercuts objectivity or open-mindedness. And, given what was said above, the lack of objectivity or open-mindedness will be partly a matter of lacking certain emotions in relation to other people's ideas and arguments. Strong emotions such as anger and contempt may undercut or block epistemic open-mindedness, but open-mindedness itself also requires certain emotions, though those emotions are arguably milder than anger and contempt.

But notice what all this entails. Intellectual objectivity requires one to be able to and in various circumstances actually to empathize with another person's intellectual or cognitive point of view; and, given what I have been saying, seeing another person's position or argument from that person's point of view means empathically (i.e., through empathy) seeing it in something like the favorable light in which the other person sees it. And that, in turn, means having a certain kind of (possibly mild) favorable emotion toward it. So being intellectually/epistemically rational and objective really does require having certain emotions (and likewise certain feelings).

But we must also remember that a theory that treats empathy and emotion or feeling as crucial to being objective or open-minded doesn't entail that the possession of these intellectual/cognitive virtues will eventually lead to agreement. As noted earlier, someone who has fully empathized with the point of view of those who disagree with her may still end up disagreeing with them. However, this often *won't* happen because getting better acquainted with the point of view of those with whom one initially disagrees may lead one to modify one's position or at least, and this is really in a way the same thing, how one defends that position.[15] Moreover, the possession of both empathy and the virtue of objectivity or open-mindedness doesn't entail that a person is entirely without intellectual/cognitive failings. If someone is obtuse about accumulating or weighing scientific or other data and ends up with a totally (in intellectual terms) unjustified theory or set of beliefs, that person will count as intellectually deficient, but that deficiency doesn't automatically show or indicate any lack of empathy for other people's intellectual/cognitive viewpoints, and the person in question may (therefore) count as objective and open minded about intellectual/cognitive issues, even if he or she is intellectually deficient *in other ways*. Epistemic rationality entails being objective and open minded, but the reverse entailment simply doesn't hold.[16] And this, in effect, means that I am not—am *not*—offering a sentimentalist account of epistemic or intellectual rationality here. Such rationality requires/involves certain sentimental/emotional elements, but it also depends on other factors that seem purely intellectual and entirely independent of emotional capacities or predilections (the tendency to commit the Monte Carlo or gambler's fallacy of thinking that red is more likely to come up in roulette after there has been a run of six blacks doesn't seem to involve any sort of emotional bias or failing). But even if I am not an epistemological sentimentalist in any strict or standard sense, I do believe that there are emotional elements in epistemic/theoretical rationality, and that is something that, as far as I know, no other *moral* sentimentalist—not even Hume—has ever claimed.

In addition to and given our conclusions about the cases I have discussed above, the presence or absence of intellectual, critical, epistemic, or scientific objectivity seems to be less a matter of how one actually acquires a given belief or viewpoint than of how one is prepared to defend one's views in the light of others' dissent from (or reluctance to accept) them. In that measure, being objective and open minded turns out to be more a *reactive* and *relational* matter than one might have initially supposed. The adage "a word to the wise is sufficient" in effect characterizes wisdom in terms of its reactive tendencies toward, its reactions to good advice, and though this may or may not be the whole of *wisdom*, it is a very important part of it. Similarly, I want to maintain, and in the light of our discussion I don't think it is implausible to maintain, that intellectual/theoretical/critical/scientific/cognitive objectivity is largely (or entirely?) a matter of how one empathically reacts or would react to what others think and say.

But does all of this imply that an objective or open-minded person can never reject any belief or assumption out of hand: that they have to be open minded, for example, about the views or viewpoints of flat earthers and people who think they are Napoleon? I don't think so. I believe there are some beliefs or ideas that even an open-minded and objective person can be intolerant of, and the two examples just mentioned serve to illustrate this point. Rejecting such beliefs out of hand is intellectually permissible in the same way that it is permissible to care less and be less concerned about someone, if he or she has done damage either to oneself or to those one cares about (which can extend to all of humanity or sentient life in general). If someone betrays me or my family, I will be angry with that person and start being much less concerned about his or her welfare. As Martin Hoffman has pointed out, such reactions are built into our empathic tendencies, and it doesn't show that someone is lacking in empathy, is a less than fully empathic person if they react in such ways. In fact, the anger one feels at those who hurt people we love or care about is based in our empathy with those people.[17] And no one supposes that a person has to be selfless and lacking in self-concern in order to count as fully empathic. Empathy normally develops against a persisting background of individual self-concern, so those who get angry and care less about someone who harms or betrays them needn't count as lacking in empathic concern for other people.

Similarly, then, a person who is entirely open minded and objective can be intolerant of the beliefs or arguments of those who are themselves closed-minded toward the views of others (including the open-minded person herself). Such intolerance involves a kind of epistemic anger, but that doesn't by itself show that the person who feels it is lacking in open-mindedness and objectivity. And since people who believe the Earth is flat or think they are Napoleon precisely show a lack of open-mindedness in regard to those opinions, intolerance toward their views need not be epistemically inappropriate and can be entirely consistent with being objective and open minded.[18] In that case and assuming that intolerance toward certain views is epistemically *called for*, we may be able to conclude further that a mild form of cognitive/epistemic negative feeling/emotion—what I have called epistemic anger—is essential to cognitive/epistemic rationality. The cognitive side of our lives therefore seems to essentially involve both positive and negative emotions/feelings: both the positive feelings involved in favoring the ideas we accept over others (and remember that one can favor a thesis such as skepticism or Popperian views about the scientific suspension of belief) and the negative feelings involved in being intolerant toward certain ideas or viewpoints. (And various lesser and greater degrees of these feelings are of course also possible.)

So rather than constitute a threat to the possibility of objectivity or to our ability to fully make sense of that notion, the fact that we reject certain beliefs out of hand, are intolerant of certain ideas can be an aspect of (our understanding of) objectivity. Objectivity and open-mindedness involve or require empathy with the points of view of others unless those others themselves show a total lack of willingness to empathize with our point of view and those of others. So our account of epistemic objectivity and objectivity itself involve both first-order and second-order empathy, but this is entirely analogous to what happens in the moral life when caring concern for others is diminished or done away with when those others are totally uncaring (or worse) toward us and/or those we care about.[19]

CONCLUSION

I have sketched a theory of objectivity, of what is required for some-one to count as being objective in some area or areas, in terms of empathy; and along the way I mentioned the problems that arise for us humans when we are incapable of being empathic with one another's viewpoints. The current state of opposition or enmity between Islam and the West (if that is an accurate description) is an unfortunate fact for humanity, or so at least I believe (others may disagree). That state prevents or works against intellectual empathy between the two sides, but it also prevents or works against empathic concern for the (nonintellectual) well-being of those on the other side. In other words, and assuming the present theory together with what I have argued in ECE, hatred and a lack of empathy make it difficult or impossible for people to be *intellectually/critically objective and open minded* about each other's viewpoints or beliefs but also make it difficult or impossible to be *morally concerned* about others' welfare or happiness. (By the same token, the presence of empathy also makes it possible to live in just and continuing peace with other people even though one doesn't agree with them about important matters.) Thus empathy is necessary to the fulfillment of both intellectual/cognitive and moral ideals or objectives, and it therefore has an even larger human role to play than I thought when I wrote ECE and focused solely on the moral implications of (developing) empathy.[20]

The idea that empathy plays an important role in overcoming or preventing hatred and conflict between individuals or (large) groups of individuals is familiar from the literature of psychology and of the specialized field of conflict resolution. And the related idea that empathy makes it easier to overcome disagreements and come to peaceable, constructive, or useful agreements is also a tru-ism of that literature.[21] But unlike philosophy and philosophers, those who write and publish in these fields don't particularly focus on the issue of objectivity/open-mindedness, so it is a distinctive feature of the present discussion that it ties empathy not merely to conflict resolution and to the overcoming of differences or disagreements but to the philosophically and, as we have seen, humanly important notions of objectivity and open-mindedness as well.

But note further that if empathy is a key ingredient in objectivity, it will sometimes be difficult to tell whether someone is being or has been objective or open minded in thinking about a given subject matter. Sometimes we can tell what someone is thinking or feeling, but at other times it is difficult or impossible to do so, and these differences and difficulties clearly carry over to empathy. Someone might seem to be taking in and seriously considering an intellectual opponent's viewpoint and ideas but actually be deeply resistant to doing so and so be either deceiving others or taken in himself about how objective he is being about some intellectual issue. And we can even more easily run into epistemological difficulties of this kind in cases of historical knowledge. When Lorentz, whose transformations allowed the difficulties in physics that eventually led to the special theory of relativity to be handled on an ad hoc basis, saw Einstein's theory, he rejected it and gave various arguments. But we may never know whether he did so for good reasons that had force at the time or whether he was simply too resistant to changing his own ideas (and giving someone else credit for solving major problems) to give Einstein a fair or objective hearing.[22] In any event, the assumption that it can be difficult to know how intellectually objective someone is being or was in the past is no more implausible than similar assumptions about our knowledge that someone is morally good or has acted from good motives, and I bring up this point not because it creates difficulties for the present approach that need somehow to be answered but because it usefully places what we have been saying within a certain kind of epistemological context.

One further point. In recent years, there has been a lot of talk, speculation, and argument about the possibility that reason and emotion (or feeling) may be inextricably linked. People outside philosophy (most famously, Antonio Damasio) and philosophers as well have begun to take seriously the idea that reason may constitutively contain or involve emotion or feeling, but there has been a great deal of unclarity here about the exact meaning of this last thesis and about the data or facts that have been said to support it.[23] However, the present chapter, to the extent one accepts its conclusions, seems to offer a clear confirming instance of this general thesis. Intellectual objectivity/open-mindedness is part of intellectual/epistemic rationality (and reasoning), and to the extent it constitutively requires empathy with the (emotionally charged) points of view of those who may disagree with one, reason and rationality also constitutively involve this kind of empathy. There may be other, even better, examples of the interpenetration of reason and emotion, but the one uncovered in these pages illustrates it very clearly and solidly, and I take that to be one of the more interesting or significant implications of the present discussion considered as a whole.

And, of course, that discussion has been, both implicitly and explicitly, a criticism of Enlightenment thinking as well. Enlightenment epistemic rationalism sees cognitive/epistemic rationality as precluding or overriding feeling and emotion, and it certainly also treats feeling and emotion as irrelevant to the very having of beliefs. (It thinks ordinary beliefs can be and should be completely or purely intellectual or cognitive.) And the present discussion has sought to show that these Enlightenment views (views shared, in fact, by many pre-Enlightenment thinkers and by many who don't regard themselves as accepting Enlightenment thought) are fundamentally mistaken. Of course, it has been known for quite a while that emotions such as fear can put us epistemically in touch with situational factors of danger that our more intellectual think-ing processes haven't yet registered and perhaps won't register until it is "too late." And this already shows a certain limitation in or to Enlightenment/rationalist views about epistemic/cognitive ratio-nality. But the criticisms of Enlightenment thinking made in this chapter and to be made in the next chapter go much more to the core of that thinking than the point about fear really does. After all, a rationalist can claim that even if fear or inexplicable hunches operate in the "context of discovering" things about the world, it cuts no ice in the "context of justifying" beliefs. But my point here has been that emotion is (on a priori philosophical grounds) an essential part of the process/state of epistemic justification and of all belief as well. This calls Enlightenment rationalism more deeply into question and does so without falling into the opposite extreme of defending any sort of epistemic *irrationalism*.

Finally, let me say something about how the preceding discus-sion—and what I am going to be saying in our next chapter—relate to Hume's philosophy. Hume was the first person in the West (there are some earlier anticipations in China and perhaps in India as well) to specifically refer to what we now call empathy, and he made use of that notion (though he employed the term *sympathy*) in some of his most significant moral arguments. For example, he recognized that we think it is generally more virtuous to help one's own chil-dren rather than help the children of strangers (when one cannot do both of those things), and he laid this opinion at the door of our greater sympathy/empathy for those who are connected to us by such associative factors as similarity and proximity. This is a great achievement in my estimation, but somehow—somehow!—Hume never thought to use the notion of empathy to explain such ideals as open-mindedness and objectivity, and although he saw and said that children pick up opinions and attitudes empathically from those they are connected to by blood, he really doesn't make much of that fact in epistemological terms. Like most or almost all Western epistemologists, he wasn't all that interested in developmental and educational/learning issues. (Perhaps that is also why he never saw that benevolence needs in some measure to be cultivated and developed [through parental interventions], that it isn't enough to call it an "original instinct" and leave it pretty much at that.)

So Hume's general epistemology doesn't make much use of childhood learning examples in order to make its general points. In fact, in various ways to be discussed later, it actually works against taking children's learning processes seriously, but what I shall be arguing in our next chapter is that epistemology has a lot to learn from (the example of) childhood learning. Such learning occurs via empathic and emotional processes that Hume, for all his emphasis on empathy and feeling, largely neglected and that others right up to the present have also neglected, processes that I believe have important lessons to teach us about the nature of human knowledge and thought. Just as people are empathically inclined to help those they know and love more than they help others, they are also partial to the opinions and attitudes of those they know and love. They are more inclined to accept what those they love believe than what (they know) strangers or foreigners believe, and this inclination is a function of the greater empathy they have for those they love, the greater ease with which they identify with them. So empathy plays a role in cognitive learning from the very start, a role that is parallel to its moral role in making us more concerned and caring about (the welfare of) those near and dear to us. In the latter case, empathy causes us to be more willing to *act* on behalf of those we love; in the former and more relevantly for issues of knowledge and belief, it makes us more likely to *take in* what those we love think or believe. This cognitive partiality is parallel to the motivational and practical partiality that we typically exemplify (and that morality tells us we should exemplify); but it is also different from this latter and much more directly relevant to issues in epistemology.[24] This will be the main topic of our next chapter—and, as we shall see, it will, among other things, lead us to some further ideas about open-mindedness and objectivity beyond anything that has been said in the present chapter.

NOTES

1. To that extent, the present book is in various ways *more* sentimentalistic than even Hume is. However, in speaking above about offering a sentimentalist epistemology in this book, I didn't mean that *every aspect* of epistemology can be reduced to or equated with sentimental factors. When one commits the Monte Carlo Fallacy of assuming that red is more likely to come up in roulette after there has been a run of black, one makes an intellectual mistake that can't presumably be traced to sentimental factors. But I do want to argue that issues about feeling or sentiment are relevant to belief, knowledge, and epistemic justification in a very general way. And I don't believe anyone has previously defended such a view.

2. It has often been said that our feelings can give us evidence for certain conclusions that we would otherwise lack: Our own fear can be a clue that there is something to fear even when more objective facts or circumstances don't seem to indicate that there is anything to fear. And feelings of guilt can indicate (to us) that we have done something wrong even when the objective details or facts of a situation don't seem to point to wrongdoing on our part. All true, absolutely true. But this is particular emotions pointing to particular (evaluative) conclusions, and I shall here be defending the more general, the entirely general claim that our conclusions about every subject matter and our epistemic/cognitive rationality in coming to such conclusions involve emotional/feelingful factors. This goes much more strongly against Enlightenment thought than merely allowing that feeling can occasionally give useful evidence for conclusions that go beyond sheer feeling.

3. Some of the conclusions I shall be reaching are similar to conclusions Sandra Harding defends in *Whose Science? Whose Knowledge? Thinking from Women's Lives* (Ithaca, NY: Cornell University Press, 1991). But we employ quite different arguments, and I emphasize empathy and its emotional aspects more specifically than she does. In any event, her work and mine here are perhaps best viewed as complementing each other. (For somewhat less closely related ideas, also see Alison Jaggar, "Love and Knowledge: Emotion in Feminist Epistemology," reprinted in A. Garry and M. Pearsall, eds., *Women, Knowledge, and Reality*, Boston: Unwin Hyman, 1989, pp. 129–55.)

4. Some recent discussions of empathy have conceptualized it as unlike sympathy or benevolence in requiring some sort of "match" between the mental state of an empathizer and that of the person or animal they are empathizing with. And this way of viewing things is no doubt supported by the recent literature on mirror neurons, which gives scientific backing to the idea of empathic matching. (See, e.g., the essays in J. Decety and W. Ickes, eds., *The Social Neuroscience of Empathy*, Cambridge, MA: MIT Press, 2009; the essays in J. Pineda, ed., *Mirror Neuron Systems*, New York: Humana Press, 2009; and A. Goldman, "Two Routes to Empathy: Insights from Cognitive Neuroscience" in A. Coplan and P. Goldie, eds., *Empathy: Philosophical and Psychological Perspectives*, Oxford, UK: Oxford University Press, 2011.) But the insistence on an actual match is, in fact, overly restrictive, given present-day usage of the term *empathy*. We wouldn't want to deny that someone was empathizing simply because the object/target of his or her empathizing was just very accurately *feigning* pain or joy, and we also want to allow for empathy with fictional characters. I think, therefore, that it makes more sense for us to understand empathy in terms of what is happening proximally rather than distally when empathy occurs: This would allow for the fuller range of cases where we want to speak of empathy. In that event we wouldn't need the idea of an actual external match in order to be able to distinguish between empathy and sympathy. And the distinction between associative empathy and sympathy can in any event be made in terms of the distinction between receptivity and reaction or response. When we are flooded by and feel another's pain or joy, we are being *receptive* to his or her psychological reality, and such paradigm empathy contrasts with sympathetic and altruistic *reactions* to the feelings of others or to their situation.

5. For an early, very extended defense of psychological altruism, see C. D. Batson, *The Altruism Question: Toward a Social-Psychological Answer*, Hillandale, NJ: Lawrence Erlbaum Associates, 1991. For those who have questioned whether humans are capable of altruism see, e.g., Elliott Sober and David Sloan Wilson, *Unto Others: The Evolution and Psychology of Unselfish Behavior*, Cambridge, MA: Harvard University Press, 1999; R. Cialdini, S. Brown, et al., "Reinterpreting the Empathy-Altruism Relationship: When One into One Equals Oneness," *Journal of Personality and Social Psychology* 73, 1997, pp. 481–94; J. Doris and S. Stich "Moral Psychology: Empirical Approaches" in the online *Stanford Encyclopedia of Philosophy*; and the introduction and chapters by Heather Battaly, Peter Goldie, and Jesse Prinz in A. Coplan and P. Goldie, eds., op. cit. Batson has responded to much of this criticism in his recent *Altruism in Humans*, New York: Oxford University Press 2011.

    For philosophical discussion of the conceptual mistake of thinking that a desire to avoid guilt is psychologically egoistic, see, for example, Joel Feinberg, "Psychological Egoism" in his *Reason and Responsibility: Readings in Some Basic Problems of Philosophy*, Encino, CA: Dickenson Publishing Co.,

2nd edition, 1971; and Thomas Nagel, *The Possibility of Altruism*, Oxford, UK: Oxford University Press, 1970, p. 80n. In the literature on whether altruism exists, only Sober and Wilson (op. cit., ch. 7) seem aware of how questionable it is to assume that the desire to be liked or approved is egoistic. And Sober and Wilson also argue for the existence of human altruism on evolutionary grounds, but don't mention that evolutionary considerations offer a reason that is independent of all the psychological studies for believing in the reality of empathy-based altruism. Empathy may very well be "evolution's way" of ensuring the learning and maintenance of altruistic motivations. Finally, Cialdini et al. argue that empathy involves such an overwhelming sense of oneness and identification with another person that consequent helping motivation and action toward that other can't really be considered altruistic rather than egoistic. In *Altruism in Humans*, Batson makes a quite plausible reply to this objection to psychological altruism, and I make a somewhat different reply of my own in my "Egoism and Emotion" (forthcoming in *Philosophia*). But I don't think I should enter into the details here.

6. See his *Empathy and Moral Development: Implications for Caring and Justice*, Cambridge, UK: Cambridge University Press, 2000.

7. See Locke's *Second Essay on Government* in *Two Essays on Government*, Peter Laslett, ed., Cambridge, UK: Cambridge University Press, 1960.

8. Carol Gilligan, *In a Different Voice: Psychological Theory and Women's Development*, Cambridge, MA: Harvard University Press, 1982.

9. I say "virtuously open minded" because someone who will automatically agree with what (certain) people tell them is in a certain sense very open to others' opinions—open, in fact, in the way that children are open to their parents' opinions and attitudes (more on this below). But such *suggestibility* is not what we are talking about when we talk about the epistemic/intellectual virtues of open-mindedness or fair-mindedness. (The notion of the epistemic broadens the notion of the intellectual in order to include ordinary contexts of knowledge/belief acquisition or maintenance. Epistemic virtues are often contrasted with moral virtues, but the line is fuzzier than one might think, and the present book can help explain why.)

10. We also sometimes speak of or question the objectivity *of some body of knowledge*, but that, again, isn't the same thing as talking about how intellectually objective someone is with respect to such a body of knowledge. I am assuming, by the way, that objective or rationally justified knowledge is possible in certain areas. Whether or not that is true, the assumption allows me more easily to make the distinctions I am interested in here.

11. See *A Treatise of Human Nature*, ed. L. A. Selby-Bigge, New York: Oxford University Press, 1978, pp. 320–24, 346, 499, 589, 592, 605.

12. In what I have been saying, I have been influenced by Michael Stocker's "Intellectual Desire, Emotion, and Action" in A. O. Rorty, ed., *Explaining Emotions*, Berkeley: University of California Press, 1980, pp. 323–38. Stocker

emphasizes the fact of intellectual sympathy and other emotional aspects of intellectual/scientific thinking but doesn't press as far in a sentimentalist direction as I am doing here. Let me just add, however, that if intellectual open-mindedness is considered a virtue, it also makes sense to think of the disposition to be intellectually sympathetic to those who disagree with one as an epistemic virtue. Now empathy is widely considered to be some sort of psychological *mechanism*, but since the tendency to empathically take in others' favorable attitudes toward various arguments or opinions *amounts to* a tendency toward intellectual sympathy, I am inclined to regard such empathic dispositions as epistemically virtuous. (I am indebted on this point to suggestions made by Nel Noddings.)

13. One might try to undercut this conclusion by arguing that, unlike talk about favoring some person over others, talk about favoring one view over others is purely metaphorical. But what motive does one have to say such a thing other than a reluctance to admit that belief and so on involve some degree of emotion or affect? Surely those who say they favor a certain theory over others don't *think* they are speaking metaphorically.

14. What also shows that belief involves an emotional element is the way we react to people who deny or question what we think is obvious. We often react with a "come on now!" that expresses a certain degree of annoyance or irritation, and that indicates that we were emotionally invested in the truth of the proposition or belief that has been questioned *before* it was ever questioned. Consider a parallel with cases where the initial emotional investment is commonly recognized. If someone hurts a person I like, I will be angry or upset with him or her, and that reaction is surely a testimony to the emotional investment that loving and even liking someone involves and that preceded the hurt/harm to the person I like. The fact that when someone questions or attacks what I take to be perfectly obvious I will also tend to react with anger, annoyance, or upset is surely by the same token, then, a sign that my belief involved some sort of emotional investment or disposition before it was called into question.

15. Objectivity may require one to modify how one defends one's position in the face of criticisms and positive ideas deployed from a viewpoint inconsistent with one's own (let us for the moment assume that we are not talking about absolutely crazy ideas such as the belief that the world is about to end). Now in the *Metaphysics of Morals (Doctrine of Virtue,* paragraph 39), Kant says that paying respect to another in conversation means understanding that there is some merit in his or her ideas. And if we accept this, it would seem that changing how one defends one's views involves acknowledging some sort of merit in another person's ideas and to that extent respecting them. But if objectivity in some sense requires respecting other people's ideas or beliefs, that doesn't in any way work against the idea that objectivity is based in empathy. In an intellectual context, I want to say, empathy with ideas or viewpoints

is (a form of) respect, and ECE similarly argued that moral respect can be understood in terms of empathy with other people's desires and states of well-being.

The present discussion, finally, also suggests a parallel between what I said about justice in ECE and what can be said about justice in intellectual contexts. Being objective in empathic terms is tantamount to doing intellectual justice to other people's points of view, and ECE argued that justice as a moral ideal governing societies internally and in relation to other societies is also a matter of appropriate forms of *empathic* concern among individuals or governments. Intellectual and moral respect and intellectual and moral justice center on our capacity, respectively, for intellectual empathy and for individual-welfare-oriented moral empathy.

16. I am indebted to Seisuke Hayakawa on the subject of the distinction between objectivity and others aspects of rationality. For the opposed view that rationality and objectivity (in science) amount to pretty much the same thing, see Nicholas Rescher, *Objectivity: The Obligations of Impersonal Reason*, Notre Dame, IN: University of Notre Dame Press, 1997. But I think treating objectivity, being objective, as just one element in being cognitively or epistemically rational comes closer to ordinary thought and usage. (*Objective* and *nonbiased* seem closer to synonyms than *rational* and *nonbiased* do.) Finally, I should mention that although both intellectual rationality and intellectual objectivity are traditionally thought of as requiring emotional detachment vis-à-vis a given subject matter, I am here arguing for the contrary idea that full intellectual/cognitive rationality and the objectivity it requires as one of its elements depend on a *certain sort* of emotional *engagement*.

17. Compare Hoffman, op. cit., pp. 96–102. Hoffman thinks the anger he describes is a form of empathic response, but what I am saying will hold true even if such anger is only *based* in empathy. I am indebted here to discussion with Justin D'Arms.

18. Many years ago when we were students in the Boston area, David Lewis told me he thought intolerance toward certain views was entirely appropriate. I didn't at the time reject what he was saying, but neither did I see any way to defend it. Now I think I do.

But let me just add, too, that I don't want to claim that everyone who is incapable of empathy with opinions that disagree with his or her own counts as a closed-minded person whose views an open-minded person needn't take into account. People of very low intelligence and perhaps some children may be *incapable* of empathy with others' beliefs, but that doesn't make them closed minded or epistemically intolerant, and it may not be at all appropriate for an open-minded person to reject their views out of hand. Such people are not unwilling to empathize or resistant to empathizing with others' opinions, merely incapable of doing so, and that difference is relevant to how it is epistemically (or morally) appropriate for us to respond to them. Further, it can sometimes be epistemically supererogatory to be open minded toward those who *are* closed minded, and such supererogatory open-mindedness may sometimes even jump-start a meaningful exchange that would otherwise have never occurred. (In making these further points, I have been responding to the very helpful suggestions of a reader for OUP.)

But, finally, what about someone who defends the theory of evolution in a closed-minded way? Can an open-minded person in that case be epistemically intolerant of the theory itself and not just of the closed-minded defense that someone has offered on its behalf? Surely not. But there is a difference here from the case of someone who thinks s/he is Napoleon. We know in advance that any adult defending the latter belief is closed minded, and we can be intolerant of his or her belief on that basis and without having to hear any arguments he or she might want to offer in its defense. But in the case of evolution, we don't know that it can't or won't be defended in an open-minded way, so we can't reject belief in the theory of evolution out of hand, even if a certain intolerance toward some ways of defending evolution can be justified. (I am indebted here to discussion with David Copp.)

19. The "profile" of objective or open-minded people involves (roughly) their being empathic with the points of view of those who disagree with them unless the latter are lacking in empathy with those who disagree with *them*. Those who believe that they are Napoleon or that the Earth is flat don't meet or manifest this profile in various ways, but it is worth mentioning two interesting, specific ways in which they may fail to do so. First, self-styled Napoleons may not so much be intolerant of (what they take to be) the beliefs and evidence of those who disagree with them but may hold rather that everyone knows they are Napoleon and that there is a universal plot to deny them their rightful status or position. And they may be closed minded vis-à-vis anyone who questions their paranoid view of things. Second, flat earthers, rather than disdain to provide counterarguments to those who say the Earth is spherical, may provide a plethora of such. In that case, they may not show the epistemic intolerance/anger toward (what they take to be genuine) dissent and disagreement that a normal and open-minded person sometimes will show, but they will presumably be closed minded toward those who question their counterarguments. However, at some point a fuller study of the relation between "crazy" views and epistemic open-mindedness (or fair-mindedness or objectivity) needs to be undertaken.

In that connection, however, let me just briefly mention Heather Battaly's somewhat related views about open-mindedness. (See, e.g., her "Intellectual Virtue and Knowing One's Sexual Orientation" in R. Halwani, ed., *Sex and Ethics*, London: Palgrave Macmillan, 2007, esp. p. 158f.) Battaly's conception of open-mindedness is Aristotelian (and virtue epistemological) in the way my own approach here has been sentimentalist (and, in effect, also virtue epistemological), and she holds in particular that open-mindedness is an intellectual virtue that lies between dogmatism and naïveté. But I don't think her view puts enough emphasis on the ways a lack of empathy and intellectual sympathy can underlie dogmatism and justify reactions of epistemic intolerance or anger on the part of others. And her view also doesn't sufficiently recognize the nonvirtuous character of certain kinds of open-mindedness. Battaly thinks of the person willing to consider the possibility that the UN secretary-general has killed a London prostitute as naïve and *not* open minded. But, as I mentioned in an earlier footnote, it seems more natural and intuitive to think of such a person as *too* open minded or, as we might say, *naïvely* open minded. In that case, even if Battaly is right about what epistemically virtuous open-mindedness consists in, she doesn't seem to have captured the notion of open-mindedness as such. (Note, too, that we can more easily talk of someone's being epistemically too open minded than of someone's being, from an epistemic standpoint, too objective or fair minded—objectivity and fair-mindedness, unlike open-mindedness, are unconditional epistemic virtues. But as we shall see in the next chapter, total epistemic virtue may be inconsistent with certain sorts of love and friendship, so this whole issue turns out to be very complex.)

Finally, I should mention that *none* of the recent virtue epistemologists who speak of open-mindedness as a virtue recognizes the empathic and emotional/sympathetic aspects of open-mindedness. Virtue epistemology, as it has been practiced so far, has been influenced by Aristotle to the exclusion of Hume, and I am therefore advocating that virtue epistemologists should start exploring the sentimental side of the virtues they treat as central to epistemic justification and knowledge.

20. As I will be arguing at much greater length in chapter 2, objectivity probably shouldn't be regarded as an absolute human ideal, because there are times when we would rather see people be loving and act lovingly than be objective. In *Morals from Motives* (New York: Oxford University Press, 2001, ch. 5), I claimed—what seems very commonsensical—that a parent, say, who genuinely loves a child won't and can't, at least initially, be entirely objective about evidence that indicates the child has done something horrible or criminal. The parent will give the child more benefit of the doubt than an objective observer knowing all the same facts would, and if one has to choose between full epistemically rational objectivity and love, love should sometimes win. (This means that the Enlightenment ideal and recommendation of critical detachment/objectivity about all beliefs and ideas has at the very least to be qualified.) Note that in a situation where one isn't objective about the issue of what one's child has actually done, one isn't going to be empathic with the point of view of an objective observer who thinks one's child *has* done something criminal or horrible. In fact, one is likely to be angry with them. But *that's love!* These ideas deserve further and more elaborate discussion—and that will happen in chapter 2.

21. For two examples of the discussion and defense of these ideas, see R. Lulofs and D. Cahn, *Conflict: From Theory to Action*, Boston: Allyn and Bacon, 2000, chs. 11–12; and J. Zubek, D. Pruitt, R. Peirce, N. McGillicuddy, and H. Syna, "Disputant and Mediator Behaviors Affecting Short-Term Success in Mediation," *The Journal of Conflict Resolution* 36, 1992, pp. 546–72.

22. Thomas Kuhn's *The Structure of Scientific Revolutions* (Chicago: University of Chicago Press, 1970/1962) stresses the ways in which scientists resist new theories that clash with ideas they have long held, and it has sometimes been said that Kuhn is (thereby) committed to a relativistic or irrationalist view of science. I won't get into the question whether this is the correct interpretation of Kuhn's ideas, but it is perhaps worth noting that if one believes there is or could be such a thing as scientific objectivity and rationality, then the widespread resistance to new ideas (as possibly with Lorentz) may only show that various motives prevent people from being as empathically objective about scientific matters as it is at least in principle possible to be. But one should be cautious about assuming that older scientists are typically less objective than younger ones. After all, even if the older scientists are resisting change, the younger ones may be so eager for change and for the glory of having brought it about that they end up treating the ideas of their elders unfairly in empathic terms.

23. See, for example, Damasio's *Descartes' Error: Emotion, Reason, and the Human Brain*, New York: Putnam, 1994. To some extent, Damasio runs together empirical issues of causation and conceptual issues of metaphysical constitution, but the argument for saying that rationality involves feeling that I have offered in the present chapter in no way focuses on empirical issues of causal explanation (e.g., on the causal interactions/relations of rational and emotional factors). The conceptual point, rather, is that rationally holding beliefs and having beliefs in general *inherently* and *on a priori grounds* involve having certain feelings.

24. In *Moral Sentimentalism* (New York: Oxford University Press, 2010), I argue that it is no accident that our partialistic empathic tendencies are seconded by our moral opinions and intuitions. I argue there that this happens because our moral concepts and the judgments we make using those concepts essentially involve empathic processes and the concept of empathy (in a rudimentary form) itself. (More on this in chapter 9 below.)

   Furthermore, Hume recognizes and explains, via empathy, our moral partiality. But he doesn't seem to recognize the existence or value of cognitive partiality, and this is somewhat surprising, given Hume's emphasis on empathy, feeling, habit, association, and epistemology itself. However, the *Treatise* (ed., Selby-Bigge, esp. p. 323) actually mentions some factors of empathic influence that *could have been used* to support the sorts of conclusions about partiality I shall be defending in our next chapter.

Chapter 2

Epistemology and Emotion

EMPATHY, TRUST, AND LOVE

I hope the rather general title of this chapter will give one a premonition of how radical its main thesis will be—though I also hope that won't make the reader stop reading. Many writers on the emotions stress their relation, sometimes helpful, sometimes detrimental, to the acquisition and retention of knowledge or epistemically justified belief. But I am here arguing for something more central, more defining, in regard to both the emotions and epistemology. In the last chapter, I attempted to show how certain empathically based positive and negative feelings are essentially involved in such epistemic virtues as open-mindedness, fair-mindedness, and objectivity and also involved in simply *having* particular beliefs or viewpoints. In the present chapter, I want to argue that empathy-related emotion and/or feeling are an essential part of the way we *learn about the world*. By showing that emotions (and empathy) play a role in having beliefs and defending them open mindedly, chapter 1 works strongly against rationalist and Enlightenment ideas about human reason(ing). But it turns out that the most important emotions involved in childhood human learning also play a central role in other aspects of our lives, and I believe that what I will be saying now about those emotions and their role in human learning and human life in general will serve to undercut Enlightenment ideals and ideas more deeply than anything we saw in chapter 1.

To do all this, I want to build on what was said about empathy and objectivity in chapter 1. Empathy with others' beliefs or viewpoints is essential to objectivity and open-mindedness vis-à-vis such beliefs or viewpoints; having a belief (or even being a skeptic) involves having a favoring/favorable attitude toward some proposition, statement, or cognitive content, and the intolerance toward certain beliefs that even open-minded people feel (and that might be necessary to having any beliefs at all) involves negative feeling, what we can call epistemic and empathic anger toward the beliefs and sometimes toward those who maintain them. What I want to argue in the present chapter, however, is that the emotional/empathic elements are here from the start. Chapter 1 was primarily about adults and what it means for them to have beliefs and/or to maintain them in an open-minded way. But positive and negative emotions also play an essential role in the way a child learns about the world, the way we *come to have beliefs in the first place.* And the way such empathy-involving emotions affect us has a decisive influence (though it is not the only influence) on whether we have epistemic justification for believing the things we do. The last chapter didn't talk about how our beliefs originally come to be justified but focused exclusively on what it is to have a belief and how beliefs, points of view, or theories can be *defended* in an open-minded or objective—and to that extent rational—way. But even if open-mindedness and objectivity are primarily a matter of how one defends beliefs, not how one acquires them, there are—or epistemologists typically assume there are— rational ways to acquire beliefs, and we tend to think that having justified beliefs depends on our having acquired them in rational ways: e.g., via justified or rational modes of data processing or inference. (I am trying to put things in a way that doesn't entail or presuppose epistemological foundationalism.)

I want to argue here that any humanly recognizable form of childhood learning is based on empathic emotions and that questions about whether certain of our beliefs are epistemically/ rationally justified essentially depend, for their answer, on what we want to say about the relation between emotion(s) and epistemic/ rational justification. Certain emotions play a decisive or crucial role in childhood learning and shape all subsequent thought and belief in important ways, as well. So we have to ask ourselves how or whether the childhood learning process makes good sense or can be justified in epistemically rational terms and also how or whether our subsequent beliefs can be seen as justified or as having been arrived at in a justified manner. Our empirical knowledge of the nature and events of childhood will, I think, help us appreciate what can be said about these issues, but the conclusions I reach will arguably be valid independently of any assumptions about the empirical facts' actually obtaining. The actual facts help us to imagine or conceive things better, but they are not what our conclusions depend on. As I have already mentioned, this is essentially Kant's distinction between knowledge that begins with experience and knowledge that depends on experience, but in the present instance the distinction is going to lead us toward questioning Enlightenment (and Kantian) views about the nature of epistemically rational thought. If cognition, learning, and knowledge are thoroughly permeated and constituted by emotional factors, this goes against Enlightenment and rationalist views in a very deep way. But what we know and can learn about the emotions involved in human learning can also lead us toward a very positive and humane vision of human knowledge and human life. So the critique of Enlightenment and rationalist ways of thinking isn't just iconoclastic but offers or leads to a definite and, I believe, attractive and realistic alternative. But which emotions am I talking about so vaguely and portentously?

I believe that children are partial to their own parents' opinions or views and that love plays a constitutive role in that partiality. Where love is absent and hatred exists, this partiality can be destroyed or distorted, and I will talk more about this possibility in what follows. But my main point is that most children love and are loved and that this makes an enormous difference to how they learn about the world. Yes, they use their senses and their nascent and increasingly developed reasoning skills to learn things they need to know, but children also rely to an enormous extent on their parents and, in particular, on what their parents tell them or believe without telling them (something that children often pick up on). Most epistemology focuses on the epistemic standpoint or predicament of individuals or on individuals as situated in a certain kind of environment. But the individuals are rarely children, and the environment is rarely (specifically) that of the family, and I believe that epistemology has more to learn from what happens to and with children in family environments than it has ever realized.

I suppose feral children can learn a lot about the world without being *told* anything, but a great deal of what normal or ordinary children learn they learn *from* their parents. And since some things their parents tell them are false, it can be more generally said that children acquire many of their beliefs (and attitudes) by being told things by their parents. If the parent tells the child that mail doesn't arrive on Sundays, or that Santa Claus won't give her a present if she doesn't behave, or that the Earth is turning and moving, or that God loves her, the child will ordinarily or frequently believe what she is told. And in the above cases and many, many others, she will do so without having any independent evidence for the beliefs she picks up from her parents.[1] When she acquires beliefs in this way, she is in a very general sense relying on her parents' authority, on their "testimony" in regard to facts they presumably know better or more intimately/directly than she, during childhood, does or will; and philosophers have had a great deal to say about (arguments from) authority and testimony over the centuries. They have even sometimes spoken of the ways in which children trust their parents, but none of the discussions points up the crucial role love and empathy based on love play in such processes. The partiality of children to their parents and/or those they love never enters the discussion, but I believe that these are precisely the factors that help us understand the character of what children do or what happens to them when they pick up beliefs from their parents. And I will argue further that our understanding of what happens in those cases affects or should affect our whole understanding of human learning and epistemic rationality—and our picture overall of what human lives are *like*.

Let's talk first about how love affects a child's willingness or tendency to believe what his parents tell him. This is precisely what previous accounts of childhood reliance on parental "authority" omit to mention, but I think it is of crucial causal and epistemic relevance. If children are partial to their parents' beliefs and opinions more than to those of mere strangers—and how can we deny that they are?—that has to do with the special relationship they have with their parents (and perhaps certain other people they are intimate with). And that partiality is therefore part of, has to enter into, the explanation of how children learn on authority or trust certain kinds of parental "testimony." So let me give you a hypothesis about how children come to rely on or trust parental testimony or authority that seems to make sense of the relevant phenomena. Once we have the hypothesis, we can and will follow out its implications for epistemology, in general, and for Enlightenment views, in particular. But first let's see how plausible a hypothesis can be offered here.

We know—at least we have been told—a good deal about how empathy works in contexts that call for practical/moral action. And as I mentioned earlier, much of the psychology literature on moral development subscribes to the idea that our altruistic concern for (caring about) others is based on and powered by the development of (increasing) empathy.[2] Studies of empathy have shown that we are more empathic in regard to people whose pain or troubles we see (or perceive or witness) than about those whose pain or troubles we merely know about at second hand (or by description). "I feel your pain" works better and happens more often when we actually see the person we then empathize with, and, similarly, we tend to react more empathically to a child who seems to be drowning in shallow water right in front of us than we do to children whose grave risk of death we merely know about by description. Given that altruism involves empathy, that is also why we are more likely to help the first child than the second. (I have argued elsewhere that there is reason to think empathy enters into our moral concepts, and on that assumption we would also have an explanation of why we think it is morally much worse to ignore a child drowning right in front of us than not to write a check for Oxfam that would definitely save the life of some child in a distant country. I will have more to say about this particular issue in chapter 9.)

But empathy also affects our actions toward those near and dear to us. The very fact that we love them (or like them a great deal) and/or are related to them and/or share a life with them makes us identify with them more readily than we do with strangers, and this greater empathy, as before, makes us more likely, makes us have a stronger tendency or motive, to help them than to help others we don't know that well. Caring concern for the welfare of others is affected, among other things, by how much one loves or likes them, and it is the connection to processes of empathy that explains a good deal of how this happens. Empathy, therefore, helps account for a great deal in the ethical universe of caring and benevolence; it affects how we *act toward* others.[3] But I now want to argue that it also affects how we *receive* others' opinions. Differences in empathy play a role in belief-formation that philosophers have tended to ignore, and once we recognize that role and see its relation to emotions like love and hatred, we will be well on our way to a very different conception of human learning and knowledge and perhaps rationality, too, from anything maintained by (Enlightenment) rationalists or, as far as I know, anyone else.

If empathy makes a difference to how much we care, it also makes a difference to how open we are to others' viewpoints, opinions, or attitudes. But a child's tendency and/or willingness to take in his parents' beliefs depends on how much love he feels toward and from them because those attitudes, as we saw in the cases of caring activity just a moment ago, make the child feel greater empathy for or with those parents. So we need to talk about how the child comes to love his parents—*and to trust them.*

Presumably, this starts with the parents' loving and showing love toward the child. The parents—and if breast-feeding is involved, then especially the mother—feed and care for the child, and if they do so affectionately, all of that will in the normal course make a difference to how the child feels about them. Eventually, and I don't think I need to try to be more precise about this, the child comes to love the parents and starts to think of what will please or help *them*. (E.g., this is why a child may clean her room or eat up his vegetables at dinner.) Such thinking will to some extent involve empathy with her or his parents, with how they look at things, with their feelings or aspirations for her/him. But as I made clear earlier, various forms of empathy depend on cognitive and conceptual development. If the child has no notion of her parents as separate beings or of their independent wishes or desires, the kinds of empathy mentioned a moment ago cannot occur. Presumably, too, the child eventually trusts his parents to take good care of him: He trusts their intentions and motives and also their competency to deal with his needs.[4] But we can ask whether that trust is epistemically well founded or justified, and there are various ways of answering this question.

Most children have seen their parents take care of them in the past, so can't their trust in the parents' ability and desire to take care of them in the future be inductively justified? And by a certain age children will (if lucky) have seen many of the things their parents have said about the world confirmed in their own experience. Doesn't that give them an inductive epistemic justification for believing what the parents tell them in the future or what they have previously told them but hasn't yet been verified within the child's own experience? Perhaps so. But even if all this is true, it isn't clearly the basis for the children's belief in what their parents tell them. We know that children are *influenced by* and tend to *soak up* their parents' opinions and attitudes, and this process seems to be of the very same kind as occurs when we feel someone's pain or (Adam Smith's example) flinch when we see someone branded, or about to be branded, with a branding iron. In these latter cases, the causal influence, the working of empathy, takes place without the consent or even the knowledge of the person who has the empathic reaction. In such cases, rather, we are *receptive* to others' feelings (this is what I earlier called associative empathy), and the two examples just mentioned illustrate that possibility very plausibly. But isn't it also plausible to hold in parallel that children are receptive to their parents' opinions and attitudes and that they can soak/pick such things up in an automatic or involuntary fashion? If pain can spread by an empathic contagion, osmosis, or infusion that doesn't require any inductive inference, why shouldn't this happen with attitudes and opinions as well? Even if someone wants to claim that inductive inference can occur unconsciously and involuntarily, there still seems some reason to hold that some transmission of attitudes and opinions can occur via the same direct empathic processes that occur when we flinch at someone's (prospective) pain—and without any need for scientific-inductive reasoning to occur.[5]

What further supports the idea that inductive inference isn't involved here is the way in which children's trust of their parents seems to go beyond anything that could be inductively justified.

When the child is told that God loves him, he has seen his parents be right about lots of *other kinds* of factual issues, but he presumably hasn't seen his parents' opinions borne out on any other factual issue *like this one*. Surely, rational inductive caution would make him at least somewhat hesitate to make an inference about this new kind of subject matter. But no, the child rushes headlong into a belief in God or God's love. If this is wishful thinking, then it surely isn't inductively rational, but presumably what happens here isn't entirely a matter of wishful thinking and depends on his simply trusting in general what his parents tell him.[6] (I am assuming parents who deliberately lie to the child only very rarely and who aren't so ignorant themselves that what they say is sometimes disconfirmed by the child herself.) Such trust, again, is not based on or a matter of inductive rationality but rather is based in or on how the child feels about his parents. He loves and trusts them in a way that he doesn't trust and love *others,* and this causes him to empathize with them more than he does with others. *Such* empathy in the present instance, then, means taking in their views more readily (and automatically) than those of others. In fact, if the child really loves his parents, he will tend to trust them even if they have sometimes been mistaken in the past. Such errors might well unseat any rational inductive argument in favor of accepting something they tell him, but they won't undercut or much undercut the child's tendency to take in his parents' views and attitudes empathically.

This kind of trust thus goes beyond the evidence, and, as has been noted in the literature on trust, trust tends, in general, to go beyond evidence, to involve belief and other attitudes that are firmer than there is any epistemic or rational justification for them to be. (More on this below.) Similarly, the sheer firmness of the typical child's belief in what the parent tells him/her goes beyond the force of any rational inductive argument, and this, too, argues for a source or basis in empathy rather than induction. But there is another possibility.

Even if trusting one's parents' opinions isn't based in rational inductive inference, it may be rational if sheer testimony or the testimony of those who have some sort of authority over one is a separate and independent source or basis for epistemically rational belief. (Of course, I am not talking here about legal testimony but about being *told* something in a serious way.) In that case, trusting one's parents' opinions could be rationally justified even if no inductive argument could be given for believing what they tell one. Such a view was held by Thomas Reid, but at this point I think we need to treat it with some caution.[7] The child who trusts her parents believes what they tell her, more firmly or strongly than inductive reasoning can support, but by the same token, who is to say that that trust-based firm conviction in what the parents tell her doesn't outstrip any justification that testimonial authority can offer as an independent source of epistemic justification or, indeed, any justification that induction and testimony/telling can *together* provide in a given instance?

Suppose someone, a benign-looking stranger, tells us that the Declaration of Independence was actually signed on August 2, not July 4, 1776, (this is in fact the case). Presumably, we have some reason to believe that people who tell us this sort of thing are fairly reliable and, if Reid is right, the sheer fact that someone is telling us that it was signed on August 2 gives us some additional reason to believe what they are saying. But surely the support for the belief here isn't all that strong, and one wouldn't be rationally justified in having a firm opinion at that point. Inductive inference and any force testimony or telling has on its own don't seem sufficient to account for the strength of children's belief in what they are told by their parents, and that gives us two options.

First, we could say that such firm beliefs are not justified in epistemic/rational terms. And we could argue that the very firmness indicates the presence or activity of some nonrational process that brings about the belief. Since feeling someone's pain occurs in a nonrational manner (i.e., it has no rational or epistemic *justification*) we might want to say that the firmness of many of the beliefs children acquire from parents indicates that those beliefs also arise in a nonrational empathic fashion. But unlike pain, belief calls for evidence or an intuitive support, so if (the firmness and strength of) beliefs acquired from parents lack such a basis and are attributable to mediated associative empathy, then they are irrational or less than fully rational in epistemic terms.

But there is another possibility. We can, in parallel with what Reid said about testimony, claim that empathy is itself a source of epistemic justification—in which case we can say that beliefs empathically acquired from parents as a result of a child's love for and trust in them have a certain (prima facie) rational justification. This would, of course, mean that a child's belief in Santa Claus or God will be justified in epistemic terms. But let's not too quickly use this against what has just been proposed. Even if the child's firm belief is rational, it may not remain rational if he is exposed to people who question that belief and it remains as firm as before. Empathy leads us to have greater concern for loved ones than for strangers, but it also leads us to have some real concern for strangers, and we might then expect that someone who loves and trusts his/her parents and who is more empathically partial to (sharing) their opinions than they are to (sharing) opinions of others would still pay some serious attention to the opinions and arguments of people who disagree with them and their parents. If no such serious attention is paid, then the person isn't open minded and counts as having an irrationally firm belief in what the parents have told him/her. All this can be accommodated by the sort of view I am now focusing on, and so I don't think the idea that empathy and empathic partiality can be and are the source of rational epistemic justifications can be rejected out of hand. (I am asking the reader to be open minded at this point.) Our earlier understanding of the epistemic virtues of open-mindedness, fair-mindedness, and objectivity also seems to favor the idea that empathy can be a separate basis of epistemic reasons or rationality. If empathy is part of what it takes to be epistemically objective/open minded and *to that extent also epistemically rational*, why shouldn't empathy also have its own role in justifying the acquisition of beliefs in the first place?

However, there are, in fact, some reasons for doubting the sort of approach I have just briefly described, reasons that have made their appearance in the course of our previous discussion but that we haven't really yet focused on. I earlier mentioned the view that trust is often irrational or less than fully rational, that it can and does involve believing and expecting things that we have no rational justification for believing and expecting. And many people have also said and believed that love is irrational: at least in the sense that it by its very nature leads us to believe things we have no epistemic justification for believing and to do things it is irrational or imprudent to do. If love and trust are often less than fully rational, then we may suspect that the beliefs that our trust in and love for our parents lead us to empathically imbibe are also less than fully rational, and that would argue against the suggestion made just above that empathy is a separate source or basis of rational epistemic justification. But this, in turn, depends on seeing whether trust and love are as epistemically questionable as has sometimes been said, and it is to that task that I think we should now proceed.

HOW RATIONAL ARE LOVE AND TRUST?

Let us begin by talking about love. Trust presumably grows out of being loved and loving in return, and what we say about love may well carry over to the topic of trust, which is a more explicitly epistemic or doxastic (belief-related) concept than love itself is. But we shall have to see, one step at a time, and it makes the most sense to start with love.

We commonly think that love is blind and/or irrational, but much of what we have in mind here is that people are irrational about who they love and how much they love them, and we need to show how or that this relates to issues of belief. It relates to such issues in the first instance, I think, because if we believe people are blind in regard to who and how much they love, we typically do so because we think they are often blind to the moral and non-moral faults or misdeeds of those they love. And to that extent, we think people irrationally overestimate their loved ones and tend to irrationally remain ignorant of what their loved ones do that is wrong, stupid, unaesthetic, or even disgusting. (The literature of psychoanalysis is full of interpretations of this "overestimation.") Someone who really cares about or loves another person won't be as ready to believe the worst of them as someone who takes a more detached (emotional and doxastic) attitude—and it is not just a question of the person who loves or cares' knowing the person better and having reason to discount evidence that points to the worst (e.g., evidence that they have committed some crime) that a more detached observer will simply lack. The love will itself—in various degrees depending on the person—make the person resist a negative interpretation of the same evidence that a more detached observer would say pointed to misfeasance, disloyalty, weakness, or some other fault or inadequacy on the part of the person one loves or cares a great deal about. (The very fact that we are inclined to describe such love-influenced thinking as showing someone's *faith* in the probity or merits of their loved one is some indication that we think there is something epistemically irrational or less than fully rational about it.)[8]

Similarly, our love for someone can make us resist believing that bad things are likely to *happen* to that person. Indeed, I would go so far as to say that someone who doesn't have these epistemic tendencies doesn't fully love or care about a given individual.[9] Impartiality, a lack of partiality, detachment with regard to epistemic matters just aren't the way of genuine love and deep friendship. But it has sometimes been argued that these tendencies are in no degree epistemically irrational, that epistemic reasonableness follows the contours of love and affection rather than opposing or going against their tendencies.[10] I think this conclusion goes against our commonsense intuitions about these matters, and that is a strike against it. But if the conclusion were granted, that would favor the previously mentioned theory that says the process of empathically imbibing parental opinions and the beliefs thus arrived at are not, other things being equal, epistemically suspect or in any way irrational. If the beliefs about the goodness of the loved one or her favorable prospects that love entails are rationally acceptable and if love is inseparable from empathy with the loved one, then it is a very short step to the conclusion that beliefs arrived at through empathy with the opinions of a loved one are also epistemically acceptable. (We could even say that the belief that a loved one has good prospects is also arrived at through empathy with the loved one, just not empathy with the loved one's *opinions*.)

So the two views—that love's overestimation of good qualities/prospects is rationally acceptable and that love's tendency to take in opinions and attitudes from the loved one is rationally acceptable—go together, but, of course, and this is the main point, the denial of both these views also constitutes a coherent whole. We normally tend to think that love's overestimations are epistemically at least to some degree irrational, and if we accept that common intuition, we have philosophical reasons to hold that the imbibing of firm opinions from parents (or others) is also epistemically at least to some degree irrational (as such and independently of actual evidence). And someone who accepts *this* view will probably also want to say that the epistemic fault here lies with empathy itself: that however good and morally desirable empathy may be, it tends to interfere with epistemically rational processes or inferences and lead people to *become* somewhat irrational or at least momentarily *think* somewhat irrationally. We therefore have a choice, an epistemological or theoretical choice to make between two ways of understanding the epistemic and epistemological significance of (partialistic) empathy and (partialistic) emotions based in empathy. *But either way empathy and feeling/emotion turn out to be of greater epistemological significance than has previously been realized.* Let me explain this a bit.

If love makes us (somewhat) irrational, both as regards the prospects/qualities of loved ones and vis-à-vis their opinions and attitudes/motives, then a life in which love exists will contain a great deal of irrationality. If we say this, then, although we are not giving up the epistemic/epistemological standards or ideals that have led Enlightenment thinkers and other epistemological rationalists to criticize the beliefs that religion and love often lead us to, we have still recognized that enlightened/epistemic rationality has a less important place in our lives than rationalists and Enlightenment thinkers have tended to think. Such thinkers have tended to hold that one should always be rational and impartial about evidence.[11] But if it turns out, as most of us now think, that love entails or constitutively involves being partial about such matters and if we hold, with the rationalists, that this means that love involves our being to some extent irrational, then we have to think we should be more epistemically irrational than rationalists and Enlightenment thinkers would like us to be and think we should be—or else we have to claim that love and friendship are less important to life than many of us now think, precisely because they entail so much irrationality.[12]

This latter thought is not really open to us nowadays. Romanticism has convinced us of the value and importance, for human lives, of passion or, at the very least, love and other feelings/emotions. So what we have said so far vindicates Romanticism against the Enlightenment ideal of total rational impartiality with respect to evidence and ideas/beliefs. It follows, then, that Enlightenment thinkers can plausibly hold on to their standards of epistemic rationality only at the cost of admitting—something they would be very reluctant to admit—that (epistemic) rationality is a lot less important to life than they have always assumed. And if the rationalists decide to move in the different direction of admitting the rational bona fides of beliefs arrived at through empathy, then they can retain their belief in the importance of epistemic rationality to human lives but will (for reasons beyond and additional to the considerations concerning objectivity and open-mindedness that were described in chapter 1) have to give up on their view that such rationality is a matter of something other than feeling and involves suppressing feeling or keeping it in rational check. And this would, again, be to give up something that has always been a vital and essential part of the rationalist/Enlightenment view of the world.

But where do I stand on the issues involved here? Do I think empathy tends to *go against* rationality or that it constitutes the basis for an often-ignored *form* of epistemic rationality? I am not entirely sure what to say, but my inclination is to agree as much as I can with common opinion here and in other areas. I think most of us think that the overestimation of a loved one's life prospects or virtues is, to some degree, epistemically irrational, and that goes with saying that opinions we take in via loved-based empathy are also epistemically unjustified.[13] Given the importance of love and friendship in our lives, that may mean that much more is irrational and epistemically unjustified in our lives than we have previously realized. But I am inclined to think that that would only go to show

how wrong the Enlightenment and rationalists have been about the importance of epistemic rationality. Their rational *standards* of belief formation and belief retention may remain at that point intact, but their overestimation of rationality itself, their *idealization* of rationality, would be strongly rejected, and epistemic rationality would turn out to interfere with much of what is important in life in ways that Romanticism clearly pointed to and that rationalism has never been able or willing to recognize.[14] (It would also turn out that empathy is *necessary to full epistemic rationality* but in certain ways also makes us susceptible to the *epistemic irrationalities* that are endemic to love, friendship, and other things we value about our lives.)

What about trust? Well, trust seems to supervene on love, and many psychologists think that the ability to trust is essential and basic to a good human life.[15] But unlike love, trust wears its relevance to epistemology on its sleeve. Trust is a tendency to believe things that someone trusted tells one (also to believe that he or she wants and is able to help one), and some people have claimed that the trust children feel toward their parents and what they tell them is justified on a rational/inductive basis. But for all the reasons given above, the sheer strength and firmness of most children's trust (or faith) in their parents argues against this kind of explanation, and it is more plausible to suppose that that trust (or faith) derives from love and the empathy that it involves. Empathy leads most of us to be epistemically partial to what our parents tell us, and the empathy is part and parcel of our love for them. But the epistemic partiality is itself just trust: It is what trust (or a certain kind of faith) is, so I am saying that trust turns out at least in part to be a love-and-empathy-based form of epistemic partiality. We saw reasons above to think such partiality is, to at least some degree, irrational, but there are also some reasons to think that the partiality of trust is just an often ignored/new form of epistemic rationality. Different philosophers have actually taken (these) different positions on the subject.[16] But my own tendency, as I have indicated, is to say that empathy-based trust and/or faith are rationally unjustified but necessary to or involved in emotions/feelings/relationships that are essential to living well. Trust and faith in people are part of our lives for better, rather than for worse; and we have to learn to live with the thought that we are and sometimes have to be less than fully rational. This may be harder for philosophers than for ordinary people—who, after all, one often finds saying things like: I believe on faith; it may be irrational, but that doesn't make me believe any the less. We philosophers may have to learn to say things like this, though we don't perhaps have to learn to say them about religion. I am far from saying that religious faith, or a self-acknowledged irrational belief in God, is part of any good life. We need love and friendship, and it is just not clear that we need religious faith in the same way.

But, on the other hand, religious faith may be a part of what makes certain lives good. We can't any more argue that its tight connection with irrationality makes faith dubious as a good thing in life—that would, according to what I am now saying, mean that love, too, isn't a good thing (for us). We clearly don't want to say that, so I see no reason to hold that epistemically irrational religious faith can't be a good thing. And in the case of the children of parents who have religious faith, the love those children may feel toward their parents can open them up to the acceptance of their parents' irrational religious opinions and attitudes. And it may well be that if children really love their parents and enjoy their parents' love, they don't have much of an option here. Perhaps when they are adults, their coming to new beliefs and to rejecting their parents' religious opinions will be consistent with loving their parents. But if a child of religious parents has a good and loving relationship with them (some religious parents are punitive and harsh toward their children), the child will almost inevitably imbibe their faith, and this will be another instance where a life good at least for a certain period of time (for constitutive reasons) requires someone to be less than fully rational. And, again, we can also imagine an adult who has imbibed religious faith in that way retaining that faith as part of his whole relationship with his elderly parents. Such a person might even admit that he was epistemically irrational, that his religious belief was based in faith, not reason. And here, interestingly, the faith and any hopes of a hereafter that it involves are based in trust that is itself based on love.[17] So Saint Paul may at least have been on the right *philosophical* track when he spoke of faith, hope, and love (*caritas*, often translated "charity") and said that "the greatest of these is love." And if the love Saint Paul spoke of is ultimately not our own but that of God herself, that, too, parallels the claim that empathically derived religious faith and hope on the part of children ultimately depends less on the children's own love than on the love they get from their parents.

Some final points. I argued in chapter 1 that we need empathy to help us be objective and open minded and, to that extent, epistemically rational about what we believe, but in the present chapter I have claimed—although somewhat tentatively—that empathy often makes us *less* objective and *less* epistemically rational. And there is at the very least a tension between these ideas. When we love, we can't be entirely objective either about the merits or about the beliefs/attitudes of the persons we love. We will be partial to the person's opinions/attitudes as compared with the opinions/attitudes of those we know less well or merely know about. So it would seem that perfect or thoroughgoing objectivity is something we cannot achieve unless our lives are starved of significant relationships, and it is also unclear that any individual lacking such relationships could ever *be taught* or *become motivated* to be completely objective about everything. (I am indebted on this last point to Heather Battaly, and I shall say just a bit more about it below.)

Nonetheless, open-mindedness (and fair-mindedness) may well be different. Even if an individual gives preference, in a less than objective way, to the opinions of those he loves or knows best, he may still be open to and respectful toward everyone's opinions—even when he disagrees with them. In moral cases, our greater empathy for near and dear isn't inconsistent with substantial empathic concern for people generally, and I think the same sort of thing can be said for empathy with other people's opinions. In that case, we can claim that someone who is open to or about everyone's views (except in the cases that understandably generate epistemic intolerance/anger) can count as an open-minded or fair-minded person, even if love makes them somewhat partial to the opinions of those they know best. Such a person isn't perhaps fully objective or fully rational in regard to everyone's views, but he may still exemplify the less extreme or demanding epistemic virtues of open-mindedness and fair-mindedness.

However, things are a bit more complicated than I have so far indicated. In chapter 1, I described the epistemic anger that another person's closed-mindedness can evoke in us, but there is another kind of epistemic anger that also needs mentioning in the light of all we have been saying in the present chapter. If someone, on the basis of an objective reading of the evidence, tells us that our sister or father has committed some crime, we may react with epistemic intolerance/anger because of the love we bear our sister or father.[18] Our epistemic anger can thus be a *sign* of a certain degree of entirely understandable, love-based closed-mindedness on our own part and not just a *reaction* to the closed-mindedness of others. On the subject of the faults, defects, or misdeeds of those we love, we may never achieve real epistemic fair-mindedness or open-mindedness—much less epistemic objectivity. But what we have said may still indicate how fair-mindedness and open-mindedness *are* possible for us *on other subjects*.

But wait! Won't many other subjects in fact be "infected" by our tendency to be closed minded in regard to the faults and misdeeds of those we love? My love of my father, say, will make me resist the idea that he is vain or has acted criminally, even when objective evidence favoring that conclusion is available to me. But won't that love then also make me resist thinking that my father's beliefs or attitudes are misguided, and won't that tend (independently of but possibly reinforced by processes of empathic osmosis) to make me less than open minded about any subject my father has pronounced upon or taken a visible attitude toward? A certain kind of epistemic *irrationality sprawl* may well be inevitable when we love (or, for that matter, when we feel hatred or antipathy), and the forces that love or feeling more generally sets in motion against epistemic open-mindedness can thus come to seem rather formidable. Still, I think the child who has been taught to venerate the Virgin Mary or Mohammed can become—under the guidance of the right teachers—the philosophy student in college who is open minded enough to consider antireligious arguments seriously and from the standpoint of those—professors, teaching assistants, or fellow students— who propose them. Irrationality sprawl doesn't have to encroach on most of our beliefs, but we need a close study of how the "forces" of open-mindedness and of closed-mindedness can and do interact in our lives. And I really have no space to do that here—though I can't resist adding that some of this will depend on whether religious or politically committed parents encourage their children to be open minded or are themselves usually open minded.

In any event, it should at this point be clear that rationality has a much less important role to play in human life than epistemological rationalists have believed. But I don't think that means that someone who is partial to the beliefs/attitudes of those they love and who is somewhat closed minded about their faults/misdeeds (with the irrationality sprawl that entails) can't count as fair minded or open minded *on the whole*. And, despite the fact that I have claimed that epistemic irrationality is to some extent necessary both to good human lives and to human life itself, it should be clear that I am not defending any sort of general irrationalism here. I have treated open-mindedness and objectivity, to the extent we can embody them, as cognitive virtues but have argued, too, that we need room for things that entail at least some degree of irrationality in our lives. Perhaps it could be said that I am advocating or even idealizing a certain kind of balance between epistemic rationality and irrationality in human life, which would then represent a kind of middle ground between Enlightenment-type and present-day rationalism and an epistemic irrationalism of the kind that is arguably attributable to Nietzsche and/or Dostoyevsky. In a later chapter, this balance or "dynamic opposition" will be folded into our discussion of the larger opposition and/or balance between rational control and receptivity. But let me, by way of concluding the present discussion, go back to some themes I raised earlier.

Above, I spoke about some issues and problems of epistemic motivation, and I would like now to say something briefly and positively about how the epistemic virtue of open-mindedness or fair-mindedness can be inculcated or educated for. (Here I am abbreviating what is said at greater length in my *Education and Human Values: Reconciling Talent with an Ethics of Care*, Routledge, 2012.) Induction à la Hoffman can empathically sensitize children or sometimes even adults to the harm or pain they have caused, and this can eventually result in a more caring attitude toward the welfare and wishes of others. But something similar can happen with open-mindedness. If a child, at home or in school, makes fun of another child's religious beliefs or of some (possibly exaggerated) claim that the other child makes, then a parent or teacher can intervene and explain how hurtful such intolerance or disrespect can be or has been. An epistemically directed inductive discipline can help instill open-mindedness (and a certain degree of objectivity), and I believe there is no reason why this virtue and its motivational underpinnings have to lie beyond our normal human powers. But, as I indicated above, sheer or complete objectivity or total epistemic rationality is another matter, and it is difficult, if not impossible, to see how someone could ever (become motivated in such a way as to) be totally objective about people's beliefs. It is not clear that even someone with no personal attachments to make them partial to certain people's beliefs could ever be motivated to become totally objective—because as various writers have pointed out, the process of induction only works if the teacher or parent doing the inducing has a good relationship with the person he or she is trying to improve or educate, and how could someone lacking in love relationships ever develop good and trusting relationships with *anyone*? And how is someone going to subliminally imbibe objectivity from others (assuming such others exist) unless the person has a close relationship with those others and is thus not going to be thoroughly objective about forming or retaining beliefs? So if we *were* objective, that would undercut or conflict with relationships we need and value, and there is reason to doubt or wonder whether any human ever *could* develop such an extreme form of humanly undesirable intellectual/epistemic virtue. But open-mindedness and fair-mindedness are different, and I believe there is no reason to think these virtues are beyond our powers or have to clash with the epistemic partiality that arises out of and is necessarily attached to certain kinds of important human relationships.

This completes what I want to say here about epistemic rationality as it is exemplified (or not) in the epistemic/cognitive virtues of open-mindedness and objectivity. But having spoken at length about epistemic rationality, its place in Enlightenment views, and the very different place it has in a psychologically realistic and ethically adequate picture of human life, we need to consider another side of Enlightenment/rationalist thinking: the emphasis on *practical* rationality and its grounding role in morality. As against such views, I want to argue that morality is based in feeling, not in practical rationality, and I will also claim some of our highest ethical/moral ideals actually run counter to practical rationality, a conclusion that doesn't at all fit with Enlightenment or rationalist thinking. We shall discuss all this in the next two chapters.

NOTES

1. I shall concentrate on beliefs rather than attitudes because (Enlightenment) rationalists are more than willing to allow that acquiring and having attitudes can essentially involve emotions or feelings (not to mention desires, intentions, and/or motives). They don't think ordinary beliefs entail or involve this sort of thing, and that is why we need to focus specifically on the origins of beliefs. Note, too, that what I am saying about parents applies with some qualifications to guardians, adoptive parents, and foster parents who love a given child, though they aren't related to her. If the child eventually realizes or is told that she isn't related by blood to these others, a factor that supports empathy will be absent: The sense and acknowledgement of common roots or origins increases empathy and partiality both in moral/practical contexts and in purely epistemic ones (to the extent they are possible). But obviously this is compatible with a great deal of love toward the child and on the part of the child.

2. See the discussion of the relationship between empathy and altruism in the main text and in footnote 3 of chapter 1.

3. When we feel others' painful feelings, we are in an important way open or receptive to them, so even when such empathy leads us to act, to be active, in regard to others, there is often or typically a passive or nonactive element in the process. However, when we take in the opinions of others, say, our parents, we are *overall* less active than in cases where empathy calls for or instigates *actions*.

4. On the relations between trust and competency, see Karen Jones, "Trust as an Affective Attitude," *Ethics* 107, 1996, pp. 4–25.

5. Hume lays great stress on the empathic transmission or contagion of beliefs and attitudes. See *A Treatise of Human Nature*, Selby-Bigge, ed., New York: Oxford University Press, 1978, pp. 320–24, 346, 499, 589, 592, and 605. But Hume himself was influenced here by Nicolas Malebranche's *Search after Truth*, Cambridge, UK: Cambridge University Press, 1997, esp. book V.

6. You might say: If the taking in of beliefs occurs via empathy with those beliefs, then how can the child swallow a belief in Santa Claus from parents who don't believe in him? Well, an extraordinarily sensitive child might hesitate to believe if she somehow empathically sensed some hesitation or guilt in the parents' statements about Santa Claus. But parents are pretty good at feigning enthusiasm and belief in Santa Claus—partly through memory of their own similar belief, partly out of excitement and joy at what they take their child's excitement and joy will be. Empathy arguably does work via certain concepts and beliefs, and someone can therefore empathically come to "feel someone's pain" as a result of seeing someone pretending to be in pain. (Too bad this couldn't have happened in the Milgram experiments, but someone might argue that the failure to stop the infliction of supposed pain was at least partly due to an unconscious sense that the subjects who seemed to be in pain were just acting. Subliminal empathy might actually have been at work here. Who knows?) In any event, and as with faked pain, if the parents do a good job of pretending to believe in Santa Claus, the child should be able to empathically pick up a belief in Santa Claus.

7. See Thomas Reid, *An Inquiry into the Human Mind on the Principles of Common Sense* in R. Beanblossom and K. Lehrer, eds., *Thomas Reid's Inquiry and Essays*, Indianapolis: Bobbs-Merrill, 1975, VI. In *An Enquiry Concerning Human Understanding* (in P. H. Nidditch and L. A. Selby-Bigge, eds., *Hume's Enquiries*, Oxford, UK: Oxford University Press, 1975, X, p. 111), Hume makes it clear that he regards it as reasonable to trust testimony only if one has independent reason to think that testimony reliable, and Reid is clearly reacting to and against Hume. But given Hume's views here, it is not perhaps surprising that Hume never claimed that any beliefs that we may empathically pick up from parents are automatically invested with some prima facie justification. Hume was antireligious, and it would probably have been galling to that side of him to have to acknowledge or hold that children can be justified in believing in miracles or God on the basis of their parents' say-so. So galling, I believe, that he missed out on or ignored the possibility that the same empathy that grounds our (sense of the virtuousness of) partiality of concern vis-à-vis others' welfare could also ground and justify partiality toward our parents' beliefs and thus give us epistemic reason to believe or at least make it understandable that we should believe what they tell us on religious matters. But we are going to explore that possibility here.

    Incidentally, I argued in *Moral Sentimentalism* (New York: Oxford University Press, 2010) that Hume's account of morality in terms, partly, of the so-called artificial virtues leaves him with a politically more conservative view of our moral obligations and of social justice than I was defending—without recourse to the artificial virtues—in that book. In the present context, however, I am consciously taking a *more* conservative position than Hume adopted. I am leaving it open that children's religious faith *may* be epistemically justified in a way that Hume presumably wouldn't have allowed.

8. In *The Limits of Loyalty* (Cambridge, UK: Cambridge University Press, 2010, ch. 2 and see esp. p. 30), Simon Keller argues that friendship can make one epistemically partial and less than fully rational but also says that *some* friendships can involve and even depend on "friends regarding each other with an uncompromising lack of bias." I think this may be true of friendships that don't involve and aren't based on mutual love, but I don't see how love can be love and still be epistemically impartial and objective. If a parent, spouse, or friend too quickly goes along with the objective evidence against his or her child, spouse, or friend, then the attribution of love to them is, I think, constitutively undermined.

9. Two caveats: Someone whose love or concern for another makes him somewhat reluctant to think that bad things are happening or going to happen to someone *may have reasons derived from his love or concern to try to counteract that very tendency.* (This also applies to the tendency to overestimate those we love.) Knowing or sensing that (my) love or concern inherently involves such reluctance but realizing, too, say, that I am responsible for the well-being of my physically or mentally challenged child, I may have reason or motive to force myself to be alert to possible problems and dangers for that child and, more generally, to work against my feelings' tendency toward wishful thinking. But no one ever said that caring about others and love were simple or easy.

Second, love may have a tendency to panic at seemingly bad news. A parent may want to think well of her child's prospects, but if the child goes off in a bus on a school picnic and news of a fatal accident involving a school bus later comes via radio or television, won't some loving parents tend to imagine/ fear/think the worst? Absolutely! But if further information isn't available for hours, wishful, hopeful thinking will also occur in such a parent (e.g., they may bargain with God). Hopefulness will tend to reverse or counteract the initial panic, and both parts of this process are indicative of love. In any event, one doesn't expect a loving parent, in the absence of further information, to settle into the firm belief that his or her child is dead. (This *might* happen if a parent were clinically depressed, but doesn't depression interfere with a person's capacity to love and care about others, to get outside themselves?) Further, if new evidence comes in that leaves the fate of the child in doubt, the loving parent will (eventually) adopt a more hopeful or optimistic attitude about (what) that evidence (shows) than detached observers would likely have.

10. See, for example, Adam Morton, "Partisanship" in B. McLaughlin and A. Rorty, eds., *Perspectives on Self-Deception*, Berkeley: University of California Press, 1988, pp. 170–82. Morton never clearly distinguishes between the view that the beliefs (e.g., in our beloved's special merits) that love leads us to are *epistemically* rational and the view that it is *practically* (or *adaptively*)

rational to allow oneself to love—even knowing that that will make one epistemically irrational—because of all the potential benefits of loving. In any event he doesn't seem entirely convinced that love's overestimations have to be considered epistemically justified. For related use of the just-mentioned distinction, see, for example, Patricia Greenspan's "Emotions, Rationality, and Mind/Body" in R. Solomon, ed., *Thinking about Feeling: Contemporary Philosophers on Emotions*, New York: Oxford University Press, 2004, pp. 129f.

11. For further description of the historical origins and character of such Enlightenment thinking and of the epistemological debates that have subsequently taken place concerning its validity, see, for example, Peter Forrest's "The Epistemology of Religion" in the online *Stanford Encyclopedia of Philosophy* and Cheshire Calhoun's "Subjectivity and Emotion" in R. Solomon, ed., op. cit., p. 111f. The present discussion, with its emphasis on the tie-in between empathy and important human relationships, provides, I believe, a quite new sort of criticism of Enlightenment thought—and one that we shall see helps move us toward a quite general critique of the Faustianism of Western philosophy.

Incidentally, the most familiar example of the Enlightenment view that we should always believe in accordance with the evidence is W. K. Clifford's "ethics of belief" (see his *The Ethics of Belief and Other Essays,* reprinted by Prometheus Books, 1999). And William James famously criticized Clifford's views in his essay "The Will to Believe" (in *The Will to Believe and Other Essays in Popular Philosophy*, New York: Longmans, Green, 1897). But although both James and I invoke emotional/sentimental factors in arguing against Clifford, I have decided not to discuss James's criticisms because they don't seem to me to be particularly convincing. I think that what we are saying here about love and other emotions has a much better chance of undermining (Clifford's) Enlightenment assumptions about epistemic rationality.

Note further, and finally, that Hume's opposition to belief in miracles and other aspects of his philosophy put him pretty clearly on Clifford's side vis-à-vis the question of whether we should always believe in accordance with the rational weight of our evidence. To that extent, Hume, for all his emphasis on the emotions both inside and outside morality, *is nonetheless in an important sense an epistemological rationalist*. Of course and unlike, say, Leibniz, he doesn't believe we can learn about the world via a priori reasoning: He is, in that sense, an empiricist rather than an epistemological rationalist. But in another sense he can be seen as an epistemological rationalist because he holds or seems to hold that we should always believe in accordance with rational evidence. And clearly I am in this sense defending an antirationalist view in this book.

12. Compare Kant's claim in the *Critique of Judgment* (J. Meredith, trans., Oxford, UK: Clarendon Press, 1978, p. 294) that "not taking in others' views uncritically is what enlightenment is all about."

13. In "Epistemic Partiality in Friendship" (*Ethics* 116, 2006, pp. 498–524), Sarah Stroud discusses the pros and cons of regarding the "overestimations" of love and friendship as having a distinctive epistemic justification. She is fairly neutral on this issue, but she also seems to place less emphasis on common opinion than I do.

14. By (epistemological) rationalism, I here mean simply the view that we should always be or try to be epistemically rational, not the more well-known view that our knowledge of the world is fundamentally a priori, the view we think of as paired with and opposed to empiricism. (Compare footnote 11.) But note, too, that what I have just been saying about the love of others may apply to what is often called self-love. If love makes us think better of our loved ones' merits and prospects than epistemic rationality would dictate or allow, doesn't our proprietary concern for and interest in ourselves also make us prone to epistemically unjustifiable wishful thinking about our own merits and future prospects? And is this any more a contingent matter than it is contingent that loving other people will make us think (overly) optimistically or wishfully about *them*? If we are really to be epistemically rational, we may have to give up on our own self-love, something that is no more possible for most of us than it is possible to give up certain feelings and relationships of love vis-à-vis others. Self-love may not have the same ethical value that love for others does, but even so, the epistemological rationalist seems to be insisting on something that isn't possible for most human beings: simply because we can't give up self-love or the love of (particular) others. So bringing in self-love makes the rationalist position seem even more unrealistic and implausible than it does when one focuses solely on issues of love toward others (or friendship). (In addition, the irrational aspects of self-love that I have just called attention to interact with the various other factors/phenomena we have been or will be discussing; but I am not going to consider those further complexities here.)

15. Erik Erikson (*Childhood and Society*, New York: Norton, 1950) is the most famous. How love helps establish trust is an interesting question we needn't speculate about. Also, children need their parents' love even if those parents are distant or harshly punitive, and taking in such parents' opinions and attitudes can be a kind of unconscious attempt to get more love (or at least *something!*) from them. This is more complicated than I can (or need) explain here: the main point being that the children of unloving parents may nonetheless reach out for their parents' love and that this sad and, one can hope, rarer form of love or need may also involve the imbibing of parental opinions and trust in what their parents tell them.

16. Compare Jones, op. cit., with R. M. Adams ("The Virtue of Faith," *Faith and Philosophy* 1, 1984, pp. 3–15), who very clearly asserts that trust involves beliefs that go beyond the evidence.

17. Of course, I don't mean to deny that faith can come about independently (and sometimes even against the grain) of parental influence. But I don't think this is *usually* the case.

18. Jane Statlander-Slote has pointed out to me that even if anger tends to separate people from each other, a willingness to tell someone that one is angry with him and to explain why may be a sign of how good one's relationship with him is. If someone tells me my sister has committed a crime and I become angry with him as a result, the relationship may not suffer grave damage if I care enough about the person to tell him how angry he is making me and why.

Chapter 3

Caring and Enlightenment

In our last chapter, we saw some reasons to think that epistemic rationality is less important than many of us have thought. A certain degree and certain kinds of epistemic/cognitive/intellectual irrationality are essentially involved in and with emotions that are central to our lives, emotions such as love and strong concern for others that form the core of many of those relationships that we find most important to our well-being and happiness. But the reasons I have just said we saw are themselves epistemic/cognitive/intellectual: They are or purport to be reasons of *theory*, of good philosophical theorizing. So cognitive/intellectual rationality in the form of philosophical reasoning and theory dictates, relative to Enlightenment beliefs, its own lesser importance in important areas of human life. And what I have just said also has the form of a skeptical reductio ad absurdum, with reason's assumption of its own powers leading to a partial, but substantial, denial or undermining of the great importance of those powers. But what I expressed and argued in the last chapter wasn't skepticism. I relied and continue to rely on analytic thought—others' and my own—to deal with and reason through philosophical issues. And I assume that a certain sensitivity to psychological and other facts on the ground can also be helpful to the philosopher.

What we have arrived at so far is a picture of the epistemic side of our lives that is willing to make very positive *claims* about that side of our lives and that seeks to accommodate, explain, and even justify some of our deepest human values by reference to epistemic/ epistemological issues. If I am skeptical about the all-important character or significance of epistemic reason in some of its aspects, an importance that Enlightenment-type rationalism has always assumed and still does, it is skepticism exercised, I hope and believe, on behalf of values that I have argued are at least as important and in relevant areas of life more important than epistemic/cognitive/ intellectual rationality and justification. I am no skeptic about the importance and validity of those values, and what I think we should replace Enlightenment assumptions and ideals with is very definite and very hopeful about human good and human moral possibilities. To favor love and friendship over epistemic rationality, given the conflict that I have argued is inevitable between them, is to tell people they should be less worried about being epistemically irrational than rationalists tell us we should be. But it is also to tell us that moral values are very important to human life. One cannot be a friend or genuinely love someone unless one cares about the person and wants to promote his or her welfare (and see the person's welfare promoted by others as well), and these are moral attitudes and goals on just about any account of what morality is. If love and friendship are important and valued in a way that hostile relationships and even merely competitive ones are not, that is at least in part because morality is so important to us. And so what I said in the last chapter argues against the overwhelming or overriding importance of epistemic rationality by adducing facts and considerations that favor the importance of morality. This isn't skepticism or iconoclasm; it's a very specific (though quite general) philosophical picture that emphasizes certain values at the expense, to some extent, of others—something we can expect any moral philosopher, not just skeptics or iconoclasts, to do.

It is very difficult to emphasize and argue for the importance of morality without favoring some values over others. No one, as I take it, had a higher estimation of morality's status and powers than Kant did, but his vision played down the value and importance of the emotions and physical desire both in life itself (remember the remarks in *Groundwork* about wishing to be free of bodily inclinations) and in the elaboration of foundations for moral thought and practice (Hutchesonian sentimentalism is criticized for offering a material end for morality [namely, human welfare] that, according to Kant, treats morality as having a less exalted status than it actually has and deserves).[1] And the sentimentalist vision/conception of morality that Hutcheson, Hume, Gilligan, Noddings, and I myself favor treats feeling and emotion as more central to the moral life and to the foundations of morality than Kant did and Kantians nowadays do. Leaving Hutcheson aside, however, we can say that Hume *doesn't* treat what we ordinarily think of as morality as having any very special status among our values. Hume famously declines to distinguish between presumably moral traits such as honesty and gratitude and traits such as wit, agreeableness, and humor that are ordinarily not regarded as moral virtues or, indeed, as virtues of any kind at all; and that, I think, is because his empiricism, his philosophically hedonistic tendencies, and his incipient utilitarian thinking led him to see all these traits in terms of whether they immediately please people and whether they lead to pleasure in the longer run. Utilitarianism has a tendency to run all virtues and values together under the rubric of producing or failing to produce good hedonic results, and, as is well known, it is even difficult for utilitarianism to treat aesthetic values as separate or fundamentally different from moral ones.[2] So utilitarianism and Hume don't treat morality as different from and having a greater value than other forms of value or evaluation, and in that respect they differ greatly from Kant.

But certain forms of sentimentalism can, in fact, treat morality as having a special status and importance, and the kind of sentimentalism I favor does precisely that. More importantly, though, if the kind of care-ethical sentimentalism I favor is on the right track, then what makes morality important is different, very different, from what Kant thinks makes it important. In some sufficiently broad and vague sense, the Enlightenment saw our capacity for reason and reasoning as central to our dignity and our lives, and that preeminent Enlightenment figure Kant was perhaps the only Enlightenment figure to mark the distinction between practical reason and theoretical/epistemic reason in a way that we can find useful today. (The distinction itself goes all the way back to Aristotle.) In the last chapter, we saw the sort of emphasis Enlightenment and other rationalists place on being epistemically rational. But Kant thought that *practical* rationality and/or reason was the basis for morality and that certain distinctions in or of practical reason (e.g., categorical vs. hypothetical imperatives) were the basis for the distinctive importance of morality as compared with other forms of evaluation and practical activity.[3] And this is another type of Enlightenment theme beyond anything discussed in the last two chapters.

In other words, Enlightenment thought holds that epistemic rationality is important, that we should always be impartial in judging things and not be swayed by emotions; but it also holds that there is another kind of reason, practical reason, that grounds (the importance of) morality.[4] Care ethics, of course, disagrees explicitly with this second Enlightenment assumption. And what I would like to do in what follows is tell you some of my theoretical or philosophical reasons for preferring care ethics over a conception of morality that grounds it in practical reason and that makes emotion less central or crucial to admirable and acceptable moral motivation. From the picture we draw and the arguments we give will then emerge a picture of moral values that makes them special and especially important in our lives. So even if we reject Kant's paradigmatic Enlightenment assumption of the importance of practical reason in grounding morality, we don't have to reject the importance of morality itself, but the importance we give it will further erode Enlightenment values and ideals because that importance will derive from the relative importance of empathy and feeling *as opposed to reason* in our lives.

Care ethics is a fairly new phenomenon—basically, it was introduced by Carol Gilligan and Nel Noddings in the 1980s.[5] And because care ethics is essential to that part of our case against the Enlightenment that questions whether practical reason is the basis of morality, I want to explain here why I believe it makes sense to think of morality in care-ethical terms and why I believe other theories of morality and especially Kantian ethics can't do as much for us. I have argued in favor of care ethics at great length in two recent books, *The Ethics of Care and Empathy* (Routledge, 2007—ECE) and *Moral Sentimentalism* (Oxford, 2010—MS), and I don't propose to repeat all those arguments here. But I do want to sketch my reasons for favoring care ethics, and some of the considerations I am going to mention will in fact involve a somewhat different emphasis from what can be found in the above two books.

In *In a Different Voice*, Carol Gilligan spoke of two different moral voices: one that approaches moral issues with such concepts as rights, justice, and autonomy and that insists on the importance of principles and rules for the regulation of moral action, and another that anchors moral questions in caring about and personal connection with other people (or animals) and that downplays the role of principles and rules in the moral realm. She associated these two voices, respectively, with men/males and women/females but didn't insist on that connection. The main point was the segregation of moral thinking into two very different, even opposed, systems of moral thought: one stressing connection, the other stressing autonomy and therefore (rights of) separateness. This latter system or voice is roughly that of Kantian/liberal moral rationalism; and the former roughly corresponds to care ethics, as it originally saw itself and as it has subsequently developed as a theoretical or philosophical approach to morality.

To the extent Kantians allow and urge us to deal with moral issues by appealing and conforming ourselves to certain moral rules or principles, they interpose such rules/principles between the moral agent and those whose welfare they are concerned to promote. This gives a sense in which such views devalue direct personal connection to or with other people. And, by contrast, the care ethicist holds that it is morally better to be directly concerned about another's or others' well-being than to refer to and be guided by principles or rules in deciding what to do about that well-being. This difference can helpfully illustrated, I think, by reference to Bernard Williams's famous example of the husband with "one thought too many."[6] According to Williams, if a husband sees his wife and a stranger both drowning in nearby water, he has one thought too many if he consults or has to consult morality before deciding to save his wife. If he has to decide that he is morally permitted or obligated to save his wife rather than the stranger, then he is far from an ideal husband (consider what his wife would think if she learned he had proceeded in that fashion!); and care ethics would say that there is something less than morally ideal about this kind of husband and this kind of love (if it *is* love) for a wife.

By contrast, Kantians can say that it would be morally all right if the husband decided to save his wife out of sheer love for/devotion to her and without any thought of what morality permits or recommends—because they can treat or accept conscientiousness as merely potential back-up motivation in those particular circumstances. But they can't morally criticize the husband if he is led solely by considerations of duty, and that is where care ethics disagrees. Care ethics is a form of moral sentimentalism that emphasizes feeling directly for others rather than rationally grounded moral dutifulness or conscientiousness (it would question whether such rational grounding is even possible), and what it says about the "one thought too many" case is much more in line with our ordinary thinking about and reactions to that sort of example than what the Kantians tell us. Kant thought that there was nothing morally problematic about emotional indifference to the welfare of others, as long as one promoted that welfare out of a rationally derived sense of duty, but care ethics will tell us that emotional indifference to the welfare of others, not genuinely *caring* about their welfare, is morally repugnant or worse, and it would apply this idea, of course, to Williams's example in a way that is more consonant with ordinary reactions to such a case than what the Kantians tell us about it. This gives us one very good reason to favor care ethics over Kantian or any other sort of rationalism.

But rationalism would claim to have its own strengths and to be superior in various ways to any sentimentalist care-ethical approach. It could claim, in particular, that it can account for deontology better than any sentimentalist view can, so let's see what care ethics and sentimentalism more generally can say in response to that possible criticism. First, let me briefly say what deontology is, so that we are all on the same page. Very roughly, it is the view that it is morally worse to cause pain or harm than to allow it; and the deontologist will say, for example, that it is wrong to kill one innocent person in order to prevent, say, the death or two or three other innocent people. So conceived, deontology is part of our ordinary thinking about morality. Almost all of us would at least initially agree that if the only way to save two accident victims would be for a surgeon to kill an innocent by-stander and harvest her organs for use to save the two accident victims, then the surgeon (morally) shouldn't do that. Any moral theory has reason to try to justify this rather basic part of our common moral thinking (the fact that utilitarianism and consequentialism more generally don't do so is usually taken to be a strike against them), and Kantianism long prided itself on its ability (through Kant's "formula of humanity" or in some other rationalistic way) to justify deontology conceived along something like the above lines. But, in fact, these Kantian defenses of deontology don't seem to work very well, and some contemporary Kantians have given up on deontology and now espouse a kind of Kantian consequentialism.[7]

I think this is unfortunate, and people with strong common-sense intuitions in this area will tend to agree. But the Kantians might then say that none of this is going to be of any help to care ethics. Kantianism may have difficulty justifying deontology, but clearly (they will say) the care ethicist and sentimentalist will have an even more difficult, indeed an impossible, time achieving that end. Deontology, they will say, sets limits on natural human feeling; it tells us that despite our sympathy and concern for the fate of two or three accident victims, we may not kill some single innocent bystander in order to save them. The "sum of feeling" might favor doing so, but something beyond or different from feeling, something presumably based in our practical/rational understanding of moral norms, tells us not to do so. And so it would seem that feeling cannot favor deontology and actually works against it; and if that is so, then care ethics can't justify deontology in the way most of us ethicists would like to see done.

But I think this Kantian/rationalist view, however plausible it initially seems, is actually mistaken, and in what follows I shall explain why and how. Our feelings or sentiments are actually sensitive to deontological ideals and distinctions in ways that are subtler than the above Kantian claims reckon with. I want to show you why this is so, but in order to do that, I need first to cast our care-ethical/sentimentalist net more widely: I need to explain how care ethics can account for numerous other non-deontological moral distinctions that certain normative approaches have a difficult time accounting for. Once we have seen how this works, we can come back to deontology and will see—perhaps surprisingly—how care ethics can account for and justify it in its own sentimentalist terms. In order to do all this or even just sketch the relevant arguments, I need to bring empathy back into the picture.

Our normal or developed empathic reactions correspond to and correlate with our intuitive or commonsense moral judgments over a wide range of issues or topics. For example, we tend to feel empathy and identify with friends and members of our own family more than with complete strangers or even co-workers, and if someone were to help a stranger in preference to helping some equally needy friend, this would go against the grain of our empathic/altruistic tendencies. And it would also seem to most of us to be morally worse than helping/preferring the friend—most of us think that in such a situation and assuming the choice is necessary, it would be morally incumbent on us to help our friend rather than the stranger. (This should remind you of the Williams example.) So there is a correlation for such cases between what we think is morally more obligatory and what we think is more in line with our empathic/reactive tendencies. And such a correlation exists in a host of other cases.

Thus, and as the psychological literature on empathy has amply documented, our empathy is more strongly and/or readily aroused by perceived pain or danger than by pain or danger we merely know about at a distance. But we also think it more *obligatory* to help someone whose pain we perceive than someone whose pain or danger we merely know about at second hand. Thus, to borrow an example from Peter Singer, if someone sees a child drowning in shallow water right in front of him, we think it would be morally worse (indeed we think it would be morally monstrous) not to save that child than for the same person not to give a contribution to Oxfam that would save the life of some distant child.[8] Singer makes an effort to show that both sorts of actions are equally immoral and ends up defending a form of utilitarian consequentialism, but common sense doesn't agree with this or with consequentialism, and the notion of empathy is arguably part of the explanation. Our intuitive sense of moral better- or worseness seems here to correlate with our stronger or weaker empathic tendencies, and this holds, as I say, in many other cases as well.

Thus what we perceive is empathically more immediate for us, but there are also cases where empathic immediacy derives not from perception but from the fact of contemporaneity. If miners are trapped underground, we may not perceive them, but the fact of their clear and present danger engages our empathy strongly. We would prefer to spend money to save those miners rather than, say, to use the same money to install safety devices that would save a somewhat greater number of future endangered miners, and that is because empathy for and the immediacy of a clear and *present* danger exerts a stronger influence on our altruistic tendencies or concerns than (within limits) sheer numbers of people potentially and probably to be saved in the future. And of course we think we *ought* to save the presently trapped miners rather than invest in safety devices.

We also think it morally worse to negligently injure another person than to negligently injure ourselves, and this, too, corresponds to empathic tendencies. We feel empathy for other people and older children learn to feel empathy even for whole groups of strangers—like the starving population of some distant country; but empathy for our ongoing selves isn't a notion that makes such sense to us or to most psychologists, so when we injure ourselves this doesn't go against a normal target of empathy in the way injuring another person does. Once again there is a correlation between what goes (more) against empathic tendencies and what is judged morally worse or wrong.[9]

All these correlations between empathy and moral judgment are evidence that empathy is part of our *concept* of moral rightness/wrongness, but before I say more about this, let me return to the issue of deontology. The examples we have already mentioned give us some clue about how a care-ethical sentimentalism that relies on empathy as the mechanism or force behind caring can and should defend/justify the deontological distinction between causing and allowing harm (killing vs. letting die, etc.). A perceived pain or danger is more empathically immediate for us than a merely known-about pain or danger and thus more strongly arouses altruistic concern or caring than occurs, typically, in the latter case. And something similar can be said about situations in which pain or danger is contemporaneous rather than highly probable or even certain in the future. But similarly, it would seem that a pain or harm one would or could cause is likely to be more empathically immediate for a moral agent than some pain or harm they would or could merely allow to occur. We empathically flinch more from harming than from letting harm occur (from killing than from letting die), other things being equal, so if our empathic tendencies have anything to do with making things morally better or worse, we can use them to explain why (we think) it is morally worse to harm than to allow harm and why harming people is usually wrong. In other words, our empathy as moral agents may be somewhat sensitive to how many people might be harmed in a given situation, may be sensitive to numbers and quantity; but it is also sensitive to how strongly, in causal terms, we relate or might relate to given harms, and if it is, then care ethics can account for deontology in sentimental terms. But this is something Kantianism has a notoriously difficult time doing in rationalistic terms and that consequentialism and recent neo-Aristotelian virtue ethics don't even attempt, so if we want to justify deontology, I have given you some reason to favor care-ethical sentimentalism over other prevalent normative approaches and over ethical ratio-nalism, in particular.[10]

I believe that the deontological empathic tendencies I have been speaking of don't in some surreptitious and illegitimate way involve our already accepting principles or standards of deontology. Far from it, legitimate and valid commonsense principles of deontol-ogy arise out of prior psychological/empathic tendencies, tenden-cies revealed in some of the processes and techniques of moral education discussed in the psychological literature on empathy. I have described those techniques in *Moral Sentimentalism* and will say something specific about them below. But the argument I have been giving in this chapter does, I think, need some immediate rein-forcing. I have tried to show that there is a correlation between our empathic tendencies and our commonsense normative judgments of right and wrong, or morally better and worse. And it doesn't make much sense to suppose this is some kind of accident. But does this nonaccidental correlation all on its own *justify* the claim I want to make that empathy and empathic concern or caring for others is the normative basis for moral right and wrong? Perhaps it does, but per-haps, some will want to say, it doesn't; and my answer or my primary answer to those who say that it doesn't is to argue—as I have both in ECE and MS—that the correlation or correspondence gives us reason to believe that the notion and/or phenomenon of empathy enters into our possession of moral concepts. If our understanding of claims about right and wrong depends on our having empathy, that would explain why the same empathy that makes us more sen-sitive to perceived pain or danger than to merely known-about pain or danger also leads us to judge it to be worse to ignore pain or dan-ger we perceive than to ignore merely known-about pain or danger. The idea that empathy enters into the making and understanding of moral judgments offers a better explanation of the particular cor-relation I just mentioned than anything else I can think of, so that correlation supports the idea that moral thought is semantically based in empathy, something Hume held but that hasn't, I believe, been held since then. This argument can then be reinforced and strengthened by applying it to others of the correlations mentioned just above. And if moral thought rests on empathy, considerations of empathy can be used to justify moral claims or judgments. What is morally wrong will be wrong because it reflects or expresses less than fully empathic concern for others, and what is right and morally good will be so because it exhibits a high degree of such concern.

Adopting the metaethical view that moral thought is semantically based in empathy helps to support and allows us to further elaborate normative care ethics. But our whole argument does assume that there is a quite general correlation between empathic reactions and moral judgments, and I need to say a bit more about that at this point. Obviously, I haven't here investigated every nook and cranny—or every broad meadow—of ordinary moral thinking, but I want to point out one area of political thought where what I have said needs to be at least somewhat qualified. Questions about social/political/legal justice are moral questions in the sense understood or intended by the ethics of care, and although both Gilligan and Noddings originally treated justice as a concept alien to care ethics and its moral "voice," things have changed since those early days. I have long argued that a care ethics that seeks to be a general approach to moral questions needs to take on issues of justice *but deal with them in its own distinctive care-ethical/sentimentalist terms.*[11] And Noddings and various other care ethicists tend nowadays to agree with this. But this means that a care ethics dealing with political morality has to be able to discuss issues in that area in plausible sentimentalist terms. I believe that can be done, and in MS and ECE directly deal with a whole range of such questions. But the issue that needs consideration now is that of correlation, and the whole idea of correlation is challenged when one realizes that care ethics *disagrees* with Kantian liberalism with respect to some very important political/moral questions. And it disagrees most particularly because the notions/theories of justice and autonomy that care ethics invokes stress our separateness from other people less and our connection to others more than more traditional and rationalistic Kantian/liberal (or libertarian) ideas about autonomy and justice tend to do.

Thus, to take one major example, care ethics has some tendency to disagree with Kantian liberalism about certain issues of hate speech. Almost everyone has heard of the town of Skokie, Illinois, because in the 1970s a group of neo-Nazis sought to march, demonstrate, and speak there and because at that time the town had and was presumably chosen because it had a large population of Holocaust survivors. The issue of whether that march and those speeches should have been allowed (for various reasons the march, etc., never actually occurred) is treated by Kantian liberals as primarily a question about respecting the rationally given autonomy (rights) of the neo-Nazi demonstrators, and the welfare of the Holocaust survivors doesn't usually get mentioned at all. The liberals therefore conclude that the demonstration should in all justice have been allowed.

But care ethicists tend to see things differently. They agree and staunchly hold that freedom of speech should be allowed and encouraged in most possible circumstances, but they are willing to make a distinction between merely offensive speech and harmful or damaging speech that the liberals don't really consider. The liberals tend to take a sticks and stones view of what speech can do or cause, but, according to the typical care ethicist, the Skokie example illustrates the difference between speech that causes offense and speech that causes damage. Because of the presence of Holocaust survivors in that town, allowing the marching and speechifying to occur there would very likely have caused psychological damage to many of the survivors, have retraumatized them in ways they would have had a hard time recovering from. Empathy can and should be very sensitive to this kind of damage and to the difference between it and merely being offended by speech or frustrated by not being allowed to speak. So the tendency of care ethics would be to question whether the marching and speaking should have been allowed. The care ethicist can grant that individuals have autonomy rights but would, for reasons illustrated in the Skokie example, argue that such rights don't necessarily trump considerations of serious damage. If many of the Holocaust survivors would likely have been psychologically damaged, retraumatized, by the event, then a really sensitive empathy would prefer to prevent such damage even at the cost of frustrating the neo-Nazis who want or wanted to march. In sentimentalist terms (and I say more about this in my two books), one has been respectful of everyone's autonomy, if one has empathized with everyone's point of view. And if such empathy or empathic caring feels the weight of the likely retraumatizations more powerfully than that of the mere frustration of the neo-Nazis, it will favor not permitting the neo-Nazis to do their thing.[12]

Similarly, the Kantian liberal will (if consistent in emphasizing traditional autonomy) be more hesitant to recommend judicial restraining orders against husbands or boyfriends who threaten harm or have harmed their spouses or girlfriends than will be a care ethicist who sees (rights of) autonomy as less absolute and separating than the liberal and who regards respect for autonomy as a matter of having full empathic concern for all parties to a given question. Such empathy, the care ethicist argues, will dictate the issuing of restraining orders in many cases where consistent liberals would recommend against, or hesitate to recommend in favor of, such orders. But if care ethicists and liberals have such different views of these matters, how can I say that the dictates or effects of full empathy correlate with our typical or commonsense moral judgments? They may correlate with the judgments care ethicists and various other feminists make about the kinds of cases just mentioned, but they won't correlate with the judgments liberals or libertarians are inclined to make about them.

What we can at least say, however, is that our empathic tendencies don't go against moral judgments that almost everyone is inclined to make and that are therefore fairly unproblematic. To that extent, there really is a correlation between empathy and (as we may call them) unproblematic moral intuitions and judgments, and that leaves the care ethicist who wants to pursue the semantics of "right" and "wrong" the option of arguing that the just-mentioned correlation is evidence that empathy is involved in moral judgment and that those whose judgments don't fully accord with empathy are making some kind of normative moral mistake. This is the kind of thing we say, most of us, about utilitarians and consequentialists who claim that deontology is invalid or that it is just as wrong not to help a distant child we are in a position to help as not to help the child we see drowning right in front of us. The defender of common sense or of empathy will want and have to show problems with the arguments consequentialists such as Peter Singer use to bolster their consequentialism (I have done some of this in ECE and in a recent online debate with Singer at "Philosophy tv"). Similarly, the defender of empathy and of its foundational role in our understanding of moral thought and judgment will have to argue that those whose normative judgments don't align with empathy—for example, the liberals or libertarians who defend all hate speech or who want to restrict the issuing of restraining orders against abusive or potentially abusive husbands—are defending their views in significantly criticizable ways. The fact that liberals such as Thomas Nagel, Ronald Dworkin, and T. M. Scanlon defend the rights of the neo-Nazis without ever mentioning the traumatic psychological damage their activities in Skokie would likely have caused is one, but only one, basis for criticizing their arguments. (For some others, see ECE, ch. 5.)[13]

The metaethically inclined care ethicist will want and need to argue, then, that Kantian liberals and even consequentialists come to certain mistaken or criticizable normative conclusions and that, as a result, they often invoke faulty metaethical views about the content of moral concepts. But this last move is no bolder or more arrogant than what *any* metaethics is forced to say. Any given theory of the meaning or usage of moral terms will clash with many other such theories and has to claim, therefore, that those others are mistaken in various ways. But it can try to back up such claims with arguments, and that is exactly what a care ethicist is and/or should be prepared to do—it is what I am doing here.

Moreover, a certain explicit normative criterion of moral right and wrong emerges from what sentimentalist care ethics says about the various examples or ranges of cases discussed above. Given our notion of empathy, a preference for saving a slightly greater number of future miners rather than miners whose lives are threatened *right now* shows a lack of fully empathic concern for others, and an ethics of care can criticize it in precisely those terms. (Such a preferential attitude will also chill those of us who are not utilitarians or psychopaths, but I won't discuss the moral signficance of that psychological fact till later, in chapter 9 of part II, where I shall have more to say about moral concepts.) Similarly, those who refuse to advocate for early restraining orders against threatening husbands or boyfriends show a lack of empathy vis-à-vis women and their welfare. And such cases and many others suggest the following general criterion of moral wrongness: An action is morally wrong if and only if it expresses or exhibits a lack of full empathic concern for others. And rightness, as I and most philosophers understand it, is simply something's not being wrong.

Now it is well known that empathy can sometimes lead us toward doing what is in moral terms totally unjustifiable. Great empathy for a criminal standing before him for sentencing might conceivably lead a judge to give him an extremely light sentence. But such empathy is blinkered and limited. It is empathy or empathic concern felt in one direction that ignores all other relevant objects of empathic concern: the convicted criminal's victims and potential future victims. And this judge is also arguably oblivious to those empathic deontological considerations that will make someone very reluctant to violate *their oath* to uphold the law. In this case and others, a care ethicist can argue (as I did at great length in ECE and MS) that the remedy for one-sided or limited empathy needn't be some rationalist or impersonalist moral standard or point of view but, rather, can simply be more or greater or fuller empathy. I therefore think the normative criterion offered above really can handle moral cases in an acceptable manner, more acceptable than what utilitarianism tells us, for example, about the miners case and deontology and what Kantian liberalism tells us, for example, about Skokie-type cases and spousal abuse.

So although I haven't given all the arguments, I think you can see some of my reasons for thinking that empathy is basic to ethics and ethical justification and that the notion/phenomenon of empathy enters into our moral concepts. But it would be nice if we could say more: if we could say *how* empathy enters into those concepts. This is something I have attempted, at length, to do in MS: In fact, it is the main thing I tried to accomplish in that book. But I propose to reserve further discussion of this topic to the second part of this book. The importance of receptivity to human life, thought, and action will be the main theme of part II, and what I will have to say there about moral concepts—about the meaning and our understanding of "right" and "wrong"—will illustrate the importance of human receptivity in a noteworthy way. But for the moment let me at least mention that the specific theory of the meaning of moral terms I will be defending and that MS defended at greater length allows moral claims to be as objective and/or valid as any Kantian, consequentialist, or Aristotelian theory permits—and as our pre-theoretical commonsense thinking imagines them to be (feels that they are). Hume's sentimentalism treated moral claims or utterances as less objective than we tend to think they are (when we say that it is wrong to torture babies, we think that that claim is valid independently of whether human beings tend to believe it is), and that is one reason why rationalists reject Hume. But the present sentimentalism can't be criticized in that fashion, and in any event, this particular issue about objectivity or objective validity isn't immediately relevant to the case against Enlightenment ethical thought because the defense of objectively valid morality I offer in MS represents an important though limited form of *agreement* with such thought.

One thing that definitely tends to *favor* care-ethical sentimentalism over rationalism, however, is that the former can make more sense of moral education than the latter seems capable of doing. By stressing the variety of ways in which empathy can operate and lead us to be more caring and moral people, a sentimentalist view of moral education can account for moral education in more clearly understandable psychological terms than Kantianism has ever been able to manage. The most elaborate and psychologically informed Kantian account of moral education is the cognitive developmentalism articulated and defended by Lawrence Kohlberg in several books and articles.[14] Following Jean Piaget, Kohlberg sees moral development and education as involving and based in increasing cognitive sophistication: the child (or some children) eventually becoming able to think in the abstract and universalistic terms that Kantian ethics treats as foundational to morality. But as is well known and Kohlberg himself admitted, it is difficult to understand how the increasing cognitive sophistication that is required for us to understand or formulate various moral rules or principles translates into moral motivation. Why should the ability to think in terms of universalizability, reciprocity, and the like lead someone to want to adhere to or follow principles formulated in such terms? Kohlberg never says, and indeed he sometimes invokes empathy as a way of evading this difficulty. But the sentimentalist can use empathy in various forms in a clear and systematic way to account for moral motivation because the idea that empathy can lead to moral or altruistic motivation makes inherent good sense to us.[15] And a sentimentalist account of moral education and moral development more generally will stress the ways children become and can be helped to become more empathically caring and thus, according to care ethics, motivated to do what morality requires of us (or even what it regards as ideal or praiseworthy and supererogatory). This account begins with the work of Martin Hoffman, and I shall begin by repeating, for our present purposes, some things I said earlier in connection with other issues.

In *Empathy and Moral Development*, Hoffman shows how the development of caring/altruistic motivation can be facilitated by the intervention of parents and others in a process called inductive discipline or just induction.[16] Induction contrasts with the "power-asserting" attempt to discipline, train, or influence a child through sheer threats (carried out if the child doesn't comply) and with attempts to inculcate moral thought, motivation, and behavior by citing, or admonishing with, explicit moral precepts or injunctions. Inductive training depends, rather, on the child's capacity for empathy with others and involves someone's, usually a parent's, noticing when a child hurts others and then in a nonthreatening but firm manner making the child vividly aware of the harm that he or she has done—most notably by making the child imagine and focus on how the child he or she has hurt is feeling. This leads the child with a normal capacity for empathy and a loving relationship with his or her parents to feel bad (a kind of rudimentary guilt) about what she or he has done.[17] Hoffman believes that if such training is applied consistently over time, children will come to associate bad feelings (guilt) with situations in which the harm they can do is not yet done, an association that is functionally autonomous of parents' or others' actual intervention and that constitutes the kind of resistance to further harming that morality, any morality, requires. He calls such habitual associations scripts and holds, roughly, that they underlie and power the use of moral principles or rules that objectify (my word) that association in claims/rules such as "hurting people is wrong."

Hoffman indicates that the use of induction in the family can be extended and somewhat generalized in school contexts and in ways that can lead to higher degrees and broader targets of empathic concern for others. The use of literature, films, the Internet, or television can make children more sensitive to the plight of groups of people they don't personally know and (if this is not prevented by local or national jingoism) make the child or adolescent more sensitively aware of how her own actions and inactions and those of her family or government can affect, for better or worse, the lives of people in other countries or poor people closer to home. As Hoffman indicates, all these things help to increase empathy and empathic concern for other people. But there are some effects of induction that Hoffman doesn't focus on and that also make an important difference to the development of empathic moral motivation.

When parents use induction, they demonstrate an empathic concern for the child (let us assume) who has been hurt by their own child, and there is no reason why the child of such parents can't take in the parents' attitude or motivation via direct empathic "osmosis." And the taking in or picking up of such empathically caring parental attitudes won't be confined to those occasions when the parent uses induction but will also occur at other times when the child notices how caring his parent is. It is often said that moral education occurs via modeling, through children's modeling themselves on parents or other figures. But the kind of modeling I am speaking of here isn't or needn't be deliberate or conscious. So even apart from any use or mention of moral principles or injunctions, both induction and modeling help strengthen empathic reactions/sensitivity and empathic concern for the welfare of others. We can see how such processes can lead to and cause greater empathic sensitivities, and the approach care ethics takes or can take to moral education therefore allows it to account for moral motivation in a way that Kohlberg's cognitive developmentalism doesn't seem able to do unless it supplements itself with a reliance on empathy and community feeling that brings it almost into the camp of care ethics.[18] Since Kohlberg has offered the most psychologically informed and comprehensive Kantian account of moral education, what we have just said and argued gives us reason to prefer care-ethical sentimentalism over Kantian rationalism.[19] Any given normative view needs, for the sake of completeness and plausibility, an account of how its normative principles or requirements can be learned and motivate us, and the theory of moral education that naturally comes with care ethics can accomplish this better than the theories associated with other normative moral views seem capable of doing.[20]

But notice one feature of moral education as I have just been describing it. I have spoken of empathy as the basis for caring, altruism, and moral motivation generally, but what I earlier characterized as associative or receptive empathy plays a much more crucial role in the process of moral development than the more active projective empathy that involves putting oneself into the shoes or the head of another person. For example, the modeling involved in unconsciously or nondeliberately taking in the caring attitudes of parents or others is clearly a process of associative, rather than projective, empathy. And, more generally, the nature of psychopathy gives us reason to think that projective empathy is much less helpful to moral development than associative empathy is. Psychopaths are notoriously capable of getting into people's heads in order to manipulate or abuse them, and to that extent they seem capable of projective empathy. But (most) psychopaths can't care intrinsically about the welfare of others, can't feel guilty about harming others, and can't empathically feel what others feel: If anything, they feel joy rather than pain at the pain of others. So typical psychopaths aren't capable of altruistic motivation, despite their capacity for projective empathy, and that gives us reason to interpret the idea that altruism depends on empathy somewhat more specifically than most of its advocates have done. It is (the capacity for) associative/receptive empathy whose development makes possible and mainly powers altruistic and moral motivation. And since such empathy involves a kind of involuntary transmission or infusion of feelings and emotions, the essential role care ethics regards it as having in moral development and education underscores the differences with ethical rationalism and the inadequacy of rationalism's picture of moral education and of morality itself.

However, most rationalists think that if morality is grounded in emotion or sentiment, it cannot be objectively valid, and they take that to at least partially justify their rationalistic approach to morality. But a sentimentalist needn't hold that morality is less objectively valid than the rationalist thinks, and so that particular objection doesn't seem to stick. On the other hand, the care-ethical account of morality just sketched seems to offer a better theory of morality than what is on offer from Kantian or other forms of ethical rationalism, and what we have said diminishes the importance, not, as in the last chapter, of epistemic/intellectual reason, but of practical reason. There may be such a thing as practical reason outside morality—concern for one's own future welfare is typically regarded as a condition on being practically rational, and I will say something in defense of that view a bit later. But if morality, objectively valid morality, is properly grounded in empathy and sentiment rather than in practical reason, that makes practical reason seem less important and all the more so if we think morality is and remains a very important and distinctive part of human life.

This, then, is a further way in which an emphasis on empathy and emotions works against Enlightenment assumptions and ideals. If love and friendship are important, then because they involve at least some degree of epistemic irrationality, epistemic *rationality* turns out to be less important and central to human life than Enlightenment rationalists have assumed. But similarly, and as we have argued in the present chapter, if *practical* reason/rationality isn't the basis of moral thought and motivation, then *another* kind or aspect of human reason is given a less important place in our lives and thought than Enlightenment thinkers and other rationalists have believed it deserves. I also said earlier that care-ethical sentimentalism can argue for the importance of morality just as strongly as Kant did. If, however, the grounds adduced for that importance are totally different from and even opposed to those suggested by Kant, that may give a further sort of reason for doubting Enlightenment values and assumptions beyond anything we have said previously. So let's now take a look at how and why the sentimentalist thinks (or can think) morality is important and see how that affects the position of Enlightenment ideas and ideals.

NOTES

1. On the undesirability of having bodily inclinations, see Kant's *Groundwork of the Metaphysics of Morals*, second section.
2. See my "Object Utilitarianism," reprinted in my *Selected Essays*, New York: Oxford University Press, 2010. Many modern-day rationalistic

consequententialists don't treat morality as important as such: moral reasons and morality are seen as fungible with other reasons and within an overall picture that stresses the idea of reasons for action more than morality itself. But other contemporary rationalists, and not just Kantians, treat morality and moral reasons as having a special kind of significance.

3. To that extent, Kant treats practical reason/rationality as equally important with or perhaps more important than morality, but we can also say that Kant used various distinctions in regard to practical reason (hypothetical vs. categorical imperatives and the "overridingness thesis" about specifically moral considerations) to *highlight* the importance of morality. Similarly, I use empathy to justify and show the importance of morality, but someone might say that I treat empathy as at least as important as morality because of the role I claim it plays in happiness, good human relationships, and epistemology.

4. In chapter 1, I noted the widespread view that feelingful associative empathy can be "mediated" by what we know. But the fact that feeling some person or group's pain or enthusiasm can involve or require certain sorts of knowledge and certain concepts doesn't undercut sentimentalism as a view opposed to ethical rationalism, because the latter treats our moral capacities and judgments as grounded in (what it calls) practical reason/rationality. Sentimentalism isn't skeptical about theoretical/epistemic rationality and allows that sort of rationality to have a role in shaping or constituting empathic reactions. But it does deny that practical reason/rationality has any grounding role in moral thought or motivation, and that is why it can be correctly seen as standing in opposition to ethical rationalism. (However, a moral sentimentalist needn't deny that there is such a thing as practical rationality outside the sphere of the moral. See my *The Ethics of Care and Empathy*, London: Routledge, 2007, esp. ch. 7.) Finally, let me just mention that most Kantians nowadays allow that the emotions and feelings can sometimes play a helpful role it getting us to do what rational morality dictates or requires, but they don't regard such emotions and feelings as morally desirable in themselves, and both sentimentalism and care ethics in particular strongly disagree with such a view of morality.

5. Carol Gilligan, *In a Different Voice: Psychological Theory and Women's Development*, Cambridge, MA: Harvard, 1982; and Nel Noddings, *Caring: A Feminine Approach to Ethics and Moral Education*, Berkeley: University of California Press, 1984.

6. See his "Persons, Character, and Morality" in *Moral Luck*, Cambridge, UK: Cambridge University Press, 1981.

7. See, for example, David Cummiskey, *Kantian Consequentialism*, Oxford, UK: Oxford University Press, 1996. But recently the distinguished Kantian scholar Paul Guyer told me in conversation that he sees no reason why a Kantian couldn't accept consequentialism and deny deontology. (Consequentialism

is the view, roughly, that an act is right if and only if it produces as good an overall result as any other act available to the agent would have produced.)

8. Peter Singer, "Famine, Affluence, and Morality," *Philosophy and Public Affairs* 1, 1972, pp. 229–43.

9. Some psychologists speak of empathy for, say, one's own sexually or psychologically abused earlier self, but that is a different matter and not directly relevant to the moral distinctions I am speaking of. Note, too, Kant's explanation of why we have obligations to promote the welfare of others, but no basic obligations to promote our own welfare. He argues, in the *Doctrine of Virtue*, that since we automatically seek our own welfare, there is no need for and it makes no sense to suppose there is a moral obligation to pursue that welfare. But as Bishop Butler had already pointed out, people do all sorts of things to thwart or undermine their own future welfare or happiness, including actions that involve negligently but unintentionally hurting themselves. We need to be on guard against hurting ourselves almost as much as we need to be on guard against hurting others, so Kant's reasons for thinking there can be no moral obligation to promote our own welfare don't really seem to apply.

10. On the neo-Aristotelians' neglect of the issue of justifying deontology, see my "The Problem We All Have with Deontology" in L. Jost and J. Wuerth, eds., *Perfecting Virtue: New Essays on Kantian Ethics and Virtue Ethics*, Cambridge, UK: Cambridge University Press, 2011, pp. 260–70.

11. See MS, chapter 9, for my most recent defense of this idea. But I have been arguing in print that care ethics needs and can have its own distinctive conception of justice since 1998.

12. The fact that the neo-Nazis' malice toward Jews will likely make a truly empathic person angry with them and less concerned about their welfare or feelings is also relevant here. But I won't go into the details.

13. All three of the philosophical liberals just mentioned have taken inspiration from the (Kantian) liberalism of John Rawls, and in regard to Skokie-type cases, Rawls's theory also commits to one skimping on the rights or interests of the Holocaust survivors. In *A Theory of Justice* (Cambridge, MA: Harvard University Press, 1971), Rawls argues for two lexically ordered principles of justice (in the context of developed societies). The first, which prescribes maximum political and civil liberties, is to take absolute precedence over the second, which, roughly speaking, is primarily concerned with people's welfare interests. Such an ordering of principles would presumably lead to a preference for the neo-Nazis' freedom of (hate) speech over the Holocaust survivors' welfare interest in not being subjected to further trauma. It would also lead to a strong reluctance to interfere with the freedom of movement and so on of abusive or potentially abusive spouses or boyfriends. And as with the arguments of Nagel, Dworkin, and Scanlon, all this strikes me as insensitive to the moral appeal and urgency of emotional/empathic considerations. (Rawls never dealt with Skokie directly or, as far as I know,

with issues of spousal abuse; but what he says about free speech in *Political Liberalism* [New York: Columbia University Press, 1993, p. 295f.] supports the present interpretation of his views.) Note further that Rawls took his first principle of justice basically from Kant, and Kantian justice therefore also favors autonomy-based liberties over welfare in a way that doesn't, I think, do justice to the intrinsic moral appeal of considerations having to do with empathy and with human feeling. But, of course and in the light of everything I am saying here, this should come as no surprise. Kant isn't willing to grant the emotions any intrinsic or inherent moral value and is generally suspicious about the emotions for reasons, I believe, having to do with his typical Western/Faustian overemphasis on rational/autonomous control at the expense of receptivity. So it is no wonder that his philosophy leads in particular toward liberal views about Skokie and about judges' not too quickly restricting the rights of (actual, potential, suspected, threatening) abusive husbands and boyfriends as well.

14. See, for example, Kohlberg's "Moral Stages and Moralization: The Cognitive-developmental Approach," in T. Lickona, ed., *Moral Development and Moral Behavior: Theory, Research, and Social Issues*, New York: Holt, Rinehart, and Winston, 1976, pp. 31–53.

15. Of course, we can in the abstract wonder why someone who empathically feels another's pain should want to help them rather than simply leave the scene and avoid the distressful empathic feelings they are experiencing. But it is still humanly understandable to us that feeling another's pain could make us want to help the person, and so a sentimentalist account of moral education based on empathy accounts for moral/altruistic motivation in a more plausible way than anything (by way of a rationalist alternative) that Kohlberg offers us.

16. Martin Hoffman, *Empathy and Moral Development: Implications for Caring and Justice*, Cambridge, UK: Cambridge University Press, 2000.

17. The tendency to resist thinking badly of those one loves that I described in the last chapter may, in some cases, make parents resist thinking that they need to use inductive discipline with their child. But much of the time a parent knows perfectly well when their child has hurt or harmed another child/person, and an empathic parent will tend in such cases to use inductive discipline, rather than threats or physical punishment, in order to change his or her child's behavior and/or attitudes.

18. Where empathy is taught in groups (e.g., in school), there will be a tendency for each child's increased empathy to reinforce that of his or her classmates—through the kind of empathic osmosis I have just mentioned. This is the upside of the unfortunate phenomenon of mutually reinforcing hostility or anger that occurs, through the same basic empathic mechanisms, in many crowds or mobs. Those who are surrounded by empathically caring people

will be more disposed to help the unfortunate than those who are not, and this works in families, in classrooms, and in society at large.

19. In recent decades, a new kind of Kantian (and arguably also Aristotelian) rationalism has taken shape based on the idea that the rational apprehension of facts can ipso facto motivate certain kinds of moral behavior. One finds this idea in Kant, but it is much more plausibly defended in Thomas Nagel's *The Possibility of Altruism* (Oxford, UK: Oxford University Press, 1970) and in John McDowell's "Virtue and Reason" (reprinted in R. Crisp and M. Slote, eds., *Virtue Ethics*, Oxford, UK: Oxford University Press, 1997). However, I believe it can be shown that this neo-Kantian approach ultimately needs to bring in associative ("I feel your pain") empathy in order to understand why and how a psychopath cannot apprehend (as salient) what a morally decent individual can. So as with Kohlberg, the rationalist cannot really account for moral education and development along strictly rationalistic/cognitivist (and Enlightenment-friendly) lines and needs to speak of ways that empathy can be taught or cultivated. I discuss this issue at somewhat greater length in my *Education and Human Values: Reconciling Talent with an Ethics of Care*, London: Routledge, 2012, chapter 3.

20. Aristotelian virtue-ethical rationalism has its own distinctive approach to moral education, one emphasizing habituation and rational insight. For reasons mentioned in footnote 19, the latter emphasis leads one toward empathy and sentimentalist ideas about moral education. And my *Education and Human Values* (also ch. 3) argues that habituation depends on what Hoffman calls power assertion and, in the light of the psychological literature on power assertion, is less educationally effective than empathy-based inductive discipline. Finally, I don't believe anyone has ever come up with a theory of moral education that goes well with and actually supports utilitarianism or consequentialism.

Chapter 4

How Important Is Morality?

H. A. Prichard taught us that our adherence to moral duty doesn't, in most of us, depend on our having a belief, à la Plato's *Republic*, that it pays, in self-interested terms, to do one's duty.[1] And in my own previous writings I have sought to compound this point, because the same considerations that led Prichard toward the just-mentioned conclusion seem to me to indicate that our sense of duty—even the sense of duty of a rationalist—also doesn't depend on our (or their) believing that we (or they) have a rational argument or rational justification for adhering to duty.[2] This is a separate point because although an appeal to self-interest is one way one may try to justify doing something, Kantian arguments for morality don't appeal to self-interest in any fundamental way but do invoke rational considerations of self-consistency and the like, in arguing for the rationality of adhering to one's duty. But I think a really moral person, even one with a philosophical bent toward ethical rationalism or Kantian ethics, in particular, doesn't ask whether she has a rational justification in self-interested or other terms in order to clear the way to or insure her doing what she recognizes to be her duty. That is a conclusion that Prichard's argument points us toward—and remember that Prichard himself was an ethical rationalist.

And the point certainly transposes—perhaps it applies even more readily or more securely—to a sentimentalist understanding of morality. The sentimentalist may allow that there are times when we face very difficult moral decisions, times when we don't know, really, what is right and what is wrong. And in such circumstances a person—even a sentimentalist—might ask questions about whether one course of action or another is really justified and even questions about which of those courses of action is likely to help them the most. But in normal circumstances, I think the sentimentalist will help people in ways that any sentimentalist morality would dictate (e.g., help a child drowning in the water right in front of them or help a friend in need even though it is going to be something of a bore and a bother to do so) without considering whether doing so ultimately serves their own interests or is rationally justified—and even without considering whether it would be morally wrong not to help. (Remember that, unlike Kantian ethics, sentimentalism of most stripes puts a moral premium on doing what is right out of "naturally" helpful rather than conscientious motives.)

Now how does all of this bear on the question of the importance of morality? Well, I think the fact that we act morally without trying to justify what we are doing in rational and/or self-interested terms shows that we think morality is quite important: important enough so that the likewise important issue of whether something is going to help us in self-interested terms is pushed or left aside. If such an important issue isn't even raised or present in our minds, that is, I think, criterially a sign of how important we think morality, or its concerns, are. Of course, there are times when we help ourselves in preference to helping others—and, as Philippa Foot has pointed out, we tend to gerrymander such occasions so that they represent or are regarded as exceptions to the moral obligation to help others.[3] So to that degree our sense of moral requirements yields to issues of what is taken to be of vital importance to the interests of the moral agent (we don't think one has an obligation to help a stranger when that is likely to lead to one's own death). This gives a sense, then, in which moral considerations aren't really *all*-important. And putting the matter in sentimentalist terms, empathic concern for others develops in most of us against a persisting background of self-interested desires and aspirations, and our moral concepts of right and wrong accommodate and are predicated on that fact. So empathy isn't always overriding to natural or developed self-concern, and present-day feminist sentimentalists don't think we somehow have to be totally selfless and self-abnegating in order to be fully empathic or morally good people. In fact, I have argued (following Carol Gilligan) that those women who become selfless and self-abnegating under conditions of patriarchy have typically become so because no one really empathized with their desires, ideas, and aspirations, because no one really and steadily listened or paid attention to their "voices" as individuals.[4] That counts as an injustice, a lack of respect, toward those women reckoned in sentimentalist moral terms. So there is no question of such a view demanding selflessness—across a wide range of cases, selflessness may only exist because *other people* aren't acting as morality demands of *them*.

Still, someone with a sense of her own worth and with genuine concern for her own well-being can also be strongly, deeply, concerned about the welfare of others. And what I said in the last chapter about inductive discipline gives some evidence of that. According to Hoffman, induction can bring about an accumulation of guilt, in relation to more than one occasion of harming others, that leads to or constitutes a *resistance to harming*.[5] And a child can also be led to feel bad about not helping when they could have, and this can help build a psychological impetus toward helping those who are in need, an impetus whose existence and at least some of whose strength are independent of self-interested calculations of the agent's own welfare. Guilt and empathy are strong forces in the mind, and that at the very least means that they can operate on their own to a substantial extent, that they don't always or even regularly operate through or by means of other considerations or the other forceful factors that operate in the mind or psyche of a given moral agent.

All of this shows, I think, that moral factors or concerns weigh heavily with us, have an important role in our psychology and active lives. And when people, even ordinary people, assume that morality is important, they may well be thinking of these facts and also, of course, *accepting them*. Hume says that our morality bears its own survey—that when we think about them, we approve our own activities of helping people and of approving or disapproving of people according as they are helpful or act harmfully/unjustly toward others.[6] And perhaps this point of Hume's can be reformulated or diverted in the direction of the following further considerations and conclusions.

Someone who is genuinely concerned to help others won't seriously ask whether they really *should* be concerned with this sort of thing. They may hear about one or another form of moral skepticism, but if they really love or are concerned about other people, they will be immune to letting such doubts infect their concerned relations or relationships with others. It just isn't open for a really moral person—where this is understood in terms of empathic concern and guilt—to start seriously wondering whether they should help that child who is drowning or likely to drown nearby, and so on, and so on. So I am saying that morality "bears its own survey" in the sense that anyone who is empathic, concerned, and moral in the way specified by (a certain form of) sentimentalism won't be seriously interested in skeptical doubts about their moral concerns and practices and will have a certain practical intolerance toward such doubts.

The liberal often tells us that every concern of ours, every relationship, should be subjected to serious critical doubt or scrutiny. But, as I argued in *The Ethics of Care and Empathy*, the sentimentalist will disagree with this. The sentimentalist will find it morally and humanly lacking and even repugnant if a mother, say, ever starts seriously wondering whether she should be concerned about the welfare of her child or children. And by the same token someone who starts *seriously* doubting the value or validity of his or her own practical concern for or about other people is to that extent a less empathic and less moral person. (Don't say that one's serious doubts can be very short in duration and won't have to interrupt one's caring for all that long—that doesn't in fact make a lot of sense. There is no intelligible mechanism for keeping a serious doubt on a short temporal leash, so there are obvious moral and human *costs* of serious moral skepticism. During a period of such skepticism, one is going to be *less* helpful and less *concerned* to help than one otherwise would or might be.) So I am saying that caring, moral people invest their concern for others with a certain importance, treat such concern as important, and don't or can't seriously doubt, much less disapprove, of these attitudes and activities. (Recall too what chapter 1 said in moral criticism of those who too quickly become skeptical about the possibility or reality of human altruism and moral motivation more generally.)

In addition, if we can empathize with the distress or pain of others, we will also (eventually) be capable of empathizing with the empathy of others, and Hume describes this tendency very well toward the end of the *Treatise of Human Nature*. He says that when we see a person acting out of warm concern for another person, we are ourselves warmed by that warmth.[7] And that seems exactly right. But if it is, then we, in effect, approve of the warm helpfulness of others (other things equal), because that is what being warmed by their warm actions effectively amounts to. (I have argued for this at great length in the book *Moral Sentimentalism* and will be saying more about this in chapter 9.) So when people act in a warm, concerned, and moral way toward others, we are ourselves warmed and approve, and that gives a real sense in which we positively approve of morality, of people's acting morally. By the same token, we are chilled by the cold-heartedness some people display in their actions or inactions vis-à-vis others, and this counts as a kind of disapproval of immoral behavior or actions. (I think we would be chilled by someone who let skeptical doubts about the objectivity or content of morality interfere with saving a child from drowning. Alternatively, such a thing might make us angry.)

Thus those of us who are empathic and concerned about others won't want to seriously *question* their allegiance to or disposition toward acting morally, and they will also tend to approve of morality or of being moral (on the part of others). And these two aspects of their psychology constitute a sense in which such people—and I hope both you and I—think morality is important. Not merely important to them but just plain important.

Further, those sentimentalists who are not skeptical about the whole idea of practical reason or rationality (as Hume arguably was) downplay the importance of such rationality in regard to the foundations of morality and moral action. The sentimentalist will want to say, for example, that it isn't important whether immoralists are as such irrational—which s/he thinks they aren't—because we can say *enough* against them or in criticism of them, by calling them *heartless*. But no ethical rationalist will be content with the coinage of *this sort* of criticism, and that gives us another sense in which rationality is overall less important to the sentimentalist than it is to the rationalist or Enlightenment thinker.[8]

In that case, the issue of whether one can be rationally justified in doing what is immoral will be less important to the sentimentalist than it is to the rationalist—and there doesn't seem to be any *other* clear notion of justification that sentimentalists want to apply to, withhold from, or question in regard to morality. Kantians hold an overridingness thesis according to which one can't ever be rationally justified in doing what is immoral, but quite apart from whether this thesis is true, the question of *whether* it is true is less important to the sentimentalist than it is to the rationalist; and there is every reason, then, too, to think that from a sentimentalist standpoint the importance of morality is a *more important issue* than the question whether the overridingness thesis is valid or true. As I indicated above, the sentimentalist sees moral individuals as placing great importance on moral considerations—that is why, for example, they don't typically ask what is in it for them, when they find themselves concerned about the welfare of some individual or group and then act in a helpful way toward that individual or group. To the extent that the sentimentalist is herself or himself a morally decent person, s/he, too, will place such importance on moral considerations and will disapprove of those who do not. And I think that someone—a sentimentalist—who automatically disapproves of those who in their lives don't place considerable importance on moral considerations is ipso facto treating the importance of morality as itself an important matter. And as more important, it would seem, than the sentimentalist tends to treat the question whether *practical reason* dictates that we should always avoid wrongdoing.

I have been using some sentimentalist theses or assumptions to argue for the importance of morality, and if that argument has been successful in its own terms, we will have shown something quite substantial and significant, even if we don't try to evaluate the overridingness thesis here. Of course, Kantian rationalists also treat morality as very important: For example and unlike Sidgwick in *The Methods of Ethics*, they regard moral imperatives as the only truly categorical ones (e.g., considerations of prudence or self-interest are not thought of as having categorical rational force).[9] But other rationalists seem to want to downplay the importance of morality—and this seems to me and perhaps would also seem to Kantians to be a fundamental mistake. Here I am mainly thinking not of rational egoists (though the point probably applies to them) but rather of those contemporary consequentialists and semiconsequentialists who say they are, or show themselves to be, less interested in moral questions as such than in questions about what we have overall reason to do. Thus both Shelly Kagan (in *The Limits of Morality*, Oxford, 1989) and his teacher Derek Parfit (in *Reasons and Persons*, Oxford, 1984) avoid focusing on questions about right, wrong, and obligation in favor of asking about what we have (most) reason to do—though, of course, and unlike ethical egoists, both these philosophers think of ordinary moral considerations concerning the welfare of others as central to the issue of what we have reason to do. Parfit recently told me that he thinks the issue of reasons is more important than questions of moral right and wrong, but this idea not only assumes a certain sort of ethical rationalism (assumes that it is irrational or against reason, for example, not to care about the welfare of others), but also, I think, downplays morality as such. For it treats specifically moral questions as fungible within an issue or issues about reasons that don't as such distinguish the specifically moral—and it is difficult to see how such a view leaves any room for saying that morality in itself or as such is important. (Incidentally, the roots of this sort of rationalism arguably lie in Sidgwick's *Methods*, where it tends to be assumed that there is no significant conceptual distinction to be made between what is morally required and what is rationally required.)

By contrast, sentimentalists such as myself think valid morality isn't based on reason and involves a deep psychological phenomenon, empathy/sympathy, that isn't typically involved in prudential or self-interested rational action—and the approach taken by Kagan and Parfit (and, originally, Sidgwick) seems to me to ignore both these considerations. That is why I favor a very different approach to moral questions and think they are making a large mistake in blending the moral into rational considerations *überhaupt*. And that mistake essentially involves the error of ignoring what is distinctive *and* important about morality. However, once we free ourselves from that mistake, it becomes much easier to view the importance of morality as more important than whether the over-ridingness thesis is true or false, and we can also see that there are different reasons for thinking morality important from those that would be given by Kant or Kantians.

Kant thinks morality important in substantial part because it exemplifies a form of universal self-legislated autonomous categorical rationality and because he thinks acting out of respect or concern for such rationality gives individuals a dignity they lack when they operate out of empirical or material motives. But following the lead of Bernard Williams (and for that matter Francis Hutcheson) the care-ethical sentimentalist finds these Kantian arguments defective and even repellent. The wife-saving husband who acts and/or needs to act from moral duty is less morally attractive than one who acts from love of and concern for his wife, and such love and concern, far from rendering us or morality less dignified, actually make it more humanly appealing and heart warming. Or so at least the care ethicist thinks.

Also, care ethicists think empathy, which binds us to others, is morally more important and attractive than a practical rationality based on a notion or notions of autonomy that mark and emphasize the separateness of the moral person from other such persons. So care ethics grounds moral obligations in considerations of empathy and forms of connection based in empathy (concern for others, love, friendship), whereas Kantian ethics grounds morality in considerations of rational autonomy. Both think morality is very important and indeed central to human life as we know it or would like it to be. But the Kantian bases that importance on the importance of self-conscious practical reason, and the care ethicist sees the importance as grounded in something other than reason and, in particular, in forms of empathy and emotion that value self-consciousness and conscientiousness much less and a deep direct connection with other people much more than the Kantians do. If the care ethicist is on the right track, then, the reasons that make morality important undercut or challenge the Enlightenment picture of the world and of human values. The Kantian account of why morality is important doesn't challenge and, indeed, constitutes a highly articulate expression of Enlightenment/rationalist values, but if care ethics is superior to Kantian ethics, then the Kantian/Enlightenment view of why morality is important has to be relinquished. And this is *another and further way* in which the emphasis this book has placed on empathy and emotion challenges Enlightenment/rationalist views.

But now we need to consider just how important morality is according to care ethics. For it turns out that given care ethics, there are limits to that importance. A care ethics that emphasizes empathy will naturally say that actions are morally wrong if they manifest or reflect a lack of full or fully empathic concern for others (animals can be included here, but I shall leave them out of the present discussion). But, as ECE argues at length, one doesn't have to be the most empathic person in the world or the most empathic person it is possible to be in order to count as fully empathic. I am fully capable of driving a car, but some drivers are presumably better at driving than I am; and I am fully capable of organizing my own activities (really, I am), but there are people who are (even) more organized than I am. Similarly, I can be fully convinced that a certain fact obtains without being *absolutely certain* that it holds. And these points carry over to empathy. Some people attain great heights (or depths?) of empathy—they are more empathically sensitive to the plight of others than the rest of us, and they are consequently willing to make sacrifices that almost no one else would ever make. But one can be a *fully* empathic person without being like that, without being as empathic as it is possible to be, without being *ideally* or *perfectly* empathic.

Let's put the matter a slightly different way. One can, given normal English, be regarded as fully empathic if one isn't seen as *lacking* in empathy (or in empathic concern for others); and we don't usually regard someone as lacking in a certain quality just because he or she doesn't possess or exemplify the highest imaginable degree of that quality. So someone can be fully empathic, not be *lacking* in empathy, even if they are not perfect with respect to empathy, not as empathic as we can imagine someone being.

If this is granted, then there is room in principle for moral supererogation according to the terms of the above care-ethical criterion of wrongness. For if the failure to perform a certain act doesn't reflect a lack of full or fully empathic concern for others, but the act is one that someone with an incredible capacity or "gift" for empathy might perform, the doing of that act will/would count as morally supererogatory, will/would count as morally praiseworthy for going beyond the call of duty. Thus consider the choice facing someone who would have to give up one of her limbs in order to save another person, a stranger, from an even worse bodily injury. (This example is ultimately due to John Taurek.) I don't think we would feel that someone who was unwilling to make such a sacrifice was automatically criticizable as being lacking in empathy. We think a fully empathic person, a person not lacking in empathy, can and typically will have substantial regard for their own welfare, and though certain sorts of unwillingness to make sacrifices for others and even strangers (giving substantially to charity is typically a kind of sacrifice on behalf of strangers) would normally be regarded as demonstrating a lack of fully empathic concern for others, the present example doesn't, intuitively, seem of that type. So if the person were, out of extraordinary empathy, to sacrifice a limb in such a case, we would regard that action as morally supererogatory and praiseworthy.

Most of us can see why someone might not be willing to sacrifice a limb in this fashion or in this kind of situation: We likely wouldn't do it ourselves, and we would stand by— not regret—such a decision once we had made it. And I think this is because most of us would regard the sacrifice of a limb in such a case as an unwise thing for us to do. Consider a similar case of supererogatory self-sacrifice. A soldier throws himself on a hand grenade in order to protect his buddies, who are all scrambling for shelter, from the explosion. If he, too, had tried to escape, they might all have avoided serious injury, but he instead sacrifices his life in order to minimize the chance of harm to the members of his squad or platoon. We often praise soldiers who sacrifice themselves in this way, but consider what the self-sacrificing soldier's mother will say or think. Like everyone else, she may well be proud of him and praise him in moral terms, but in her heart of hearts she may also say: You fool(ish boy) to have thrown your life, your whole future, away like that!

The point of bringing in this further example is to indicate how natural it is in the further example and in the first case we described to apply epithets that are commonly associated with irrationality. What it is unwise or foolish to do, it is in practical terms presumably irrational to do, so even if we think of the self-sacrificing soldier and the person who gives up a limb as morally admirable and as having acted in a supererogatory fashion, we also think they have acted in a somewhat irrational fashion. We also find it hard to understand them: Their motivation is mysterious to us, and what they do seems from a rational standpoint to be inexplicable. But all of this is consistent with our admiration for them, and that admiration is paid out through the coinage of empathy: We empathically warm to the warm-heartedness they display; we see them as exhibiting an extraordinary degree of empathy and concern for others. And that is the basis of our high moral opinion of them or of what they have done.

So we are in fact of two minds, most of us, about the kinds of cases just mentioned. We praise the supererogatory actions they involve but ourselves shy away from doing similar things—and we don't regard that strong reluctance to be a matter of weakness or irrationality on our part (like delaying a visit to the dentist). On the contrary, we see the opposite and self-sacrificing choice as less amenable to rational justification or explanation, and that is shown by the fact that we regard it as at least to some degree foolish or unwise for someone to do such a thing.[10]

However, these examples also show that there are limits to the importance sentimentalist care ethics places on morality and on empathy. Such an approach tells us that we aren't morally obligated always to do what exhibits the highest possible degree of empathy. It holds that there are cases where considerations of self-interest can set a limit on what we are morally obligated to do and on what can be characterized as showing a *lack* of empathy. But in this respect Kantian ethics seems basically the same. Kant says that we can on a given occasion, and for reasons of self-interest, fail to help someone we are in a position to help and yet not be doing anything morally wrong. Our duty or obligation to promote the well-being of others is an imperfect one, according to Kant, and in that measure he holds that there are limits to what can be morally required of us.

But as far as I know, Kant never claims that it would be irrational always to act against one's own self-interest when that was necessary to helping others. I don't see him saying that the soldier who meritoriously throws himself on the hand grenade or the person who sacrifices a limb has acted contrary to practical reason, but that is precisely what I am inclined to say and what, as I indicated above, it is natural and intuitive to say about such cases. If we assume as much, then it follows that being practically rational is of more limited importance than Kant—or Enlightenment thinking more generally—realized. There will be times when someone is morally praiseworthy not only despite the irrationality of what they do but also, as we might want to say, because what they do involves their *making a sacrifice* of their rational interests. We find it hard to understand the soldier who throws himself on the hand grenade rather than try to save himself, and I think a certain sense of what we might call rational mystery enters into our awe and admiration for what he does. But in any event, if what I have said above is correct, then such acts of self-sacrifice are *essentially* both morally praiseworthy/good/admirable and unwise/foolish/ill advised, with the moral goodness and the practical irrationality being inextricably linked in the particular instance.

Thus our care ethics has led us to limit the importance of reason/rationality in still another way. There will be times when it is morally praiseworthy to act in a way that is precisely not practically rational, and this is something that neither Kant nor Enlightenment/rationalist thought, in general, will be very comfortable with. And as I said earlier in this chapter, there is also the further point that the importance of morality seems to be much more connected with sentimental factors and considerations than anything that would be acceptable to Kant or other Enlightenment thinkers. It is time, however, to consider some criticisms of Enlightenment thought that come from an entirely different direction from anything we have discussed so far.

NOTES

1. H. A. Prichard, "Does Moral Philosophy Rest on a Mistake?" in his *Moral Obligation*, Oxford: Clarendon Press, 1949.
2. See my *Morals from Motives*, New York: Oxford University Press, 2001, p. 193ff.
3. See her *Virtues and Vices*, Oxford, UK: Blackwell, 1978.
4. Gilligan, *In a Different Voice*, Cambridge, MA: Harvard University Press, 1982.
5. Martin Hoffman, *Empathy and Moral Development: Implications for Caring and Justice*, Cambridge, UK: Cambridge University Press, 2000.

6. See *A Treatise of Human Nature*, Selby-Bigge edition, Oxford: Clarendon Press, 1958/78, p. 619f.

7. Hume, *Treatise*, p. 605.

8. But if sentimentalists think it important to show that morality isn't based in practical reason or rationality, doesn't that in and of itself prove that they consider practical rationality to be important? Not in the least. It only proves that the sentimentalist thinks it important to show that rationality is *less important* than rationalists believe. And that is an entirely different matter.

9. For the record, I agree with Sidgwick's view (in *The Methods of Ethics*, 7th edition, Indianapolis: Hackett Publishing, 1981) that imperatives of self-interest have categorical rational force. Hume may have denied that self-interest is rationally mandated, but it is quite possible for a moral sentimentalist to hold both that immorality isn't automatically irrational and that a lack of concern for one's own welfare *is*. This seems to me to be quite commonsensical, and I have defended such a view (on those grounds) in *The Ethics of Care and Empathy*, ch. 7.

10. Pace Sidgwick, this illustrates a dualism not of the rational, but of and within the *ethical*. See my "Ancient Ethics and Modern Moral Philosophy" in my *Essays on the History of Ethics*, New York: Oxford University Press, 2010.

Chapter 5

The Impossibility of Perfection

Enlightenment-type rationalism, both in its eighteenth-century and its present-day versions, has treated human reason as central to the good life but also as central to what we as human beings simply—or perhaps not so simply—are. Our capacity or capacities for reason are, according to such thinking, the highest and best thing about us, and emotions, feelings, and sentiments that interfere with or undercut our reason and cognitive/intellectual accomplishments detract both from life and from what is best or most admirable about us. Romanticism, of course, called these ideas into question, but Romanticism was (*also*) a very extreme philosophy. For example, most of us are not persuaded that passion in artists or other geniuses can justify moral transgressions on their part, a view that is associated with Romanticism and that has been asserted in its name. Nor, further, are most of us convinced of the almost total disparagement of reason that one finds some practitioners of Romanticism expressing and attempting to justify.

Still, most of us are convinced that feeling and emotion are much more important or central to our lives than Enlightenment rationalism ever allows, and our ability and tendency to believe such things is surely in substantial ways due to the historical and persisting influence of Romantic art and thought. However, one can see how much more important feeling and emotion are than the Enlightenment ever granted, without recognizing the implausibility of certain very specific philosophical assumptions that have been and continue to be made by Enlightenment/rationalist thinkers; and the past four chapters have been an attempt to call a number of such specific assumptions into question.

For example, rationalists hold that we should always be impartial about evidence, and it is important to see—and we have here added to previous attempts to show—that we needn't and shouldn't always be epistemically impartial if emotions like love are important to us and important to our lives. Similarly, one can recognize the value of emotions in our lives without seeing the important role they play in determining what beliefs and attitudes we take in from our parents or others—our "normal" cognitive processes are trammeled with emotional/empathic factors in ways that we have been largely unaware of, and I have sought here to make the case that such emotionally charged cognitive processes are essential to life as we know it and to any good life we can believe in. This, too, undercuts Enlightenment thinking in a specific new way.

We have argued further that a sentimentalist care-ethical approach to morality also undercuts the Enlightenment/rationalist belief that a specific use or kind of reason, practical reason, is the basis for that enormously important part or aspect of our lives, and we have also seen that the importance of morality needn't depend on a connection with (practical) reason but can be a function, rather, of emotional factors. And our last chapter also pointed out that some of the traits and actions we find most morally admirable, rather than exemplifying (the glory of) reason, actually run counter to or *baffle* reason. Again, this puts reason in its place in a way that Enlightenment thinking has never allowed or envisioned. So our previous arguments pinpoint specific implausibilities in various Enlightenment views or assumptions, and in philosophical terms at least, this is an advance over simply holding the "general Romantic thesis" that emotions are more important and reason less important than Enlightenment thinking allows. The general thesis may be true, but our arguments here put a good deal of new philosophical flesh on those bones of contention.

All our previous criticisms specify ways in which Enlightenment thinking overestimates the value or importance of reason, but in addition to its belief in the all-importance of being rational (and knowledgeable), Enlightenment thinkers also typically subscribed to a belief in the perfectibility of man (sic). Like the ancient Greeks and like certain Romantic philosophers who came after them (e.g., Rousseau), Enlightenment thinking tended to assume that perfection both of human lives and of human character was possible in principle, and this assumption cuts across (is orthogonal to) the belief in reason because, as I just indicated, certain Romantics also believed in it. Nevertheless and despite the admittedly widespread acceptance of this idea, I believe it is mistaken. Following Isaiah Berlin but attempting to nail down his views with more arguments than he ever gave us, I believe that perfection either of happiness or of (the) virtue(s) is impossible in principle—and not just for us humans but for any intelligent creatures that can be imagined.[1] If true, this works against Enlightenment thinking in a very deep way, though, as I indicated, it comes at Enlightenment thought differently from the way we have so far been criticizing it.

Now in another book, *The Impossibility of Perfection*, I have spelled out a defense of Berlin's impossibility thesis at considerable length and, basically, for the sake of its considerable intrinsic philosophical interest.[2] But even if Berlin's thesis is of great philosophical importance in its own right, I am not going to give all the arguments presented in that book here. Our main purpose has been and remains to critique the Enlightenment view of things, so I shall rehearse only so much of the earlier book's arguments as I think necessary to make a plausible case against the side of Enlightenment thinking that says perfection is possible (and to be striven for). Enlightenment thought contained an ethical picture of the world according to which (putting things at the most general level) all our ethical values can be harmonized and subsumed under the aegis of reason or rationality. We have previously argued against the "aegis of reason" part of this philosophy, and I hope now to convey my main reasons for dissenting from the harmonizing part. Our ethical values in regard to happiness/living well and ethical admirability/virtue not only don't exemplify a harmony but actually conflict with one another. And this conflict or inconsistency involves not merely a pluralism of mutually inconsistent or conflicting goods and virtues but the impossibility of any sort of ethical perfection, however pluralistically such perfection might be understood. We shall see later how these different theses vary in strength and substance, but the main point is that I shall, in what follows, be defending the strongest of them, the claim that perfection is impossible. That will or would serve to undercut Enlightenment (and Greek and Romantic) optimism in a very deep way—though from a quite different direction, as I said, from anything we have argued thus far. And in the second part of this book, we shall also see that the Enlightenment belief or *any* belief in the possibility of perfection is not only criticizable in itself but may also indicate an unfortunate lack of receptivity to one's own life or to human life itself.

But to begin our discussion, I would like to talk about some issues in feminist ethics that I think are very interesting in themselves but that also advance us toward the main thesis of this chapter: the claim that perfection—whether of happiness or of the virtues—is impossible in principle. The considerations I shall be discussing in what immediately follows were the actual entry point of my thinking on the subject of perfection, and we shall see how they naturally or inevitably led in that direction. But along the way, we shall also have reason to engage and criticize Aristotelian views about happiness, virtue, and perfection, and these criticisms will, indeed, form the basis for the diametrically opposed conception of happiness, (the) virtue(s), and perfection that I will be describing and defending—somewhat briefly—in these pages.

Ethics in the largest sense not only asks about moral right and wrong and moral good and evil but also considers questions about the good life (what kinds of life are good for us or make us happy) and questions about various virtues that lie partly or wholly outside morality proper. Thus, when we praise resourcefulness and strength of purpose as individual virtues, we don't necessarily think of these qualities of character as specifically moral. For a resourceful person can be a moral scoundrel; but most of us, nonetheless, think of resourcefulness as a virtue, an admirable and praiseworthy quality of character. And similar things can be said about strength of purpose (or stick-to-itiveness or perseverance).

I mention these other, nonmoral aspects or foci of ethics for a reason. More perhaps than anyone else, Carol Gilligan (in *In a Different Voice*) brought issues of gender to questions about morality; but gender issues also arise with respect to questions about the good life or human good and questions about what sorts of character traits count as either moral or nonmoral virtues, and these latter gender issues arguably bear on the question of whether ethical perfection is possible. (For simplicity's sake, my discussion won't take in issues about gays, lesbians, and the transgendered.)

To begin with, traditional/patriarchal attitudes and opinions about what is good for people and what counts as admirable or a virtue are very broadly contoured to considerations of gender, and we need to recognize that fact before we can move beyond such thinking in a way that feminism (or I myself and most readers) would find acceptable and toward an understanding of why perfection is impossible. Now some human goods and virtues are and always have been considered important for everyone, male or female. No one disputes that patience and wisdom are virtues in women or that kindness is a virtue in men; and both women and men have always been supposed to enjoy and derive some good from the aesthetic contemplation of beautiful things. However, in other cases, patriarchal or sexist attitudes involve thinking of certain goods as good only for men and certain virtues as virtues only in men.

Let's begin with the personal good of security. Even if it has always been understood that both men and women want or can want security in their lives, the good of security is in fact more traditionally associated with women than with men. Adventure is the opposite of, or inconsistent with, security, and men are traditionally supposed to be interested in or to need adventure in a way women *aren't* supposed to. So to that extent, men are traditionally thought to require security less than women do. And what has just been said about the way patriarchal or sexist thinking conceives certain goods as in some sense gender-relative also applies to questions about what counts as virtue, as an admirable trait of character. If patriarchy sees adventure as a good thing only in *men's* lives, it also sees adventurousness as a character trait that is appropriate for men but not appropriate, not a virtue, in women.

But feminism, contemporary feminism, thinks very differently about these matters. It thinks adventure and adventurousness are as relevant to women's lives as to men's, and so it also thinks security and the related virtue of prudence are as relevant to men as they are to women. However, if we assume that feminists (and I am a feminist) are correct about this, some important things follow about the possibility or impossibility of perfection. For example, philosophers often use the term *prudence* to cover the entire range or great swaths of human practical rationality, but in its ordinary sense, it implies or entails a concern for long-term well-being (usually one's own) and a tendency or need to play things safe. In other words, if one is concerned with one's long-term well-being, one isn't supposed to take big chances; rather one is supposed to insure against risks to such well-being, and all this, I believe, is part of the meaning or connotation of the ordinary English term *prudence*. But then someone who is prudent can't be a bold risk taker and can't really, therefore, be *into adventures*. By the same token, someone who values adventure as a human good is likely to think that risk-taking boldness is not only acceptable but admirable, a virtue; and since prudence as ordinarily understood is inconsistent with such boldness, the typical or traditional male or contemporary female who values adventure will regard prudence as less than fully admirable.

But what about the goods themselves: What about adventure versus security? Well, in the first place, they are mutually inconsistent. If one is leading an adventurous life, then one cannot be leading a life of security. (One can be adventurous in one's thought or writing—as Flaubert once advised—but if one is merely adventurous in one's thought or writing, then one is not really having adventures: One's life is not, even temporarily, a life of adventure.) But according to feminism (though not according to sexist thinking), both adventure and security are in some measure or in some way good for both men and women. So however one lives, at least one of these good things will be absent or missing, and we should now ask what this entails in relation to issues of perfection.

The answer is: not very much taken on its own or in isolation from other considerations. Having a great Chinese meal for dinner may be inconsistent with having a great French meal for dinner, but we don't for that reason conclude that it is impossible ever to have a perfect evening. These goods may be inconsistent, but that may simply mean that there are or can be different kinds or styles of perfection. A "Chinese evening" may be just as perfect as a "French evening": There may be nothing less than perfect, nothing at all regrettable, about either kind of evening, and so the fact that certain goods are incompatible or conflict needn't entail that an evening or a life in which one of those goods occurs and the other doesn't has to be less than perfect. (The fact that one can't live a full life as an architect and also a full life as a scientist doesn't entail that either life needs to be less than ideal. The ethically intelligent scientist doesn't have to in any way regret the fact that he or she couldn't also be an architect.)

But this "different styles of perfection" understanding of how one spends an evening (or of the kind of career one chooses or has) doesn't fit the case of adventure versus security very well.[3] If we are really open to both values, really value an absence of risk and danger but also really value the excitement of adventures that involve risk and danger (we are not necessarily talking about someone who *courts* risk), then I think there is going to be something to regret whichever way one's life goes. If one has security, then something will be missing and felt as missing and as less than ideal about one's life; and similarly, I think, for adventure. If one is having adventures, one is running risks and facing dangers, and one will be neither safe nor secure; and I think (and I believe most of us would judge that) there will be something less than perfect about such a person's situation or position in life. So the conflict between security and adventure illustrates Berlin's idea that perfect happiness, a life that is totally ideal with respect to happiness, is impossible.[4]

And this argument transposes to the associated virtues. We see someone who is prudent as *lacking* in something we also admire or think well of, and we view someone who is adventurous as also lacking to a certain degree. There is something narrow and dull about the character of a prudent person and something a bit lacking in seriousness, sobriety, caution, and/or self-concern about someone who is really adventurous. So in each case, there is something less than ideally admirable about (the character of) the person in question, and that means that perfect admirability with respect to character or the virtues is impossible in principle.[5]

Let me illustrate the impossibility of perfect/ideal admirability with a further example. Everyone recognizes that the virtues of frankness and of tact stand in some kind of opposition.[6] They are naturally seen as paired and opposed because there are so many situations in which a choice has to be made between being tactful and being frank, situations in which one cannot exemplify both of these qualities of character. But an Aristotelian take on such issues would want to hold that whenever there is a choice between tact and frankness, there is a completely *right* choice in the matter. That is (at least in part) because Aristotle and many Aristotelians accept a doctrine of "the unity of the virtues" according to which one has to have all the virtues in order to possess any single one of them.

However, I don't believe that what we regard as virtues are as well behaved as the unity doctrine and other aspects of Aristotelianism assume, and I think the issue of frankness versus tact helps illustrate this point. On the Aristotelian view (and speaking rather roughly), frankness and tact never clash *as virtues*. In any case, where tactfulness is called for, frankness or being frank wouldn't count as virtuous or praiseworthy—quite the contrary. And in that case, when one acts tactfully in response to situational ethical requirements, one's lack of frankness will simply not be open to ethical criticism. Now recent discussions of moral dilemmas and moral cost should make us suspicious of these Aristotelian ideas; but I would like to articulate my own suspicions by mentioning a case where it seems to me the Aristotelian take on frankness versus tact doesn't hold water.

Imagine that you have a friend who is always getting himself into abusive relationships that eventually turn sour and become intolerable for him. You have previously pointed this out to the friend; but he says he has no idea what you are talking about and enters into new and abusive relationships without seeming to have benefited in any way from what you or other friends have told him. (He also isn't willing to talk to a therapist about his problems.) So imagine further that your friend comes to you after his latest relationship has broken up and deplores the awful bad luck (as he puts it) that has led him once again into an unhappy and unsuccessful relationship. But he has no idea how abusively he has been treated in this relationship or the others and simply asks you, implores you, to tell him why you think this sort of thing is always happening to him. "What am I doing wrong?" he asks. However, you have told him in the past that he has a tendency to accept abuse, and you don't believe there is any chance he is going to change his ways or his thinking. (Assume he is an older man.) So what do you say to him?

Well, since he is imploring you to tell him what you think, you might once again be frank with him and explain the role he himself plays in bringing about these disasters (e.g., by accepting abuse, from the start, in the relationships he enters into). But you have every reason to believe (let's assume) that if you say this to him, it won't really register with him or make any difference to his future behavior; whereas, *if you just commiserate with him and say that you don't understand how he can be so unlucky*, he will feel much relieved or consoled by what he takes to be your understandingness and what is clearly your sympathy vis-à-vis his situation. So what do you do? I don't think there is a right answer to this question. In other cases, there is reason to choose tact over frankness or frankness over tact, but in the present case I think ethical considerations are finely balanced, and one's eventual choice of either the tactful or the frank thing to say may show more about oneself than about the ethical issues operating in the particular situation I have described.

Moreover, and this is the main point, whatever choice one makes will be less than ethically ideal. If one is tactful, one will have compromised one's frankness with a friend who is imploring one to be frank, and to that extent one is open to the (mildish) criticisms that what one has done is less than ideal and that, more particularly, one has shown oneself to be somewhat lacking in the virtue of frankness (or even of truthfulness). By the same token, if one is frank, one will have acted in a way that isn't entirely kind (or tactful), and, once again, what one has done will count as less than ethically ideal. Or so at least it seems to me. But if this take on the situation I have described is correct, the doctrine of the unity of the virtues is at the very least called into question; and more importantly for present purposes, we have another illustration of the impossibility of perfect admirability, of perfection with respect to ethical virtue, to set alongside our earlier example of adventurousness versus prudence.

Perhaps the most interesting illustration of the Berlin thesis comes, however, from an issue that we haven't yet mentioned and that is of central importance to feminism. We are nowadays familiar with (having) the choice between career and family, but of course in the bad old days no one thought there was anything difficult about that choice. Women were to choose family over career and men were supposed to put more emphasis on their careers than on their families, if they had one. But nowadays we think both women and, increasingly, men need to juggle or balance career and family, and there is a certain tendency to blame oneself or to blame society or other individuals for the attendant difficulties and frustrations. But I believe the difficulties and frustrations are, in fact, inherent in the values that are at stake here, and that this whole issue, suitably generalized, gives us a prime illustration of the impossibility, in principle, for humans or any other intelligent beings of perfect happiness or a perfect life.

I say "suitably generalized" because I think the deepest sort of choice that is at issue here doesn't depend particularly on the notions of career and family. We think having a family can make one's life richer and better, but we also think that that is true because human beings are better off having deep and intimate personal relationships. And not everyone faces a choice between career and family because not everyone wants a family or can have one. Similarly, we think of careers as adding to the quality of lives to the extent they involve meaningful creative accomplishments and self-fulfillment (not to mention certain professional relationships). Emily Dickinson didn't have a career and neither did Marcel Proust, but we tend to think their achievements made their lives richer and better, even if the value of what they had accomplished wasn't recognized in their lifetimes. So insofar as we think they are relevant to human happiness, the choice between career, on the one hand, and family, on the other, is best and most universally construed as a choice between creative self-fulfillment/accomplishment and deeply fulfilling intimate personal relationships. And I want to say that however one makes the latter choice, one's life will be less than ideal from the standpoint of happiness.

If one doesn't make much out of either the creative/career side or the personal relationships side of one's life, then of course one's life isn't perfect, far from it. But if one works hard and achieves great and self-fulfilling things, one will have to have devoted oneself to some area or areas and persevered in regard to problems and obstacles along the way. If things come too easy, the (sense of) accomplishment is less (actually, even Mozart had to work hard), and the corresponding enhancement of the life one leads or has led will consequently be less. But the kind of perseverance and devotion that is involved here is inconsistent with the physical and, more importantly, the psychic energy that a person who gets *the most* out of personal relationships has to "invest" in such relationships. By the same token, someone who is so completely and emotionally devoted to his friends and family as to be able to get the greatest possible fulfillment from those relationships won't be able to achieve (through struggle and concentrated hard work and great stick-to-itiveness) the most that it is possible to achieve. And in that respect, the person's life will seem less than an ideally good one— even if it can perhaps been seen as on the whole *satisfactory*. (For reasons mentioned in *The Impossibility of Perfection*, it doesn't help

matters to divide a life up into an earlier period devoted to achievement followed by a period devoted to relationships. In such cases,
there will be something lacking about both periods.)

So, what feminism has taught us helps move us toward recognizing the impossibility of having an absolutely perfect or ideal
life. Once we see that career/creative accomplishment and close
personal relationships are relevant to and good for both men and
women, we may be made aware of how difficult it is to combine
them satisfactorily—and this is what the juggling of career and
family sometimes teaches us. But the present argument seeks to
show that the difficulty and frequent frustrations of the juggling are
symptomatic of a philosophically deeper problem or result: the fact
that creative self-fulfillment and deep relationships cannot be separately realized or brought together in any imaginable life that that
we would regard as perfect.

From the standpoint of contemporary society and its thinking, this last example may be the most interesting and significant of
those we have mentioned as illustrating and supporting the argument for the impossibility of perfection. But for purposes of criticizing Enlightenment assumptions and those of ancient Greek thought
about the harmony or harmonizability of all our ethical values, I
think they all do equally well, and as a group they help us make a
strong case against Enlightenment views. Those views not only place
an inordinate amount of emphasis on reason and its supposed role
in grounding our ethical values but fail to recognize how messy and
unharmonious our values really are. To be sure, pluralists have been
making this kind of point against Enlightenment and Greek thought
for years, even decades. But the/our argument for the impossibility
of perfection makes the case against Enlightenment more deeply or
strongly than arguments based on pluralism alone can. Pluralism
leaves open the possibility that all our diverse values can coexist and
even be realized together in some perfect manner, and though this

may not count as harmony, it is certainly not the opposite of harmony either.[7] Pluralism can also allow for different styles of perfection and this permits and permits us to praise *different styles or forms of harmony*. But when we deny the possibility of perfection altogether and do so because certain conflicting values cannot either separately or in some kind of diluted combination make for a perfect whole, then we are denying the possibility of harmonizing our values in a much more thoroughgoing way, and this way of taking issue with the Enlightenment ideal of harmony is more complete or thoroughgoing than anything pluralism (as such) offers us. Thus I believe our present arguments more strongly undercut Enlightenment or Greek assumptions about harmony and perfection than anything else to be found in the recent or previous literature of philosophy or ethics.[8] And taken together with everything I have said against Enlightenment views about the role or importance of rationality, the argument of the present book may represent a more philosophically serious and systematic indictment of Enlightenment thought and attitudes than has previously been articulated or available.

And what I have said about Enlightenment thought—about its rationalism and also about what we might call its perfectionism—will also serve as grist for the mill of what we have to say, more overarchingly, about the previous failure of Western thought on the whole to recognize the importance, the value, of receptivity. But before we proceed to that discussion, we should take some more stock, and we will be doing that in our next chapter.

NOTES

1. See Berlin's "The Pursuit of the Ideal" in H. Hardy and K. Hausheer's collection of his writings titled *The Proper Study of Mankind*, New York: Farrar, Straus and Giroux, 1997.
2. New York: Oxford University Press, 2011.

3. On the idea that a conflict of values/virtues/goods may entail only the possibility of different styles of perfection and not necessarily undercut the idea and possibility of perfection as such, see A.D.M. Walker, "The Incompatibility of the Virtues," *Ratio* VI, 1993, pp. 44–62. *The Impossibility of Perfection* argues specifically against Walker's "styles of perfection" interpretation of conflicts like that between tactfulness and frankness.

4. Some lives contain adventure early on and then taper off into something much more secure and less exciting. Those who lead such lives often feel— and on my view it makes sense for them to feel—that something is lacking in their later lives. For example, in the film *National Velvet* (in which the preteen Elizabeth Taylor made a rather startling early film appearance), the stay-at-home mother expresses regret for her exciting earlier life in approximately these terms.

5. Here is another example of how an ideally good or perfect life is impossible that arises out of feminist criticisms of patriarchy: Many contemporary young women think sexual adventuring can be a good thing both for women and for men, but most of us are also inclined to think that sexual activity that takes place on an emotionally secure or committed basis is also a good thing. However, these two forms of sexuality are incompatible (I have more to say about why in *The Impossibility of Perfection*), and it is plausible to hold that both men and women are missing out on something if they only have sexual adventures but also missing out on something if they have an emotionally committed and secure sexual relationship and thus no exciting sexual adventures. This example is presumably an instance of the general impossibility of perfect happiness vis-à-vis the goods of security and adventure, but it illustrates that impossibility in a very specific way that is particularly relevant to present-day values and choices.

6. Berlin, op. cit., mentions this, and so do many others who have discussed virtue and the virtues. But I believe that the example of frankness versus tact mentioned in the text above is more specific than anything that has previously been described in the literature of the virtues.

7. In *The Virtues* (Cambridge, UK: Cambridge University Press, 1977, pp. 160–68), Peter Geach maintains that the virtues don't conflict among themselves but also can't be completely harmonized and unified. Many people have questioned Aristotle's doctrine of the unity of the virtues in a less radical fashion than I am doing here (or than Walker does in his article).

8. However, what has been said here isn't nearly as complete as the argument against the possibility of perfection that takes up most of *The Impossibility of Perfection*.

Chapter 6

A New Picture

I have been criticizing Enlightenment/rationalist ideas from a number of different directions; and I hope the criticisms have been philosophically clearer and more cogent than much of what has recently been said, especially by the postmodernists, against Enlightenment thinking. But this first part of the larger book is titled "Beyond Enlightenment," and to be true to that title, and to what I actually think, I need to say more about the positive vision or picture that I believe should replace the rationalist/Enlightenment thinking that still largely dominates the scene in Anglophone philosophical ethics and epistemology. Of course, given what I am going to say in the second part of this book, what I say here is going to be partial at best, but I think it makes sense to take stock of the positive results that our criticisms of Enlightenment have so far allowed to accrue.

What can be said positively at this point certainly grows, and grows directly, out of the various criticisms I have made about Enlightenment assumptions and the Enlightenment worldview, and I have no intention of offering or describing some total post-Enlightenment worldview either here or later in this book after our discussion of what one can usefully call Faustianism. That would not only be presumptuous but also premature. Rationalism is still so influential and even dominant in the field of philosophy that it is no easy task to see things in a way that is free of the central assumptions and methods we have criticized, and, of course, there is much that I haven't challenged and, in fact, agree with in the Enlightenment view of things. However intolerant it may have been of religion as such, the Enlightenment moved Western culture and politics as a whole toward greater religious tolerance and religious freedom, and that is only one of its great accomplishments. So I see us as needing to go beyond Enlightenment thought but not as rejecting it altogether; and that is why this part of the present book is called "Beyond Enlightenment," not "Against Enlightenment."[1]

I have also sought to describe ethical issues without caving in to pressures toward relativism, emotivism (the view that moral utterances express emotions and lack real validity), and postmodernism, and that is because (like Socrates) I believe that we shouldn't too easily give up on our desire to correctly understand ethical values. The postmodernists and others who would deny the possibility of a correct, or an increasingly insightful, ethical picture of things offer us less than strong arguments for doing so, and I am saying that we in any event have good intellectual/philosophical reasons not to give up (yet or too soon) on our quest for philosophical truth and understanding about ethical matters that affect all our lives and that more people than one might suspect, are interested in. Kant speaks of science as being committed to finding the causes or causal explanations of things that happen in the world, and why should philosophy not likewise keep looking for ethical truths? We may not have reached any universally agreed-upon answers, but there have certainly been positive developments in the field of ethics over the past two or three centuries (perhaps they amount to something we can call progress). Even if we don't agree on answers, most analytic moral philosophers agree that we need the distinctions (e.g., between categorical and hypothetical imperatives, between *das Gute* and *das Wohl*) that Kant was arguably the first person to make clearly.[2] And however important Henry Sidgwick's work and influence have been, there are issues about consequentialism versus deontology (e.g., the issue of "side-constraints") that he didn't appreciate and we today do.[3] So we are more sophisticated in many ways than our philosophical forebears, and I see no reason not to hope and strive for more sophistication, more clarification, more ethical understanding, in the future.

That is why my arguments against rationalist/Enlightenment views about rationality and harmony are made in an analytic spirit I share with (recent) rationalists. I believe that sensitivity to linguistic and emotional nuance should have a greater role in philosophical discussions than rationalists allow them (I think many analytic philosophers would have only a vague notion of what I am talking about here). But I am, nonetheless, convinced that one has to argue for ethical and metaethical claims and that the arguments have to be of a kind that one's opponents, the rationalists, will recognize as respectable arguments—even while they may reject their conclusions or some of their assumptions. But what then can we take positively from our criticisms of Enlightenment (and Greek) thought?

One positive (though you may wonder about that characterization) implication of what we have been saying here is that religion and religious beliefs are less weird and outré than we as analytic philosophers have tended to think (I include here my earlier self). Most of us have thought of belief in God or an afterlife as unsupported by any decent arguments and therefore as a sign of intellectual weak-mindedness, confusion, laziness, or just plain stupidity on the part of those who have such beliefs. We have thought such belief should be discarded—and certainly not relied on as a basis of how one lives one's life. And in the light of what we know about the weaknesses of all the traditional arguments for God, we are, many of us, intellectually intolerant of religious belief, and I am not going to tell you that such intolerance shows a lack of open-mindedness. Religious belief may not be as unfounded or closed minded as the assumption that the Earth is flat, but there may well be no good epistemic/intellectual reason for accepting such belief or even for viewing it tolerantly.

But intolerance of beliefs is a kind of anger toward those beliefs that tends to spill over onto those who hold the beliefs, and I would like to persuade you that we really shouldn't be (intellectually) angry with those who accept God's existence or the existence of an afterlife. Many of these people got these beliefs from their parents or their community, and we have seen that religious belief may well be inevitable, or at least very likely to occur, when it grows out of love and trust for loving and caring others. Do we really expect these believers to stop loving their parents?[4]

Well, you say, they can be exposed to valid criticisms of religious belief in philosophy classes, and shouldn't they at least then give up what they have previously accepted on faith (sic) from their parents? Well, some of them will give up religious beliefs at that point, but (as I pointed out in ch. 2, above) one should at least expect some resistance to doing so on the part of those who have good relations with their parents, and I think most philosophers would be uncomfortable with and displeased by such resistance, even if it is eventually overcome. But I am saying we shouldn't be *so* uncomfortable or displeased, given the not very controversial facts/ideas I have just been rehearsing with you. And there is all the more reason for this conclusion when one considers that *everyone* who has an emotionally close relationship with another person is subject to epistemic irrationalities. If *you* love someone in a fairly unambivalent way, you will be inclined to discount and disbelieve evidence of criminal or otherwise morally blameworthy activity on his or her part in a way that others will tend not to do. And the difference, as I explained earlier, will not just be due to one's greater acquaintance with (facts about) the person in question. (In fact, that greater knowledge might in many cases make a less involved person be more suspicious of your loved one than they otherwise, in their relative ignorance, would be.) We are all disposed to be somewhat epistemically irrational if we are lucky enough to be involved in close personal relationships or even one such relationship. As Frederick the Great said: We are all the sophists of our passions.

Therefore, we should perhaps be more humanly tolerant of people who "cling" to religious beliefs in the face of valid philosophical criticisms.[5] Our success as philosophers in having discarded the religious beliefs with which we were raised (if that is what has happened) may be partially due to a lack of good relationship with our parents, a lack that gave us the space to think about the issues in an epistemically rational fashion. Or the discarding of the beliefs may, in certain cases, be a sign of the open-mindedness of one's own loving parents even as regards their own religious beliefs. And in that case, one is fortunate to have had and to have such parents both from an emotional standpoint and as regards the epistemic/intellectual capabilities that they didn't discourage one from having and may have made it easier for one to acquire. Or one may be, quite on one's own, a rebel in the name or under the banner of epistemic/theoretical rationality. But whatever may be the origins of one's own epistemic rejection of or even intolerance toward religious faith, I think we have mentioned some reasons for greater tolerance of those who have such faith. *They are more like us epistemically rational types than we have thought.*

And their faith may also betoken a close and loving personal relationship with parents that many of us would have reason to envy or at least appreciate. But we have to be careful here. The child of religious parents who withhold love and who at some level make the child feel both angry and rejected may seek to gain that love by submissively accepting his parents' beliefs. Not all bad parenting leads to rebellion—some leads to frustrating and ambivalent submission to the parents in question. (Think of the way girls raised in patriarchal circumstances fall in with their parents' prejudices while presumably, at the same time, harboring some resentment for the way they have been treated.)[6] But where faith is the fruit of close and satisfying personal attachments, it is a sign that things are in a certain important respect going well for the person in question. They may not be as epistemically rational as a philosopher; but they may have a wonderful personal relationship with their parents or community, and we philosophers ought to be broad minded enough to respect that. So our critique of Enlightenment thought does support a more tolerant view of or attitude toward religious belief and/or believers than most philosophers (including Hume) have been accustomed to. And this certainly counts as a positive element for any post-Enlightenment picture of ethical phenomena.

But, of course, our earlier arguments lead even more directly to a positive view of the emotions, in general, that can and presumably will form the central panel in such a post-Enlightenment picture. This is by no means an entirely new or unprecedented way for an Anglophone philosopher to argue. Michael Stocker and Bernard Williams and many, many others have asserted the importance of the emotions to human life and to morality against the contrary, rationalist views of many previous philosophers, and much of what the people who have spoken about the importance of the emotions have said would need to be part of the overall post-Enlightenment picture that we can hope will eventually emerge. But the present book offers new arguments for the importance of the emotions, and some of them more directly bear on and against Enlightenment ideas than other suggestions and arguments that have recently been made about the emotions.

For example, Williams and Stocker have stressed the importance of emotions to and in the moral life, but they haven't directly argued for *grounding* morality in emotional factors. However, care ethics does exactly that, and such *alternative foundations* for morality cut more deeply against rationalism than somewhat piecemeal claims about the emotions tend to do. Thomas Kuhn tells us, roughly, that it takes a theory to beat a theory, so by providing a systematic alternative to giving morality a rational basis, we offer more philosophical reason to reject or discard rationalism than the piecemeal criticisms really provide.[7] After all, as long as rationalistic foundationalism is the only theoretical game in town, the points that have been made about the emotions can be accommodated on an ad hoc basis (as were the astronomical facts that at the end of the nineteenth century caused problems for Newtonianism—until Einstein came up with a *theory* that could better account for them). But once we have care ethics, a clear theoretical alternative exists for the grounding of moral claims (I assume that secular philosophers aren't going to take something like a divine command theory seriously in intellectual terms).[8] So the positive picture or conception of the ethical that emerges from the present book is one that at least in part contains a theory of how morality can be based in empathy and emotion.

But that centerpiece of the positive picture has penumbral aspects that are also worth remembering. If morality is based on emotion, then reason is less important to our lives than we have thought, and we earlier mentioned and discussed a number of different ways in which emotion turns out to be more important than reason. These specifics are also part of the positive picture, which I think at this point is filling out somewhat and giving us something definite and interesting and plausible to say about what ethics and our world look like in the wake of rejecting the Enlightenment worldview.

Finally, let's talk about empathy. We nowadays live in what Frans de Waal has called "The Age of Empathy": Everyone (even presidents) talks or chatters about empathy, and the notion has become central to our cultural consciousness, at least in the United States, in ways it never was in the past.[9] As I mentioned earlier, the term *empathy* wasn't introduced into English until early in the twentieth century, and after it was, it took quite a bit of time for the term/concept to become so much focused on. (That didn't, in fact, happen until the latter part of the twentieth century.) But nowadays some school systems have initiated empathy training, often as a means of stopping or preventing bullying, and we think of intelligence as involving empathy—as per the notion of emotional intelligence—in a way we never did before. And the present book will hopefully add to the crescendo of interest in empathy.

We have argued that empathy is involved in open-mindedness and thus plays an important role in epistemic and intellectual rationality. But we have also seen the important role it plays in making or letting us be epistemically irrational in ways that are necessary to and often enhancing of our lives. We need empathy to arrive at our epistemically best understanding of the world, but on the other hand and working in an opposite direction, empathy is basic to feelings, emotions, and relationships that make us less likely to understand the world in an epistemically rational manner or to care about the fact that we don't. So moving and moving us in different directions, empathy is a very important part, perhaps even the *most* important part, of the world picture that comes naturally out of the arguments we have given against rationalism.

But our arguments not only call the rationalistic side of the Enlightenment worldview into question but make us realize how oversimplified its view of ethical values and of a world understood in the light of such values really is. Not only are our values plural, not only are some goods or good lives incompatible with others, but our values also cannot in principle be harmonized or integrated into a coherent vision of any kind of ideally good/happy life or of any kind of ideally admirable character. And the impossibility of these two forms of perfection undercuts the Enlightenment *Weltanschauung* more deeply than conclusions merely about values pluralism and about differences between ethical styles ever could.

It is perhaps not surprising that the Greeks and the philoso-phers of the Enlightenment believed in an ethically harmonious universe and in the possibility of perfection. They lived in less com-plicated times, times when multiculturalism was not an issue, when feminism had gained little or no foothold, when human psychol-ogy hadn't been very much explored, and when humanity hadn't yet begun to systemically destroy huge groups of its own members and to threaten our whole species (and every other) with extinc-tion. Feminism offers some of our best examples of how and why a perfect life is impossible, so the side of our argument here that stresses the impossibility of perfection and total harmony owes a great debt to the feminist critique of sexist/patriarchal values. But the argument against harmony and against perfection makes use of other evaluative issues that may show the complexity of human life or intelligent living generally but do so fairly independently of the considerations and ideals on which feminism has been based.

However, if the need for greater complexity than Enlightenment thought allows reflects the greater complexity of our times but also points toward some universal truths that characterize intelligent life generally, the same may be true of the emotion-emphasizing part of our arguments and of our positive view of things. The greater atten-tion to and emphasis on empathy that we have seen in recent times may be some sort of response to the complex and ethnically/reli-giously pluralistic character of typical modern societies and of our common world. Certainly, empathy is more needed when interna-tional activities and organizations become more central to our lives and when the incredibly complex variety of and differences among the world's ethnicities/religions/nationalities finally dawn clearly on us. But, as I suggested in the introduction, the greater empha-sis we now place on empathy may also reflect the unprecedented and widely known history of large-scale human atrocities that have been committed over the past hundred years. Empathy now seems more necessary to our future than it has ever been or seemed before. The importance given to empathy *here in this book* may also reflect the greater complexity and diversity of our common world and the incredible atrocities of its recent history as compared with earlier periods; and if the rejection of Enlightenment and the substitution of a world picture that places positive emotions squarely at its center is the fruit, or natural consequence, of such a very different world, that can only give us further reason to reject the overall Enlightenment picture and see things in some of the new ways I have been talking about here.

Note, in addition, that the terms *reason* and *rationality* contain no suggestion of a desire to reckon with (human) diversity. Kant himself didn't believe that different people could have seriously different moral opinions; and reason is in fact typically seen as unified and universally applicable in a way that emotions or social customs are not. Nor does the term "virtue" imply any willingness to deal humanely with diverse and differing opinions. As Jerome Schneewind has pointed out, the Aristotelian emphasis on the ideal of a virtuous individual made that ethical philosophy ill suited to deal humanely or humbly with the diversity of opinion and allegiance that characterizes the modern world.[10] And that, according to Schneewind, is one reason why Aristotelianism went into decline in the eighteenth century: It left no room and gave no reason for the virtuous individual to respect other people's different views and so was ill suited to an increasingly diverse and complex world in which people have to learn to accommodate and tolerate and even respect one another despite their differences in moral and other beliefs.

Now even the concept of emotion carries no hint or suggestion of accommodating and tolerating diversity. Anger and intolerance are, after all, very strong paradigmatic emotions, and empathy for other viewpoints is notably absent when these emotions are present. However, we have seen that empathy is the basis or one basis for positive and valuable emotions like love and (civic or private) friendship, and the term *empathy* clearly does suggest a willingness and a desire to deal humanely with diversity, conflict, and difference in general. So it is no wonder that empathy—rather than reason, virtue, or sheer emotion—is so central to the Enlightenment-rejecting worldview that I have begun to describe. In fact, even some of our arguments for the impossibility of perfection make an indirect appeal to empathy, because the idea that women can benefit from careers/individual self-fulfillment but also gain a great deal from raising families or from their deepest personal relationships requires one to take the advice of feminists and try to understand the desires and aspirations of girls and women from *their* particular standpoints. So the replacement of the Enlightenment worldview with the positive vision I have been sketching rests to a large extent on an acknowledgement of individual human differences that is itself largely grounded in a more empathic and emotionally open and accommodating view of our values and our world.

But now one final point. Above, I praised the Enlightenment for the positive effect it had, overall, on religious freedom and religious tolerance. But doesn't what I have said about epistemic anger threaten religious freedom and toleration? If I have a high opinion of my parents and someone who questions their faith is, in effect, suggesting that I shouldn't have such a high opinion of them, won't that make me angry with the questioner and leave me intolerant of their religious thinking and practices? (I mentioned something like this point previously in a footnote, but it now deserves our complete attention.) Doesn't empathy at that point therefore threaten religious liberties rather than constituting the basis for open-mindedness about others' beliefs and practices? How can religious tolerance be justified on the basis of empathic considerations if such considerations, in fact, are ambiguous in their import: with an empathy-based open-mindedness toward others' opinions in tension or clashing with an intolerance of anything that too immediately or deeply questions the merits of those whom we empathize with and love and who have decided opinions/attitudes about religious matters? But our moral criterion in this matter, or others, shouldn't be empathy as we all too typically find it but a more capacious or fuller empathy that it takes *moral education for empathy* to develop.

We tend to imbibe our opinions about religion and many other matters from our parents, and if these manifest intolerance, then the children will inherit that intolerance. And the tendency to want to think well of our parents may, for the reasons just mentioned, reinforce the tendency toward intolerance where parents are themselves intolerant. So love and empathy may present difficult obstacles to or for moral education, and the moral education that occurs in schools may have a very hard time mitigating or overcoming that intolerance through moral-educative processes making use of literature or films or student role playing, and so on. Indeed, parents will often fight hard to prevent schools from making their children more empathically tolerant of other faiths than they (the parents) are.

So love and empathy have many unfortunate consequences along with all the good ones. And this will be true no matter what one thinks about the moral issues. Whether one thinks religious liberties rest on rationally derived rights or depend on issues of empathy, we need to see how much of an obstacle our own psychologies present to our acting morally. In a way, I am saying that the situation is worse than many have thought because of certain normal consequences of love that neither rationalists nor care ethicists have really attended to. Therefore, even when love and empathy run contrary to morality's dictates, their importance in and for human life is underscored in a way that has not previously been recognized. And on the issues of morality and justice, my main point is that at least there are forces that if properly marshaled can counteract the intolerance children imbibe from parents. And the child's desire to think well of his or her parents is also subject to countermeasures—one fact of growing up is learning that one's parents aren't always right. So even if empathy for and loyalty to parents might make children/students at least somewhat intolerant of those who disagree with the parents and whose disagreement may constitute an implicit challenge to one's good opinion of one's parents, a larger or fuller or more developed empathy would counteract that tendency. That is why we need moral education, and care ethics shouldn't and doesn't make people's actual empathy the criterion of what is right or wrong but says, rather, that an act is wrong or unjust or a character trait deplorable if it shows someone to be *lacking* in empathy in the sense of being less than fully empathic.[11] But our discussion here should show how difficult, at least in controversial areas such as religion, it can be to cultivate, instill, or manifest fully empathic right actions and attitudes. No one ever said the moral life was easy. But if care ethics is correct, that difficulty, and the issues of justice surrounding religion, can best be dealt with in terms of the idea of fully realized empathy, and we don't, for example, have to invoke the reason-based abstract right to autonomously practice one's own religion as the basis for the moral requirement that one be allowed to worship as one chooses. (I shall say more on this last point in chapter 9, below.) But our examination of empathy, at the same time that it offers us a criterion of morality, also helps explain why it is difficult for people to fulfill that criterion and how moral education can or might make it easier for them to do so.

NOTES

1.   Nor is the first part of this book or anything to be proposed or defended subsequently any kind of argument for Romanticism. Romanticism à la Rousseau believed in the possibility of human perfection as much as the Enlightenment did; it romanticized immoral (but presumably glorious) actions on the part

of the hero or artist in the way no care ethicist would or could; and it certainly didn't advocate a *balance* or *tradeoff* between rational and emotional factors, a theme that will emerge later in this book.

2. See my "Kant for Anti-Kantians" in my *Essays on the History of Ethics*, New York: Oxford University Press, 2010.

3. See Robert Nozick, *Anarchy, State, and Utopia*, New York: Basic Books, 1974, p. 30n.

4. If we need to be more accepting of beliefs, whether religious or otherwise, that are imbibed from parents or one's surrounding culture, then we also need to take another close look at the Burkean gradualism that criticizes the Enlightenment tendency to believe that the whole world can be rethought and remade, at a single time, in accordance with reason. I am indebted here to a column titled "Two Theories of Change" by David Brooks that appeared in the *New York Times* on May 24, 2010. Brooks, in turn, indicates a debt to Juval Levin's University of Chicago dissertation, "The Great Law of Change," and to Gertrude Himmelfarb's *The Roads to Modernity*.

5. Of course, children also imbibe contempt and intolerance for other people's religions from their parents, and this is or can be a lot more dangerous and socially divisive than sheer differences in religious beliefs. But just as professors or graduate students in introductory philosophy courses can try to wean students from the unquestioning acceptance of their parents' belief in God, schools can try to help children overcome prejudices and forms of intolerance they have imbibed from their parents or other sources. Much moral education in schools aims specifically at such a goal; and sometimes it tries—somehow—to involve the prejudiced parents in this process in the hope that this will help more effectively counteract the children's prejudices. Perhaps we needn't be or feel quite as benign when someone inherits feelings of contempt and hatred as I have argued we should be in regard to putatively harmless, though irrational, theistic beliefs, but the process of morally educating for greater tolerance is a difficult and complex one, and it might well be helpful to that process if those who were trying to educate weren't totally negative about those they sought to educate.

6. I am indebted here to unpublished work by Kristin Borgwald.

7. Thomas Kuhn, *The Structure of Scientific Revolutions*, Chicago: University of Chicago Press, 2nd edition, 1970.

8. Care-ethical theory is actually more heterogeneous than my discussion of it so far in this book has indicated. For example, Virginia Held (in *The Ethics of Care: Personal, Political, and Global*, New York: Oxford University Press, 2006) holds that personal morality can be understood in sentimentalist care-ethical terms, but that in the political sphere liberal ideas that aren't reducible to care-ethical terms have a certain importance and validity. She (along with certain other care ethicists) thinks that these different ideas or approaches can be harmonized or integrated, but I wrote the book *The*

Ethics of Care and Empathy primarily in order to show that such integration is impossible: that liberalism and care ethics are irrecusably at odds even in the political sphere. This has, I argued, to do with the fact that care ethics emphasizes connection with others and liberalism autonomy vis-à-vis others: How could such opposed emphases fail to yield disagreement and a lack of harmony about particular ranges of moral cases? And it is also worth noting that both Carol Gilligan (in later printings of *In a Different Voice*) and Nel Noddings (e.g., in *Starting at Home: Caring and Social Policy*, Berkeley: University of California Press, 2002) *don't* think political thinking/reality should be governed by liberal principles and hold that it should, instead, be understood in terms of the same caring notions that operate in personal morality. And that is an idea I have myself been defending since 1998 (see "The Justice of Caring," *Social Philosophy and Policy* 15, 1998).

In addition, both Noddings and Held (but not so clearly Gilligan) hold that care ethics must focus not only on the help we should give to others but also and somewhat independently on the preservation and enhancement of caring relationships. I haven't myself stressed this aspect of care ethics, in part because I believe what I *have* said accommodates the ethical importance of relationships in appropriate ways but also because I think that the two just-mentioned philosophers put *too much* stress on relationships. As I point out in *The Impossibility of Perfection: Aristotle, Feminism, and the Complexities of Ethics* (New York: Oxford University Press, 2011, ch. 5), contemporary feminism wants to accord as much importance to people's having career fulfillment as to people's having good personal relationships; so the care ethicist who speaks, as Noddings and Held do, of promoting good relationships but who doesn't give equal weight to promoting (women's) achievement-oriented fulfillment is arguably too traditional minded and not sufficiently *feminist*.

9. Frans de Waal, *The Age of Empathy: Nature's Lessons for a Kinder Society*, New York: Random House, 2009.
10. Jerome Schneewind, "The Misfortunes of Virtue," reprinted in R. Crisp and M. Slote, *Virtue Ethics*, Oxford, UK: Oxford University Press, 1997.
11. Remember that "fully empathic" doesn't mean "as empathic as it is possible to be." I am a fully capable driver but not the most capable driver in the world.

PART II

RECEPTIVITY

It is time to shift gears. We have so far steadily focused on the ideas and values of the Enlightenment, ideas largely centering on assumptions or conclusions about the pervasive and foundational importance of both practical and epistemic reason and about the possibility that the values reason grounds for us can all be harmoniously accommodated or integrated into a unified picture of what is valuable in life. But as I mentioned in the introduction to this book, an emphasis on reason is typically an emphasis on being ethically active rather than passive. And so the Enlightenment also exemplifies a tradition of thought that is much older than itself, one that goes back at least as far as ancient Greece. This tradition emphasizes the importance of being active and in control rather than passive and under someone else's control, and because Goethe's *Faust* both discusses and illustrates this notion, the tradition I am talking about can conveniently be and often is characterized as Faustian.[1]

But the Enlightenment and its ideas and values aren't the only major illustrations of Faustianism to be found in the history of thought in the West. (I won't be discussing Eastern philosophies very much here.) There are historical notions and attitudes not immediately associated with Enlightenment that very well illustrate the Faustian tendencies of Western thought, and I shall begin discussing them now. I am going to talk first about the Rawlsian/ Aristotelian suggestion that one live one's life according to a life plan, an idea that I think perfectly illustrates the Faustian tendency, and I will also talk about the liberal notion that every element in one's life—one's habits, emotions, beliefs, relationships, and so on—needs to be rationally questioned and scrutinized. And I will criticize those notions in the light of a value or virtue that hasn't yet or ever received enough attention, the idea that we should be *receptive* in regard to people, events, ideas, and a host of other things.

I will then discuss how the ideal of receptivity also allows us to identify what is most deeply appealing about "green values" (or deep ecology) concerning the environment; and after that I will look back into the first part of the book to see whether the criticisms it makes of Enlightenment values and the positive picture it offers of what is valuable in life don't also illustrate and help to justify belief in the importance of receptivity. Finally, I will deal with a number of theoretical and conceptual issues concerning the concept of receptivity and use the results to illuminate the nature and limitations of Western notions of autonomy. There is much to be said in favor of being autonomous, but some of the ideas and values associated with and endemic to that notion work against what is valuable about receptivity, and the book will close with a discussion of how its own second part helps supplement and fill out the positive picture of human values that the first part began to sketch.

Chapter 7

Receptivity to Life

I am going to begin our discussion of receptivity by considering the value it has as an attitude toward life or certain aspects of (one's) life. I want to begin by talking about the idea, defended by Rawls, Aristotle, and many others, that one should live one's life according to a life plan. I will argue that both this recommendation and the actual having of a plan of life show an undesirable and not particularly sensible lack of receptivity toward one's own life. I will then speak of some ways in which philosophical liberalism, too, commits one to being less receptive toward (one's) life than it is desirable for people to be.

LIFE PLANS AND RECEPTIVITY

In recent decades, the concept of a life plan came into prominence largely as a result of the work of John Rawls. Rawls drew many of his ideas from Aristotle, but others have followed both Rawls and Aristotle in arguing or assuming that life plans display, in a high form, the virtue of practical rationality.[2] Most significantly for our purposes here, those who have described and advocated life plans treat the having and following of a life plan as a reasonable and desirable way for individuals to live.

None of those discussions has pointed out how inappropriate it is or would be for a child to (already) have a life plan. And they also tend to neglect the possibility that it may be advisable for an adult to do without a life plan altogether until certain sorts of relevant information become available.[3] A forceful example of this latter possibility arises in connection with couples who want to pursue distinct careers. An academic woman with a nontenured position in the same town where her husband has tenure may well worry about the possibility of not receiving tenure. Should she perhaps then plan for that contingency, deciding, in advance, whether, in the event of being denied tenure, she should look for employment elsewhere (and, if necessary, spend much of her time away from her husband) or should stay with her husband (even at the cost of remaining unemployed)? Of course, other relevant factors may require her plan(s) to be more complicated than I have just suggested, but in addition to the issue of appropriate complexity, there is the further, important consideration that the very having of such a plan may actually impoverish the choice it eventually leads our woman to make.

If, for example, she decides in advance to live apart from her husband if that turns out to be the only way she can pursue her career, may that decision not make her slightly withdraw from him during the period of uncertainty about her tenure, so that it becomes easier for her to follow her plan if and when she is denied tenure? By the same token, if she decides in advance to stay with her husband, may that not affect the seriousness or the energy with which she pursues her career during the period of uncertainty about tenure? If we assume that plans can have emotional repercussions in this way, then there will be excellent reason for the woman *not* to make an advance decision about what to do if she doesn't receive tenure. For even if she eventually does receive tenure, the woman is likely to cramp either her career or her marriage by deciding what to do in advance, and if she does not make contingency plans, then although her eventual decision may be full of storm and stress, she will not at least have limited herself *unnecessarily* or *prematurely*.

I think many of us would agree—and for reasons of the sort just mentioned—that it would be better for the woman not to decide in advance. But we would also find it understandable that anxiety about tenure might make her rush into a decision about what she should do in the case of nontenure—as if intense anxiety over an event could somehow be allayed by imposing certainty about its effects on one's actions. However, I think we would agree that the woman would do better to contain, or learn to live with, her anxiety rather than allow it or herself to force an issue that is better delayed. Of course, if the decision *is* delayed, then both her career and her marriage may flourish in the interim, and her decision between them, if it comes to that, become all the more difficult to make. Indeed, a certain awareness of that fact may be part of what pushes or impels the woman toward an early decision. But such a decision would nonetheless be premature: It is worth waiting for a possible, more difficult, later decision, if that difficulty would be largely due to the greater richness of the then available alternatives.

Now one of the chief attractions of the notion of a life plan is that it seems to allow one to be active in determining one's fate; that it permits one (in a phrase that Rawls and others have used in this connection) to "take charge of one's life." But even if this is sometimes or even often a valid and rational motive, the above case suggests that this is far from always being so. Sheer suspense about whether she will be given tenure, sheer tension (and anger?) about having to be passive before the decision of others, might induce our woman to (re)assert some measure of active control over her life by at least having a plan about what to do in the event of not receiving tenure. But in her situation this is likely to be the prudentially wrong thing to do, and a sign, actually, of her weakness in the face of anxiety. Rather than unhelpfully and to a certain extent artificially trying to impose a kind of control on her own part over her situation, it would be better if she had a more *open* and *receptive* attitude toward the possibilities and eventualities that her life or situation may bring her way.

Rawls tells us that one's desires and capacities are affected by which life plan one adopts and follows: What one does according to the plan eventually makes a difference to the kind of person one is. But in the case of the academic woman, it is clear that the adoption of a life plan for certain eventualities may have adverse effects even before those eventualities arise and before one follows what the plan dictates with respect to them. This suggests some very significant limitations on what is appropriately the subject of life plans or planning in general; but our example also shows how and why a desire to control or impose control on (conditional events in) one's life can be counterproductive and also express or exhibit a certain weakness (and irrationality?) on the part of the person who seeks to assert or impose that control. It would in every sense be better if the woman could have and act from a more receptive attitude toward her life's possibilities, toward what life was in the future going to bring her way.[4]

Let me now mention yet another respect in which too much has been included within the scope of life plans through insufficient appreciation of the importance of a certain kind of receptivity or openness, that of waiting rather than taking charge or trying to be in control, in various areas of our lives. Those who advocate life plans typically hold that the basic goods of human life properly figure as ends or goals to be optimally or sufficiently catered to within rational life plans or schemes of conduct. But to think of personal goods as ends figuring within life plans is to regard them as things to which one can take means, as things one can try to achieve or obtain (or else as things under the immediate control of the will). And it seems to me, rather, that some of the most basic goods of life are precisely not things that it makes sense to think of pursuing or controlling in this way.

I have in mind here not merely assets, like a strong constitution or high intelligence, that one either has or lacks throughout one's life but also certain goods that come or do not come during the *course* of a life: in particular, the goods of friendship and love. Because love, or the state of being in love, is generally recognized to be largely outside our rational control, people do not usually take steps or exert efforts to attain it. Yet we tend to think of love as an important human good, as something that makes or can make an important contribution to human flourishing or happiness. And so it makes little sense in human terms for the good of love to feature among the ends catered to in life plans that dictate the means to, the best way of achieving, those ends. Thus although many young and not so young people hope and expect to get married someday, it would be odd for someone with no particular person in mind to say he *planned* to get married someday, and the reason, I assume, has to do with the fact that marriage is thought to presuppose love and that we cannot reasonably plan to love. So if anyone talks in the odd way, they are expressing a desire for control over what (if they thought about it) it makes no sense to think of controlling; and such a person thus lacks the kind of receptive attitude toward certain aspects and goods of life that it makes sense and is desirable for human beings to have.

To the extent that the advocates of life plans think of such plans as taking in or encompassing all of life's major goods (and evils), they have stretched that notion and the more general idea of planning beyond its actual usefulness and beyond what it makes sense to include within it. Some goods cannot sensibly be treated as goals of a plan of action, and anyone who thinks or tries to think of those goods in that way is expressing a desire for control over his or her life and a lack of receptivity toward the eventualities of their life that make no sense for human beings.[5] There is something not only futile but also ethically unattractive or offputting about such attitudes. But let me now mention some qualifications and caveats.

In saying what I have just being saying, I haven't intended to deny that love may sometimes require a certain amount of "stage setting" (e.g., joining an Internet dating site); and if one really wants or hopes for love to figure in one's life, one will avoid setting obstacles in its way (e.g., by signing up with the French Foreign Legion). But none of this needs entail that we can sensibly plan to fall or be in love—or plan to fall or be in love when certain conditions like financial security obtain. Nor does it entail that we should take means to this good rather than waiting—in some sense receptively—for it to occur and expecting, in the light of some knowledge of human nature and one's own "assets," that in due course it probably will.[6] I do not, however, mean to suggest that one must be entirely passive and/or receptive during love's genesis. Clearly, love can develop out of the activities of an ongoing relationship, but these activities are not, I believe, typically directed toward creating the love that grows out of them. The fact that we do not pursue the condition of loving means that we are in some sense passive, or at least receptive, vis-à-vis its coming; but it does not follow that we are passive or exclusively receptive in every relationship out of which (we hope) it may eventually grow.

All the above seems to be true not only of love but of the mutual affection of friendship, which thus constitutes another exception to the life plan theorist's assumption that the various major goods of life figure as goals within the life plans (and just plain plans) of individuals. It also represents a further good illustration of the idea that, at least in certain respects, a receptive and open attitude makes sense in our lives. A desire to control or be completely active with respect to the good of friendship makes no more sense and is just as unattractive as we have seen similar desires with respect to love and love relationships clearly to be. Rawls tells us that we are happy when we are in the way of successfully carrying out a rational life plan; but if important goods escape the net of such plans, then even if the lack of love or affection may not interfere with the fulfillment of what sensibly can occur within a life plan (or any plan), it may still prevent the happiness of an individual who is doing all she has planned for (and could reasonably hope to plan for). Rawls and some of the other advocates of life planning explicitly claim that acts and relations of love and friendship are among the ends we pursue and are thus among the goods that must be balanced off or orchestrated within life plans. And they also hold that love and friendship involve the pursuit of certain ends such as the well-being of the loved one or friend. But it is one thing to say that love *involves* (the having of) ends of action, quite another to claim that love is *itself* an end of action, and even if it makes sense to accept the first of these claims, the above discussion may help to explain why the second should be rejected.

All in all, the Rawlsian/Aristotelian emphasis on and advocacy of life plans seems to put too much of a premium on controlling our lives. With respect to some or many of life's important goods, a more receptive and open attitude makes more sense and is ethically much more attractive.

LIBERALISM AND RECEPTIVITY

There is a certain resemblance between the idea that we should live according to a life plan and the familiar liberal notion (discussed briefly in chapter 4) that nothing in one's life should be accepted uncritically, that everything—beliefs, relationships, habits, attitudes, emotions, commitments, ideals—should be at least at some point subjected to serious critical/rational scrutiny in order to determine whether it should be accepted or one should continue to accept it in(to) one's life. (It is no accident, I think, that Rawls, who pushed the idea of life plans so hard, was also a political liberal.)[7]

But if we should never just accept the feelings we find ourselves having toward others or certain relationships (as with siblings and parents) that we just find ourselves in, then a certain sort of receptivity toward what life has to offer us is (as in the case of life planning) being ruled out a priori and independently of the nature of what life actually brings our way. Feminism has taught us that certain relationships and feelings can be subject to gross abuse, and in the all-too-familiar circumstances of patriarchy, therefore, there is a case for women to be critical or more critical of certain of their relationships. But the typical contemporary liberal in effect translates these particular, but very familiar, historical/sociological reasons for critical doubt and hesitation into a need to question every feeling and/or relationship irrespective of whether there is any reason in advance to suspect or be wary of it. And this entails a very general or universal lack of acceptance or receptivity toward life and toward one's own life.[8]

I have argued at great length against this aspect of liberalism in my *The Ethics of Care and Empathy* (London: Routledge, 2007, ch. 5); and if that argument is on the right track, then the kind of critical vigilance (as I characterized it) that liberalism recommends is inconsistent with what is arguably a healthier, more receptive attitude toward one's own feelings and relationships. Obviously, one should scrutinize and be critical of relationships that are one sided or abusive, but that doesn't mean one should be looking for problems before they turn up or even threaten to turn up. And if one isn't looking for problems but is willing and able to consider and confront them if they *do* turn up, then one is receptive in a desirable way that liberalism clearly fails to appreciate.[9]

But notice, too, how all this compares with the issue of life planfulness. Someone with a life plan shows a certain lack of receptivity toward what their life will bring them in the future, but those who act as liberalism recommends and automatically subject the relationships they are in and the feelings that naturally attend those relationships to rational/critical scrutiny show a lack of receptivity toward what their life *has brought them*. So there is a difference of temporal modality and/or direction between the receptivity desirably involved in *not* having a life plan, on the one hand, and the receptivity desirably involved in *not* subjecting everything in one's life to rational scrutiny, on the other. Each of these forms of receptivity illustrates a different way in which life calls for receptivity and a different way of being receptive *toward* (one's) life. And understood together, what I have said about them constitutes a general illustration of how very important receptivity can be in any life.

But let's be clear. The forms of receptivity I have spoken of in this chapter both involve receptivity toward one's life in one or another of its aspects. And receptivity with this sort of "intentionality" (i.e., psychological content) is important to and in our lives. But other forms of receptivity are also important to and in our lives, forms that don't particularly involve any intentional attitude toward (one or another aspect of) one's own life but whose intentional objects or targets are more specifically or at least differently given. If, for example, one has a receptive attitude toward the natural world, then the immediate intentional object of one's receptivity is nature, not one's own life or life, in general, or any part or aspect of one's life. Now there may be a correlation between receptivity toward nature and receptivity toward one's own life. I don't know, and for all I know that correlation might even be established a priori. But I have no idea myself how one might be able to do that, so I shall assume that when we talk, say, of receptivity toward the environment or toward nature, we are talking about a different kind of (virtuous) receptivity from those forms of receptivity *toward (one's) life* that I have been discussing in this chapter. But these other forms of receptivity are very important *to* and *in* our lives even if their intentional focus isn't *on* (one's) life itself, and a full picture of the value and importance of receptivity therefore needs to take in a consideration of many different kinds of receptivity. We will be working toward that goal in our next chapter when we consider receptivity toward nature, but we shall subsequently be examining a variety of other forms of receptivity we haven't yet mentioned in this part of the present book. The discussion of part I, however, turns out to illustrate the importance of receptivity in several important ways, and after we talk about the environment and environmental ethics, I shall return to several topics discussed in part I and show how they (too) illustrate and illuminate the importance and virtuous character of being receptive.

NOTES

1. The Enlightenment wasn't the first movement or tradition to emphasize reason in the West—after all, all positive Greek ethical thought was committed to ethical rationalism. But as I mentioned earlier, the most important Greek philosophers weren't interested in or alive to those skeptical issues about human reason that preoccupied much of Enlightenment thought, and the criticisms I made in part I about Enlightenment views concerning (the importance of) epistemic rationality aren't so immediately relevant to ancient Greek or Roman philosophy. That is why part I focuses mainly on the Enlightenment and its influence; but the issues raised in part II will, in fact, occupy a somewhat wider swath of Western philosophical rationalism.

2. See, for example, Rawls, *A Theory of Justice*, Cambridge, MA: Harvard University Press, 1971, esp. pp. 398–449, 550–63; Charles Fried, *An Anatomy of Values*, Cambridge, MA: Harvard University Press, 1970, pp. 1f., 98–101, 156–75, 234; David A. J. Richards, *A Theory of Reasons for Action*, Oxford, UK: Clarendon Press, 1971, pp. 29–46; and John Cooper, *Reason and Human Good in Aristotle*, Cambridge, MA: Harvard University Press, 1975, pp. 94–127. These books contain pertinent references to and discussions of Aristotle's views, especially in book I of the *Eudemian Ethics*, on life plans and life planfulness.

3. Richards, op. cit., is a partial exception, but he never, in fact, mentions the specific kind of example I will describe in the text above. My own discussion here substantially follows what I have written in an earlier book, *Goods and Virtues*, Oxford, UK: Oxford University Press, 1983, chapter 2.

4. Rawls and others allow that there may be reasons to revise a total life plan during the course of one's life, but I don't think this affects what I have just been saying about the woman who prematurely makes plans about what to do if she doesn't get tenure and can't get another job in the city or area where her husband has tenure. Nor does it affect the other objections to life planning that I will be mentioning in what follows.

5. I have been putting things as I have because I want to allow the possibility that someone should care only about their own creative goals/fulfillment and have little or no interest in love or relations of close friendship. (As chapter 5 argued, such a life would necessarily be less than perfect, but it doesn't follow and it may not be true that such a life has to be less than a good one.) But, then, unless Rawls and the other defenders of life plans wish somehow (and on what basis?) to exclude love and friendship as basic or important goods in human life, they shouldn't recommend having a life plan as a way for *everyone* to go about living their life. A life plan has to focus on what can be considered to be major life goods, and it makes no sense to plan to fall in love or to have close friends. In addition, great creative achievement, if and when it occurs, is also a great good in life, but does it make sense even for an artistic, philosophical, or scientific genius to *plan* to make an important contribution? Is such a thing really that much under her or his control? Can it even be predicted? I am inclined to answer such questions in the negative, and in that case both the having of close relationships and the creative self-fulfillment I characterized in chapter 5 as mutually clashing, but important, goods can't reasonably be planned for. And that gives us all the more reason to reject the notion of a life plan.

6. Even getting therapy in an effort to become more capable of love is more plausibly regarded as a clearing away of obstacles to falling or being in love than as a means to or part of a plan for falling or being in love.

7. Liberalism has some of its roots in Enlightenment thought and in ancient Greek philosophy (compare Socrates' idea that the unexamined life is not worth living). But I haven't found any places in the literature of eighteenth-century Enlightenment philosophy where the specific idea that everything should be subjected to rational scrutiny is advocated or even mentioned, whereas it is quite easy to find examples of this idea in the literature of or surrounding liberalism. See, for example, Martha Nussbaum, *Sex and Social Justice*, New York: Oxford University Press, 1999, p. 74ff.; and John Christman, *The Politics of Persons: Autonomy and Socio-Historical Selves*, Cambridge, UK: Cambridge University Press, 2009, p. 121.

8. In chapter 4, I argued that someone who seriously questions his or her own desire to help those who are in need of help (and this especially applies to their own friends and family) will to that extent be a less caring, moral, and altruistic person. So if liberalism tells us to be seriously skeptical about our own moral "commitments," it is telling us to be less moral than we otherwise

might or morally *should* be. This is or would be an unfortunate implication of the liberal position, but I am not at all convinced that liberalism is committed to *this* kind of individual self-doubt. However, if it is not, one then wonders how the liberal can plausibly or consistently tell us to question everything *except* our morality. Moreover, not everyone has good moral character, and those who do not probably *should* question their own character. Only one then doesn't know how the liberal can make a principled exception for those people who in actual fact *are* decent and caring (possessed of good moral character).

9. If the liberal is committed to seriously questioning everything in his life, perhaps he should question his own commitment to the liberal idea that one ought to question everything. And perhaps the argument offered here can help the liberal to do just that.

Chapter 8

Green Thinking

The Faustian attitude involves a controlling and even a dominating attitude toward the world and even toward one's own actions. As we shall see more clearly in what follows, this kind of attitude antedates the Enlightenment in the West—indeed, its roots and its predominant influence go at least as far back as ancient Greek thought and culture. But the examples of Faustianism described in the last chapter are not familiar as such. No one or almost no one thinks of the preference for life plans and/or the insistence on subjecting everything in one's life to serious critical scrutiny as examples of the/a Faustian attitude, and yet they really are that, and our previous discussion shows, I think, how objectionable Faustianism is in those particular instances. It shows, in particular, that the forms of Faustianism we discussed in the last chapter demonstrate a deplorable or criticizable lack of receptivity in the relevant attitudes toward the world and one's own life and actions. Receptivity has long been underappreciated in Western philosophy, but the attempt to show what is wrong with Faustianism makes us see the importance of receptivity in and to our lives. As I shall argue at greater length later in this book, receptivity is a virtue, and any attempt to understand our ethical values needs to understand the role receptivity plays in relation to other ethical values.

There is, however, one place in recent ethical thought where the importance of *something like* receptivity has already been appreciated. Even though the term itself hasn't been particularly emphasized, recent advocates of green environmental values or of deep ecology have certainly attacked and criticized the (Faustian) attitude/motivation of active control and domination over nature that has historically characterized our treatment, in the West, of the environment. And the term *receptivity*, in fact, helps us in our attempt to describe what is or has been *lacking* in Western attitudes and behavior toward the environment, just as it helps us to say what is lacking about the effort to live in accordance with a life plan and about the insistence or recommendation that we should subject every feeling and relationship to critical scrutiny.

According to green thinking, Western thought has tended to equate maleness with being active and rational and femaleness with being passive and emotional; and along with those equations, of course, has gone the assumption that male, rational activity is (ethically) superior to female, passive emotionality.[1] Since controlling or even dominating and exploiting the environment seems to be the most active way of dealing with or treating the environment, it has been assumed that it is rational and sensible to treat the world around us in this fashion. But green thinking and/or deep ecology questions these assumptions. Aside from the invidious attitude toward things female that the assumptions express or embody, green thinkers question whether it is always or even usually best to approach matters—not just the environment but other things as well—in an active or dominating manner. What about just *appreciating* or even feeling awe at the beauty and diversity/richness/complexity of the world around us? Isn't this not only appropriate but *called for* in the light of how beautiful and awe inspiring the natural world actually is.[2] And even though, as I said, green thinking hasn't emphasized the notion or phenomenon of receptivity, that notion, that phenomenon, seems very relevant to what I have just been saying.[3] To be willing and able to appreciate nature, rather than always having to dominate, exploit, or control it, is to have a somewhat receptive attitude toward the natural world, and I believe green theorists should and would be willing to accept that thought—and use it to help make their case against Faustian values.[4]

And in this respect we can also see that *receptivity* is a better word for what greens or deep ecologists want and recommend than is the term *passivity*. To be sure, Western thought has drawn comparisons between emotionality, femaleness, and passivity and between rationality, maleness, and activeness/activity/control; but when it comes right down to it, green opposition to these comparisons doesn't entail the recommendation that we be passive or more passive toward the environment. Appreciating the beauty and diversity of the environment and leaving it to some extent alone needn't and probably shouldn't be described as involving passivity or a passive attitude toward the environment—that seems too extreme a claim, an exaggeration. What the green thinker should, I think, want to say is that we need a more receptive attitude toward the environment, and so I think the term/notion of receptivity gives the green thinker a good further way to criticize Faustian attitudes toward the environment and state what they themselves think our attitude ought to be. In effect and in metaphysical terms, receptivity vis-à-vis the environment lies somewhere between a totally dominating attitude and total passivity vis-à-vis the environment, and I think the green thinker should say that this more moderate or "medial" attitude is superior to each of those extremes.

But this is not—is *not*—intended as a criticism of those forms of Eastern thought that stress wu-wei in regard to the environment and more generally. The Taoist term *wu-wei* is sometimes translated as "nonaction," but many commentators have argued that this risks treating the term as implying more sheer passivity than it actually does, and for some such commentators, therefore, "natural action" or some other such expression is a better translation.[5] But even if the notion of natural action approximates what Taoism is speaking of here, that is clearly not the same thing as receptivity. The two may be related, and there may be no immediate inconsistency between the Taoist doctrine of wu-wei and what I want to say here about receptivity toward the environment, but receptivity is a very specific notion, and it is my purpose here to call attention to it and to highlight its special importance for environmental thought and, more generally, in and for our lives.[6] I don't believe the notion of wu-wei would allow us to make the same arguments because in itself it doesn't really *distinguish* between passivity and receptivity and doesn't allow us, therefore, to say that receptivity is valuable even if or when passivity is not. This is something that we should want to say and that I am, in effect, now saying in my own voice; and so although a further examination of wu-wei and a further comparison with receptivity would almost certainly be worthwhile, it would take us away from our main purposes if we did that here.

By the same token, the Chinese notion of yin, as contrasted with or complementary to yang, is often thought of as involving *both* the idea of receptivity *and* the idea of passivity (and perhaps the idea of nonaction and of the negative, in general, as well). And for that very reason the notion may be too broad to be of much help to the green environmentalist cause. As I have already mentioned, the green thinker should want to recommend receptivity *rather than* passivity toward nature; and the notion of yin is too unspecific, too general, too vague to serve that purpose. In fact, the overall critique of Enlightenment and Faustian Western values that I am making here in this book can only be made by distinguishing between passivity and receptivity and showing the value and importance of the latter notion. The more general (or metaphorical?) idea of yin cannot do that, and that is why the more specific notion of receptivity has been and will be the main basis for my general argument.[7]

The distinctive idea of the present book, therefore, is that the specific notion of receptivity can be used as a general corrective to previous Western thought and attitudes and constitutes an essential and pervasive (though hardly exclusive) basis for what we do or should find valuable in our lives. In effect, then, I am saying that we need to be more *receptive to receptivity* than we have previously been. In the last chapter, receptivity turned out to be important for clarifying and correcting our views about what is important in or to our lives. And I am now saying that we need the particular notion of receptivity to help us account for and even justify our values vis-à-vis the environment. I say "our values" here because I assume that the reader will appreciate the force of the views that I have so far attributed to the green philosopher. But green thinkers sometimes make other or further claims that are worth discussing in the present context (though I won't talk about the pacifist element in some green political thinking). Green thinkers have questioned the all-encompassing focus on rationality or sentience within the main moral theories advocated by Western moral philosophers, and they have urged the independent relevance of environmental values to a proper ethical understanding of what is valuable and important. I think we need to consider some of this in order to understand how the care ethics discussed in the first part of this book fits into a larger ethical picture, but let me start our discussion by focusing briefly on what other ethical traditions have said about the non-human and nonsentient environment.

Kantian ethics regards us as having moral obligations only toward other rational beings—thus leaving both lower animals and the environment or surrounding ecosystem as basically outside our proper moral concern. Of course, the Kantian can say that a concern for animals that altogether lack reason, can, as a matter of empirical fact, have implications for what we do with fellow rational creatures and with creatures that are *to some degree* rational; and to that extent they can allow that there are ethical considerations that favor treating nonrational creatures (or, for similar reasons, the environment more generally) in certain ways. By contrast, the green thinker and many utilitarians and sentimentalists can hold that the welfare of completely nonrational fellow creatures is of intrinsic moral concern to us, and this fits better with our present-day ethical views.

But the utilitarian and care-ethical sentimentalists like Nel Noddings see sentience as the basis for intrinsic ethical concern, and this means that they, too, don't accord any fundamental ethical relevance to green environmental values.[8] If something damages the environment but has no possible or likely effect on any sentient being, they will say that the damage done cannot and will not involve any moral or ethical disvalue, and, of course, many green philosophers would strongly disagree. But care-ethical sentimentalism may actually be able and may, indeed, want to side with green thinking on these issues: There is at least one way of naturally extending care ethics that I think may and should move care ethics in the direction of green thinking. What I have in mind is not—what may have occurred to some of you—that we should extend or expand our ideas about empathy to allow for empathy with plants and nonliving things or systems. I don't see this idea as all that promising and think we should move in a somewhat different direction.[9]

Care ethics places great value on caring about others, but clearly people who are cared about need not only the material/physical goods that care givers provide but are also often needy of and emotionally responsive to the caring attitude that motivates someone to provide such goods. In the case of maternal or parental caring, this amounts to a need for love, and although care ethics has been more than willing to acknowledge such a need, it hasn't particularly emphasized that need in relation to its own ethical values—hasn't stressed, for example, how much the value of caring relationships depends on fulfilling someone's basic need to be loved or at least liked. Where such a need *is* emphasized is in the work of Abraham Maslow.[10] In contrast with the behaviorism and Freudianism that dominated psychological thought at the time he wrote, Maslow held that the desire for love and for esteem and for being liked are basic instinctual needs. He also spoke of a higher need for "self-actualization," but what is most relevant to our discussion of environmental ethics is what he had to say about another supposedly basic need, the desire/need to belong.

Now I don't think we need to get into the question of how deep the desire for love or for belonging goes in our psychological repertoire. But even if these things aren't exactly instincts, they play an important role in human life, and that is all I need to say for present purposes. The idea that we need or want to belong, in tandem with the idea that we need or want love, expands or extends care ethics, but clearly does so in a direction that its emphasis on love and caring itself encourages. Part of the value of caring comes from the way it answers our human neediness, and the desire to belong shows itself perhaps most strongly in those caring familial relationships that answer our need for love and that have collectively functioned, for care ethics, as the very paradigm of caring. So how does the need to belong help us with or toward green ethical values?

Well, to begin with, our sense of what belongs and our need to belong extend far beyond families and close personal relationships. Nationhood involves citizens or subjects having a sense of belonging together and belonging to a larger whole, the nation or the country, that includes them all. And the sense of belonging also involves a sense of obtrusiveness, of what doesn't belong, and of bereftness when what does belong is destroyed or taken away. During World War II, when a great number of American soldiers were stationed in Britain as preparations were being made for the Normandy invasion, the British had a saying about them. The Americans were "overpaid, oversexed, and over here," and that expression was clearly giving vent to a very general feeling that, despite the necessity of their being there, the Americans were an intrusive or obtrusive element, that they didn't belong where in such great numbers they temporarily were.

But consider, too, the suggestion that was once made that we should try to blow up the moon in order to prevent the disasters that will invariably result from increasingly higher high tides here on Earth.[11] Surely, we'd feel utterly bereft if such a thing were done or occurred through natural processes like the lunar impact of an enormous asteroid, and that is because the moon *belongs*. It belongs to our larger human habitat and we feel, don't we?, that we and it belong together within that habitat. The words *environment* and *ecosystem* are too impersonal to convey this sense of what belongs with or in what, and although we could naturally and expressively say that the moon belongs to our "world," in that non-scientific usage that we are all familiar with, the word *habitat* is perhaps more specific and less metaphorical in its ability to convey what we mean by belonging in such cases. The idea of a common habitat conveys a sense of the familar and of what belongs, a sense of things/people whose absence would leave one feeling bereft and somewhat alienated and a sense, too, that some things can be intrusive or obtrusive because they are so unfamiliar. Thus just as the moon belongs in the sky, the sky itself in the colloquial sense of the term belongs to our world, our human habitat; and, on a smaller scale, the river that runs through a small town will seem to its inhabitants to belong there, so that if it is dammed upstream to create a reservoir, it will typically be over the objections of the local citizenry and of the environmentally minded. To that extent, that river and the sky and the moon all belong where they are or where they have been.[12]

Now let's be a bit more specific about the ethical implications of what has just been said about the sense of and impulse toward belonging. We seem to want to belong to various larger habitats or groups or communities, and to have a sense of what does or does not belong with us in those larger units. But I have claimed that nonliving things or entities can either belong or not belong, and I think we need to say more about how one *thinks* about something that is regarded as belonging with one. Much of what I say will also apply to plants and animals, and in the first instance what is thought of as belonging, what is felt to belong, is seen as having a certain intrinsic importance. We don't regard the river that flows through our town and the moon simply as means to human or other purposes, and this thought is certainly reminiscent of what Kant and many Kantians say about how we should think about and treat other rational beings. But the twist in the present context, what the idea of belonging allows us to do, is to make that idea of intrinsic importance relevant to environmental thinking and values in a way that Kantianism as such never sought and may be unable to do.

Of course, many green environmentalists are more than willing to say that we shouldn't treat inanimate things and ecosystems as mere means and to claim that such entities have an intrinsic importance or are even "ends in themselves."[13] It can be said, for example, that the sheer existence of asteroids or inanimate natural systems can be valuable in itself, and such nonutilitarian consequentialist thinking can certainly lead us toward green environmentalism's idea that we should preserve such entities for motives or reasons that are independent of how they serve the purposes of human beings or other sentient creatures. But if we buy into the care ethics that was defended earlier, we will reject the moral impartialism of consequentialism in favor of an emphasis on how we empathically, and of necessity therefore partially, relate or ought to relate to others. And my point here is that such an ethics of care naturally extends to green environmentalism when one recognizes the importance of the need for love to any care ethics and sees that the need to belong is also basic to our human perspective. In relation to that perspective and to our needs as humans, the despoliation and destruction of natural objects and habitats runs counter to our sense of what belongs and ethically offends against our sense that certain things aren't just means to the fulfillment of our purposes and are intrinsically important to us. And such thinking and such values derive principally from our desire for and sense of belonging. To destroy the moon or the river that runs through our town is to treat these things as lacking the importance that we all think they have, and we simply don't want these things to happen. But then, when I consider how such destruction affects or would affect those I live with and care about, more traditional or familiar sentimentalist care-ethical considerations also kick in and support an ethical concern for certain inanimate things, for whole habitats, and for flora both individually and considered as a whole.

But this discussion has taken us away from our main focus on receptivity. It shows the resources a suitably expanded care ethics has for dealing with green environmental values and so indicates a direction in which what was said in part I ought probably to go. But having said as much, I think we need to reconnect with our discussion of receptivity. In particular, we need to say how our whole discussion and criticism of Enlightenment/rationalist values in part I helps to illustrate and make the case for the importance of receptivity as a phenomenon and as a value, and I will say a great deal about this in our next chapter.

NOTES

1. On these "equations," see the very interesting discussion in Andrew Brennan and Yeuk-Sze Lo's article, "Environmental Ethics," in the online *Stanford Encyclopedia of Philosophy.*
2. In speaking as I have, I have been treating human beings as *relating to* an environment, rather than as being part of ecosystems that *include* both human and other elements. The ways I have spoken may, to some degree, lead toward thinking that we should control the environment, because an environment is something that stands *over and against* human beings. And thinking in terms

of ecosystems might encourage the thought that "we are all in this together," a thought that would make it easier to understand and appreciate the force of what green thinkers have been saying about the harmfulness and inappropriateness of a largely dominating attitude toward nature. But having acknowledged this point, I shall allow myself to speak less carefully or accurately in the main text.

On the receptivity involved in aesthetic appreciation generally, see Nel Noddings, *Caring: A Feminine Approach to Ethics and Moral Education*, Berkeley: University of California Press, 1984, p. 21ff.

3. It isn't just green environmentalists who neglect the notion of receptivity in relation to environmental issues. One also sees this neglect in some of the best work that has been done on the ethics of the environment from the standpoint of traditional ethical theorizing. See, for example, Rosalind Hursthouse's (Aristotelian) "Environmental Virtue Ethics" (in R. Walker and P. Ivanhoe, eds., *Working Virtue: Virtue Ethics and Contemporary Moral Problems*, Oxford, UK: Clarendon Press, 2007, pp. 155–71) and Thomas Hill's (Kantian) "Ideals of Human Excellence and Preserving Natural Environments" (*Environmental Ethics* 5, 1983, pp. 211–24) for work that emphasizes the virtues of respect for nature and humility toward nature as antidotes to the desire to dominate nature, but that doesn't discuss (the similar role of) the virtue of receptivity toward nature. Nontraditional green thinkers also sometimes advocate greater respect for and/or humility toward nature, but somehow (again) the useful notion of receptivity toward nature tends to get lost in the shuffle. However, for a relatively rare exception, see Peter Marshall, *Nature's Web: Rethinking Our Place on Earth*, New York: Paragon House, 1994.

4. Many environmental ethicists (not just "greens") think it is important for us to see ourselves as part of nature, but I don't think such an attitude or belief directly involves being receptive toward nature in the way that the appreciation of natural beauty *does* seem to be a form of such receptiveness. However, both seeing oneself as part of nature and a receptive appreciative attitude toward nature stand opposed to a dominating or controlling attitude toward the natural world and so have at least that much in common.

5. See, for example, Roger Ames's article, "Taoist ethics," in L. Becker and C. Becker, eds., *The Encyclopedia of Ethics*, 2nd edition, New York: Routledge, 2001, esp. p. 1683. Incidentally, the Taoist notion of wu-wei, like the Buddhist emphasis on enlightened nondesire, can at the very least call our attention to the value and/or virtue of self-sufficient contentment with what one is and has. The Buddhist and the Taoist view such a state or states through the prism of certain metaphysical assumptions, but we needn't make those assumptions in order to see virtue/value in a "Buddhalike" sense of contentment and (at least temporary) nondesire. I have argued at great length for viewing things this way in my *Beyond Optimizing*, Cambridge, MA: Harvard,

1989; but I don't think a further examination of self-sufficiency and of moderation in one's desires or "satisficing" would much affect the issues between Faustianism and the ideas I am trying to put in its place.

6. I say no immediate inconsistency because, as was just mentioned, the Taoist notion of wu-wei is usually deployed against the background of certain metaphysical assumptions about the illusoriness or disunity of the self, assumptions that are not presupposed by anything I say in this book and that may, indeed, turn out to be inconsistent with the necessary metaphysical underpinnings (who knows?) of what I am saying in this book about our values and our lives. But I don't want to go any further into metaphysical issues about personhood and identity here and will, at most, simply rely on what seem commonsense assumptions about such issues.

7. To the extent yin also connotes the negative (with yang suggesting the idea of the positive), it is even more inappropriate for the arguments we want to make here. No one or almost no one is ever likely to think there is some virtue in the negative or negativity as such; but a case can and will be made for the virtue status of human receptivity, and that will have important implications for how we see the main tradition(s) of Western philosophy.

8. See Noddings, *Caring*, chapter 7. A nonutilitarian consequentialist can hold that the preservation of nonsentient parts of nature can have ethical value in itself, and to that extent green thinkers can also be consequentialists. However, there are other aspects or implications of consequentialism that are questionable in relation to green thinking. Consequentialism accords no basic moral relevance to our relationships with particular individuals (or things)—saying, for example, that we have no greater basic obligations toward those we know and live with than toward strangers, and so on. And I would think this sort of impartialism wouldn't sit well with a green philosophy that puts so much emphasis on our *relations with and to our own environment or habitat*. What I shall be arguing for below does, however, allow us to accommodate and justify such an emphasis.

9. Some Confucian thinkers seem to have believed we can feel empathy for broken tiles and other material objects, but more recently R. M. Hare has claimed that we can feel empathy for plants and mountains. (See his reply to critics in D. Seanor and M. Fotion, eds., *Hare and Critics*, Oxford, UK: Oxford University Press, 1988, p. 283.) For forceful criticism of Hare's view here, see Richard Holton and Rae Langton, "Empathy and Animal Ethics" in D. Jamieson, ed., *Singer and His Critics*, Oxford, UK: Blackwell, 1996, p. 212ff.

10. See, for example, his *Motivation and Personality*, New York: Harper and Row, 1954.

11. I am indebted for this rather shocking example to Rosalind Hursthouse, "Environmental Virtue Ethics" in R. Walker and P. J. Ivanhoe, eds., op. cit.

12. In "Building, Dwelling, Thinking" (in *Poetry, Language, Thought*, translated by Albert Hofstadter, New York: Harper Colophon Books, 1971) Martin

Heidegger speaks in something like these ways of the sky and of our common world, and the relevance of Heidegger's views to green environmental ethics has long been recognized. (See, e.g., M. E. Zimmerman, "Toward a Heideggerian Ethos for Radical Environmentalism," *Environmental Ethics* 6, 1983, pp. 99–131; and his "Implications of Heidegger's Thought for Deep Ecology," *The Modern Schoolman* 54, 1986, pp. 19–43.) My main point in the text above, though, is to highlight the instinctual or deep psychological aspect of our sense of belonging, and I shall use this in furtherance of specifically ethical thinking in a way that Heidegger and others have not, to my knowledge, done.

13. For references and discussion, see the article "Environmental Ethics" by Andrew Brennan and Yeuk-Sze Lo in the online *Stanford Encyclopedia of Philosophy*.

Chapter 9

From Enlightenment to Receptivity

The first part of this book, "Beyond Enlightenment," argued at great length that Enlightenment ideas and values distort our deepest sense of values and how we view our lives. The discussion went forward without the use of the specific notion of receptivity, but it turns out that this notion can help us make better sense of and justify most of the criticisms that were made earlier of Enlightenment thought. I say most because what was said in part I about the impossibility of perfection doesn't in any immediate or obvious way relate to issues about receptivity. The idea that perfection is impossible certainly goes against the Enlightenment view of things, but what I showed or argued was wrong with the Enlightenment (and ancient Greek) idea of human perfectibility didn't bring in anything that readily relates to the idea or ideal of receptivity. (Later, in our conclusion, I will have more to say, however, about how the impossibility of perfection connects with what I have said about the value and importance of receptivity.)

But if we leave the issue of necessary imperfection to one side, there were still a number of other topics discussed in part I that relate to what I have been saying about the importance of receptivity. And it will be my purpose here in this chapter to show you how various of the criticisms of Enlightenment thought in part I can be further clarified—and *justified*—by connecting them to a larger and positive ethical view that highlights the virtue of receptivity. Let us begin with what was said in chapter 1 about the epistemic/rational virtues of fair-mindedness, open-mindedness, and objectivity.

In chapter 1, it was argued that these virtues depend on our capacity for empathy with others' points of view (or beliefs or arguments); and this clearly means being to some degree receptive toward what may very well be very different from what we ourselves think or want to argue. There are limits to this, of course, and as I mentioned in chapter 1, if someone else shows no sign of being open or willing to listen to what one has to say, a certain intolerance (and unreceptiveness) toward his or her ideas may be not only appropriate but understandable in terms of the way empathy itself tends to work. But in any event and to the extent open-mindedness is an epistemic virtue, so, too, is epistemic receptivity. And this is a point that even virtue epistemologists who have stressed the virtue of open-mindedness (in a way traditional epistemology hasn't really done) have missed. Even though they emphasize the virtue status of open-mindedness, they haven't recognized or spoken of the virtuousness of the more general trait of receptivity (to ideas) that underlies it.

Moreover, since such receptivity, as we have argued, involves a capacity for seeing and a tendency to see others' viewpoints (the propositions they assent to, for example) in the favorable light in which they appear to those others, it has an emotional or feeling-ful component, and so the objection to Enlightenment thought, made in chapter 1, that it fails to recognize an important emotional component in the epistemic values it recognizes and emphasizes, can also be put in terms of receptivity. A certain emotional receptivity is an/one important aspect of epistemic rationality, and the Enlightenment philosophy, by treating the emotions as something irrelevant to and, if possible, to be banned or isolated from the epistemic/intellectual realm, can be criticized for failing to see the virtuous character of receptivity, of being receptive, in that realm (or in any other).[1]

In chapter 2, I described the epistemically irrational tendencies that I claimed were attendant on and actually essential to certain sorts of emotional attitudes and personal relationships. If we love another person, we tend to take in their ideas, attitudes, and values in a nonconscious and nondeliberate way, and such a taking in or imbibing of other's traits or views is clearly a form of receptivity. Chapter 2 argued that a certain amount or degree of epistemic irrationality is important to many of the things—like love and love relationships—we value most in life, and it criticized the Enlightenment and those who today tend to think mainly in Enlightenment terms for failing to see how important it is actually to *be* epistemically/cognitively less than fully rational in certain ways. The Enlightenment tells us basically that we should always be epistemically (and otherwise) fully rational, but, as chapter 2 pointed out, this simply doesn't sit well with what our deepest and most irrecusable values actually are. But having now pointed out the importance of receptivity to our lives and values, we can usefully reframe what was said about epistemic rationality and irrationality in its terms. If certain feelings and relationships are central to (what is valuable in) our lives, then the receptivity that those feelings and relationships require or involve is also shown to be a central value in our lives and in our thinking about what is of value in our lives. And the still very influential Enlightenment idea that we should always be cognitively/epistemically rational can therefore be faulted for its failure to acknowledge or recognize that value.

In chapter 3 of part I the focus moved away from epistemic virtues and values to a concern with normative morality. Care ethics was defended as a view of right and wrong against rationalist theories of morality that treat our emotions as, at least at a fundamental level, irrelevant to normative questions of moral obligation and moral goodness. But, as the recent psychology literature by and large indicates, caring seems to depend on the development of our capacity for empathy, and sometimes that empathy involves and has to involve a tendency to feel what others are feeling that works in an automatic fashion. However, that tendency, the capacity for unself-consciously taking in what others feel, involves a high degree of receptivity, and so what I said earlier about normative care ethics can be reconfigured as a way of illustrating and emphasizing the importance of receptivity to leading a morally good or decent life.[2] (What I said about inductive discipline in chapter 3 also moves us in the same direction, but there is no need to say any more about that at this point.) By contrast, Enlightenment-type ethical rationalism essentially represents a failure to see how important receptivity is to the moral life. The moral rationalist thinks (practical) rationality is or can be an adequate basis and motive for morality, and since morality thus conceived doesn't essentially involve and isn't inherently subject to "passive" human emotions, it can be viewed as essentially under our control. But this downplays or ignores the receptivity that morality and the moral life require of us, and that, I think, is the most basic reason why care ethicists and others who think emotion and feeling are central to the moral life should regard ethical rationalism as fundamentally misguided.[3]

And let me illustrate the difference, as it favors such sentimentalist approaches, by the following two examples. Kantians and other rationalists treat respect for other people as essential to the moral life, but they regard such respect as largely a matter of rationally acknowledging or appreciating the rational nature or dignity of other individuals and don't see that respect also requires emotional attitudes or responses. Thus the parent who imposes a career on a child without paying any attention to what the child wants—and who says that he or she is doing so for the child's own good—shows a lack of respect for the child as an individual and also demonstrates a lack of empathy for the child's point of view. (For example, if the child says he would like to play baseball sometimes rather than always practice the violin in order to become a concert violinist, the parent will often insist that he doesn't "really" want to play baseball and waste all the money that has been spent on his musical train-ing—or the child is told: you can't really be as ungrateful as you are sounding.) Moral respect for others requires us to see things from their standpoint (a parallel point was made for epistemological con-texts in chapter 1, above); and therefore, far from being a matter of sheer rational/intellectual acknowledgement along rationalist lines, respect for others requires us to be open and receptive to their reality.

Rationalists also fail to appreciate this point in regard to politi-cal/social contexts. They often say that respect for others' right to freedom of worship involves a rational acknowledgement of such a right that makes one, in practical and legal terms, tolerate the beliefs and practices even of those whose beliefs and practices one views with disgust, distaste, or hatred. But, ideally speaking, respect involves more than this: It involves an effort to understand the views of those one deeply disagrees with (let's not talk about cases where these others are themselves preaching hatred and intolerance), and this means being receptive to their point of view even if one strongly rejects it in the end. Thus ethical rationalism with respect to various rights and liberties fails to appreciate the receptive element in the fullest or most ideal kind of respect for others, and it would seem that the emphasis on sheer reason or rationality (understood rather narrowly) is what prevents this deeper and more ethically adequate understanding of what respect for others involves.[4]

In chapter 3, I also said that the correlation that seems to exist between our less controversial normative moral judgments/intu-itions and our empathic tendencies points toward the metaethical conclusion that empathy enters into our moral concepts, into our very understanding of claims about right and wrong.[5] But I said that I wanted to delay going into further detail until such time as the bearing of these metaethical facts on the importance of recep-tivity could be highlighted, and this is that time. So let me briefly say why I think empathy enters into moral claims or judgments and then say how that fact bears on the importance of receptivity. (The idea that empathy enters into moral concepts and judgments is defended at much greater length in my book *Moral Sentimentalism*.) Sentimentalists such as Hume and myself think moral claims of right and wrong are semantically grounded in independently understandable emotional attitudes of approval and disapproval, and, following some remarks Hume makes late in his *Treatise of Human Nature* but dissenting from his official theory of what approval and disapproval consist in, I want to say (very roughly) that emotional approval basically involves being empathically warmed by the warm-heartedness some agent displays in her actions or attitudes toward a third party or parties; and that emotional disapproval involves being empathically chilled by or at the cold-heartedness someone displays toward a third party or parties.[6] And when you think about it, this is a rather intuitive idea of what approval and disapproval, at their most basic level, consist in.[7]

Moreover, sentimentalists have typically said that moral judgments or claims express, describe, or project hypothetical or actual attitudes of approval and disapproval, but these traditional approaches force one to treat moral claims as less objectively valid than rationalists and most ordinary people think they are. So in MS I made use of Saul Kripke's notion of "reference-fixing" to argue that the meaning of moral claims is *fixed in relation to* empathic attitudes of approval or disapproval, but that moral claims in no way *take in or describe such attitudes as part of their actual subject matter.* This arguably allows claims of right and wrong and of moral goodness to be objectively valid or true, but for present purposes the most important point is that whether or not it allows for moral objectivity, any sentimentalist view of the meaning of moral claims/utterances that sees them as based in empathic approval and disapproval gives receptivity a central place in our explicit moral *thinking* (and not just in what as decent people we unself-consciously *do*).[8] If moral judgments and claims depend on our capacity for approval and disapproval, then they depend on our capacity for empathically taking in the warmth that we see others expressing in their actions or attitudes and the lack of warmth or coldness that those who are indifferent or malicious toward third parties exhibit in their actions or attitudes. And to be warmed or chilled by another's warmth or coldness is not to do something deliberately, but to be to a high degree emotionally receptive to what is going on around us. So on the view just described, receptivity lies at the heart of moral judgment and moral belief and is therefore essential to a very important part of our life and thought.[9] Thus, receptivity may play a role not only in the epistemic rational virtues of open-mindedness and objectivity and in the epistemically less than fully rational attitudes and beliefs (and acquisition of such) that are characteristic of important relationships and feelings such as friendship and love, but in acting morally and in thinking about morality as well.[10]

Given the above, we can now see that the philosophical arguments that I used in part I to *question* Enlightenment thinking also and in a variety of ways help to establish the positive importance of receptivity as part of our lives. And, reciprocally, when we think of receptivity as central to our values, we are also supporting the particular positive and negative conclusions I arrived at in part I. For example, if we (at least in the West) have a general tendency to value and emphasize control and activity at the expense of openness and receptivity, then it becomes more understandable that so many moral philosophers (again in the West) would prefer rationalism to sentimentalism and be uncomfortable with the kind of discussion of and emphasis on empathy-based and receptive emotions/feelings that is so characteristic of moral sentimentalism. (Remember, though, that love and empathy can lead to forms of intolerance, and this then applies to receptivity as well—so receptivity can in some ways be important for the obstacles it presents to morality. Still, intolerance represents a failure to be really receptive to others' views, and so a full receptivity to others represents a virtue even if lesser degrees of receptivity deployed in certain directions can be ethically negative in their import.) So much of Western normative ethics has been rationalist in character (intuitionism, Kantianism, contractarianism, ancient virtue ethics, and various forms of consequentialism are all good examples) that one might well wonder whether sentimentalism has any chance of surviving and thriving in contemporary philosophy. But the specific arguments that were given in chapter 3 and here in the present chapter (and more fully in MS) do support a sentimentalist view of morality, and I am saying that my general critique of Faustian assumptions helps further support such an approach because it makes the previous *rejection* of moral sentimentalism seem part of an *all-too-familiar pattern of errors*.[11]

Similarly, what was said in chapters 1 and 2 about epistemic rationality tends to show that such rationality is less important than many philosophers have thought, but most or many philosophers will be uncomfortable with and resist these conclusions. We philosophers like the idea of being epistemically or theoretically rational.[12] We think that if we are rational in that way, then emotion won't play a role in what we think and our actions will be more under our control than they otherwise would be. And that idea pleases many of us a great deal. But the strong emphasis on control and on rationality (conceived as not involving emotion or feeling) distorts and, in effect, seeks to subvert the very real and essential role receptivity plays in our lives. So what is being said here in part II supports our earlier conclusions about epistemic rationality by situating the rationalist views that were criticized in part I within a newly recognizable pattern of errors or bias. In effect, the conclusions of part I argue in favor of the general picture I am painting in part II but also find further support themselves by being part of that hopefully persuasive larger picture.

However, we can also see at this point that the value of receptivity extends far beyond the problems we have found with the Enlightenment philosophy in part I. In chapter 7, we saw that a certain philosophical view about the value of life planning is misguided precisely because of its failure to reckon with and acknowledge the importance of a more receptive attitude toward our lives. In addition, I argued that the liberal's insistence on subjecting every feeling and relationship to rational/critical scrutiny and control also constitutes a failure to properly value receptivity in regard to our own lives. Then, in chapter 8, we saw that receptivity is an important and perhaps even a necessary antidote to the ethically repugnant dominating attitude toward nature that characterizes the historic Faustianism of Western thought and culture. These uses of receptivity don't engage with or work critically against any specific Enlightenment theses or attitudes, and so they show, and we have seen, that receptivity has a value and significance beyond any engagement with or against Enlightenment thinking and that it, at the very least, potentially holds the promise of being a central element in any post-Enlightenment and post-Faustian general picture of what is really valuable in and about our lives.

And one further point. What I have said about Faustian attitudes toward the natural world suggests and more than suggests that we in the West have long overemphasized control and domination at the expense of receptivity. And Enlightenment-type ethical rationalism and epistemological rationalism also exhibit and express an inordinate desire for control, inordinate because, once again, they are unwilling or unable to acknowledge or reckon with the value of receptivity and of emotions that involve it.[13] Similar things can be said about the insistence on life planning and on questioning everything in one's life that I described in chapter 7. So if I have illustrated the importance of receptivity in this second half of the present book, I have at the same time also demonstrated how philosophically one sided or debilitating the desire for control (or domination) has been and can be. If receptivity is the great virtue being recommended here, then by the same token control or the inordinate desire for control is the besetting philosophical sin of our entire Western tradition, and any new large-scale picture of our values needs to emphasize these facts or conclusions.[14]

However, I have not yet finished with *describing* receptivity, and that is the task I will be taking up again in our next chapter.

NOTES

1. Enlightenment thought and contemporary epistemological rationalism can accept, I think, the need to be perceptually sensitive and, to that extent also, in a sense, receptive to the world around one, if one is going to learn useful and important things about that world. (This is not true of typical "Continental rationalists," such as Leibniz, who downgrade the role of sense perception in coming to know about the world; but as my colleague Elijah Chudnoff has pointed out to me, Cartesian rationalism clearly *does* recommend a kind of receptivity in relation to intuitively clear and distinct ideas.) However, in leaving no room for empathy in our coming to know or have rational belief about the world, the Enlightenment-type rationalist denies the role and value of *this* sort of receptivity—even if the receptivity of sheer sense perception (or rational intuition) is in fact allowed for. And note two further things. As Otávio Bueno has pointed out to me, many empirically minded epistemologists think we are more passive than receptive in the process of perceptual justification or knowledge (perhaps sensitive is neutral between these two concepts), and if they are right, then receptivity may not really apply to the sphere of perception (though it might still hold for rational intuition). But, further, even if and where receptivity is granted to characterize the process or results of perceptual knowledge, no one has thought of such receptivity as itself an epistemic virtue. Our traditions, even when they allow for receptivity, have, *in general,* failed to appreciate its role as a virtue.

2. In "What Do Women Want in a Moral Theory?" (reprinted with a postscript in R. Crisp and M. Slote, eds., *Virtue Ethics*, Oxford, UK: Oxford University Press, 1997, pp. 263–77) and in other writings, Annette Baier discusses or

refers to care ethics but also offers an ethics of trust as an alternative conception of morality. Her ethics of trust hasn't caught on in the way care ethics has, but it is worth noting that receptivity vis-à-vis others is a common underlying element of both caring and trust (as we described it in chapter 2).

3. As I mentioned in chapter 1, empathy is more a matter of receptivity and sympathy of reactivity, and to that extent, an ethics of care that emphasizes empathy as the basis of sympathy and altruistic caring sees receptivity as even more important and central to the moral life than any sentimentalist view that highlights sympathy and caring without arguing for a grounding in empathy. To relate morality in an essential way to emotion and feeling is certainly to repudiate the rationalist emphasis on control—and, in contrast with ethical rationalism, it involves a recognition and valuing of receptivity *to a point*. But bringing in empathy as a foundation stone of morality involves a *further* or *greater* degree of emphasis on the importance or value of receptivity.

4. This critique of rationalism's treatment of its own favored notion of respect doesn't assume moral sentimentalism and doesn't by itself show that we have to *be* sentimentalists. Some mixed or hybrid view might conceivably be preferable. But I hope the rest of what we have been and are saying here will convince the reader of the promise and plausibility of care-ethical sentimentalism as a general theoretical approach to morality.

5. We have seen cases where rationalism and sentimentalism make opposing moral judgments, so no theory can consistently account for all our particular moral judgments. But I have given you some reasons for thinking that sentimentalism gives a better answer to normative questions on which it disagrees with rationalism (e.g., in regard to extreme hate speech, restraining orders, and, now, religious toleration and respect), so I think it is entirely proper (and other theories make parallel moves) to propose a theory of the meaning of moral terms that accounts for cases where there is widespread commonsense moral agreement and that treats the cases where there is normative *disagreement* as indicating a certain kind of mistake or bias on the part of those whose judgments don't align well with the sentimentalist theory of meaning being proposed here. That means, for example, explaining away the tendency to treat respect as requiring only toleration for those whose views one hates, as due to a failure to appreciate the receptive element in respect. And it also means saying that those who want to strongly limit restraining orders against husbands on the basis of traditional views about autonomy and autonomy rights are not empathically sensitive enough to what is at stake in such cases. A woman's need for security and physical safety is surely more important than any desire for totally untrammeled freedom of movement, and most of us now are capable of seeing that. So care ethics appears to have the normative upper hand vis-à-vis the cases where it disagrees with rationalistic liberalism (and

with an American public that has imbibed the traditional American political emphasis on rights and liberties rather than on the general welfare); and I am willing for my account of moral meaning to be hostage to that claim's turning out to be correct.

6. Some philosophers have criticized my view that emotional disapproval is fundamentally a matter of chill and coldness, arguing that we often are angry with those we disapprove of and that it makes more sense to think of anger with someone as constituting our disapproval of that person. (See, for example, Justin D'Arms's "Empathy, Approval, and Disapproval in *Moral Sentimentalism*" in the *Southern Journal of Philosophy* [Spindel Supplement: Empathy and Ethics], vol. 49, 2011, pp. 134–41.) But the opposition between chill and warmth helps make sense of what we take to be the oppositeness of approval and disapproval, and it isn't easy to think of some feeling that opposes anger and that can plausibly be regarded as constituting our basic attitude of approval. In addition, although we are often angry with people who are (eventually) objects of our disapproval, anger is typically hot, and the locution "hot disapproval" is both odd and unfamiliar. By contrast, we do, very idiomatically, speak of the "chill of disapproval," and all this supports the idea that emotional disapproval involves coldness or chill rather than anger. That means that the anger we often feel toward those who do injurious or immoral things has to die down or intermit in order for actual disapproval to occur; but this isn't counterintuitive. Doesn't hot anger have to die down in order for us to feel or attain the *distance* that the idea of disapproval clearly connotes?

Note, too, that psychopaths don't take in the feelings of others and so aren't capable of moral approval and disapproval as I have described them. (We may be chilled by the cold-hearted acts and attitudes of a psychopath in a way that another psychopath cannot be.) And to the extent that emotional/empathic approval and disapproval are viewed as essential to moral judgment, the present approach has the implication that psychopaths cannot make real or full moral claims. The psychopath is thus like the congenitally blind person who cannot make full judgments about the color of objects, but that conclusion seems rather intuitive and commonsensical.

7. I am not saying that we have to be actually feeling empathic warmth or chill whenever we can be said to approve or disapprove of something: Someone who is asleep can still be said to disapprove of racism, and there may be a habitual element to disapproval or approval that doesn't require actual momentary feeling in order for it to occur. There can also be a more formal sense in which moral approval can be said to be the expression of an inner moral judgment to the effect that something is morally acceptable or good. But even so, and as MS argued at some length, the more primitive or basic attitudes of empathic warmth and chill don't require moral judgment, and

because such attitudes can, for various reasons, be respectively characterized as positive and negative, it makes sense for a sentimentalist to try to understand moral judgment itself, with its positive and negative poles, as grounded in them.

8. Some philosophers and others have claimed that the moral distinctions we ordinarily make are innate in us, rather than due to the operation of empathy and reference fixing. But unless they bring in the idea of God (and probably even if they do), the innateness hypothesis doesn't really explain or justify the objectivity of moral judgments (something most of us would like to preserve or accommodate), and it also doesn't explain as much, do as much explanatory work, as a sentimentalist view that grounds moral judgment in the development of empathy and the historical semantics of reference fixing.

And it is also important to note that a view that fixes the reference of terms such as *right* and *wrong* in relation to empathic phenomena needn't say that men and women mean different things by these terms just because they tend to differ with respect to their empathic capacities or tendencies. There is evidence that testosterone interferes with empathy and that men are more subject to the effects of testosterone than women are, but even if this means that the moral education of girls may be more easily accomplished than the moral education of boys, boys and men are capable of a great, great deal of empathy. And men and women have a common understanding too of what it is to be fully empathic. Thus Hoffman has noted that someone (a man) seeing a person injure a third party might angrily chase after the offending party rather than stay and help the person who has been injured; and this may be an effect of testosterone. But both women and men, at least after the fact, are capable of seeing and judging that the person who chases after the person who has injured someone typically shows a lack of fully empathic concern for the person injured, so if, as I have argued, our moral concepts are fixed by reference to the idea of fully empathic concern, there is no reason to think they aren't shared by both men and women.

9. Judgments about human rights and social justice are generally considered to involve moral thinking, so I am saying that receptivity is central to our understanding of political morality, despite the fact that many philosophers and ordinary citizens (especially in the United States) are strongly inclined to think that our rights of free worship, free speech, and so on are (rationally) self-evident and independent of anything having to do with human feeling and emotion. In fact, liberals often say that human feeling and emotion can't, for example, guarantee common rights of free worship because those (e.g., the Spanish Inquisition) who attack our rights of free worship often do so in the name of a concern for people's welfare—as when they say that they have to torture heretics for the sake of their souls' salvation. But John Locke in his *Second Essay on Government* wisely noted that the "dry eyes" of the torturers

give the lie to any claim that they were concerned about the welfare of those they persecuted and tortured. And I believe that the right of free worship is most intuitively and humanely understood, not by invoking a rationally self-evident right, but by seeing the lack of empathy for and receptivity to others' points of view that is involved in religious persecutions and also seeing the hatred and contempt—rather than positive concern—that essentially underlies religious persecutions. I have discussed this and related issues in both ECE and MS, and my general thought and conclusion is that at its most plausible, the legitimate invocation of political rights has to engage with our receptive empathy vis-à-vis others' points of view and our (often empathically based) epistemic anger with those who can't or won't receptively empathize with such different viewpoints.

Finally, let me tie this discussion up with what I said earlier in chapter 3 and just above in footnote 5 about mistaken ideas concerning one's own political/moral concepts. The fact that most Americans think of rights of free speech or worship as independently and rationally intuited may give them an initial reason to resist the sentimentalist idea that receptive empathy—rather than traditional rational autonomy—offers a grounding basis for those rights. But if the emphasis on traditional autonomy gives us normatively mistaken conclusions about Skokie-type cases, spousal abuse, and so on, and if we can be persuaded of that, then we also have to acknowledge that our "American intuitions" about the nature of rights and about what "justice" and "rights" mean are arguably mistaken, and a sentimentalist account of those terms might well then be correct. This doesn't mean abandoning the notions of autonomy and respect for autonomy, but it does mean reconceiving them in sentimentalist terms that conform more to our most considered normative judgments about when autonomy isn't being respected: For example, when a husband who threatens violence is put under a restraining order, that needn't show a lack of respect for him or his autonomy, but, rather, a morally relevant sense of the greater importance of a wife's need for security and safety in a given set of circumstances. On these points, see ECE, chapters 4 and 5; and MS, chapters 8 and 9.

10. Hume assumed that our basic moral (or other) concepts can be unpacked, analyzed, in terms of their felt/experienced phenomenology, but this idea has for a long time now been in disrepute. Frege and Wittgenstein helped bring that about, and I have no desire to argue that the full associationist/ empiricist/sentimentalist/phenomenological project can successfully proceed along its original lines. For example, as Philippa Foot and others have pointed out, pride can't reasonably be thought of as some distinctive feeling (felt in the breast) because to be proud of something one has to *believe* that one owns or has created the thing in question or is associated with it in certain other familiar ways. Nonetheless, the account we have given of approval

and disapproval as second-order empathic warmth and chill does conceive these states as having a distinctive felt phenomenology, a possibility that many recent philosophers have explicitly denied. Similarly, our discussion has indicated that first-order empathic concern for others is characterized by a kind of warmth and that a lack or the opposite of such concern has a cold feel to it (we think of it as cold-hearted, cold-blooded or chilling). And our extramoral discussion of fair-mindedness and objectivity (to the extent we are capable of the latter) argued that these epistemic virtues also carry with them a certain phenomenological "feel." To empathize with the point of view of others, one has to see things in something like the favorable light in which they see them, and that means there has to be at least a temporary "whiff" of positive feeling, of liking, of sympathy, in one's attitude toward their views or arguments. And, of course, those who favor a particular argument or position have to have a more substantial positive attitude or feeling about the given argument or position. We also saw earlier that epistemic intolerance of the intolerant can be thought of as a form of epistemic anger, and anger, too, has a phenomenological feel about it. If fear can be thought of as typically cold, anger, as I have already mentioned, is commonly conceived as hot; so we see or are beginning to see how much phenomenology actually attaches to many of our concepts and (notions of) virtues. This constitutes at least a partial vindication of the phenomenological emphasis of sentimentalists like Hume against latter-day critics like Frege and various others. And we can also see in the long-standing tendency to downgrade phenomenology some of the same thinking that leads philosophers to be rationalists. Rationalists are averse to allowing emotion an important place in the moral life, and we have been saying that this stems from a desire for control that is inconsistent with ordinary levels of human feeling and emotion, from a failure, therefore, to recognize the need for and value of receptivity. But the long-standing unwillingness—and I can only call it that—of most Anglo-American philosophers to look for or acknowledge the role of phenomenology in the epistemic and moral parts or aspects of our lives and to refer to that reality in philosophical discussions of ethical and epistemological notions or topics also seems to me to represent a lack of receptiveness, a failure to pay attention to, acknowledge, or appreciate how things feel that stems from a lack of receptiveness to the way things actually do phenomenologically feel.

11. Kantians and other rationalists often stress rational agency as a condition or central element of personal identity, but receptivity to others (especially those we are close to) is also crucial to the formation and nature of personal identity. Our whole book has been an argument for that conclusion, but this (I hope) compelling idea seems to be pretty much totally ignored by Kantians/rationalists. On the other hand, the idea of receptivity as central to personal identity is congenial to, and may even be implicit in, Nel Noddings's

care ethics, which stresses our personal relationships as crucial to our identities and emphasizes receptivity as essential to caring. Other care ethicists often haven't really picked up on the idea of receptivity, but I think there is no reason why they shouldn't.

12. I am attempting to give epistemically rational arguments in this book, but there is no inconsistency in using rational arguments to question the supreme importance of giving rational arguments or of being rational more generally. Nor is it inappropriate for someone committed to rational argument to advocate more receptivity, empathy, and sensitivity in the way we do philosophy or live our lives—see "Men's Philosophy, Women's Philosophy," the apprendix to my *The Impossibility of Perfection*, New York: Oxford, 2011.

13. Recent Kantian ethicists have been willing and sometimes even eager to grant that (the cultivation of) various emotions can help us act morally. But to acknowledge such instrumental usefulness is not to treat/regard the emotions as having any *intrinsic moral importance*, and the usual Kantian insistence that the exercise of reason can by itself suffice to ensure moral/dutiful action and the highest degree of moral merit seems to be a very good example of the misguided Faustian emphasis on control.

14. Some previous work in care ethics has pointed to the role of receptivity in caring but hasn't noted (the philosophical importance of) the opposition—or sometimes just tension—between receptivity and control. Note, too, that if empathy powers altruism, then the receptivity it involves is geared to benevolent activity and action. A genuinely caring person is both open/receptive to other people and their feelings and at least partly on that basis motivated to actively *do* things for other people. (All the more reason to think of empathy as receptive rather than passive.)

Chapter 10

The Virtue of Receptivity

I think we should regard receptivity as a kind of virtue, but if it is one, it certainly hasn't featured in any lists or accounts of the virtues that have previously been proposed. I believe that is because those making the lists or offering the accounts have accepted Enlightenment or Faustian assumptions that would preclude seeing receptivity as a virtue or even thinking at all about it as a character trait, whether virtuous or not. In my opinion, this has been a quite tremendous loss—if, and as I have been arguing here, receptivity is central to the things we most deeply value in our lives. But, of course, the notion of receptivity has in some sense been in the background "haunting" green discussions of environmental ethics and psychologists' and philosophers' descriptions of how empathy works. When the green thinker deplores our dominating, controlling, or highly activistic attitudes and actions toward the environment, s/he clearly thinks we should be acting and thinking differently, and even if and when the term *receptive* isn't mentioned (and I haven't checked every environmental-ethical discussion of this topic one could look at), that term fits or would fit the stance vis-à-vis the environment that is being implicitly or explicitly recommended. Similarly, when Hume speaks of the sympathetic/empathetic contagion of feeling from one person to another and Hoffman speaks of associative processes of empathy that are largely or entirely involuntary, their claims presuppose a certain receptivity on the part of those who are empathically *affected* in the ways they describe—even if the term *receptivity* is never used or mentioned.

Thus receptivity is or has been the virtue "that dare not speak its name." No one has spoken of it as a virtue because there has been an overarching and predominant rationalist mindset that has precluded seeing it as a virtue, and even those who have moved in a somewhat different ethical direction haven't seen the full measure of what the previous mindset has made it impossible or difficult to recognize. They have spoken "around" the subject of receptivity and have sometimes even mentioned it, but they haven't put receptivity in the spotlight in the way I have been doing here.[1]

But now that I am putting or attempting to put it in the spotlight, we need to see and say more about the nature of receptivity. And we can best do this through some philosophical comparisons. To begin with, I think I need to mention the stark contrast that exists between everything I have been saying about the virtue of receptivity and Aristotle's metaphysical-cum-ethical views. Aristotle holds that what is most active is automatically highest and best, and he (therefore) sees God, the Unmoved Mover, as pure active intellect. His views here may seem, in some sense, to be at odds with the predominant Faustianism of Western civilization and culture because the Unmoved Mover's activity was supposed to be purely intellectual and in no way involved acting physically on the physical environment. But if one dissents from Aristotle's assumption that pure intellectual activity constitutes the highest possible degree of being active and substitutes the idea of dominating and controlling what is outside us, nature, as the best example of what it is to be truly active, then one arrives at Faustianism and effectively preserves Aristotle's idea that more activity is better. The idea of dominating over nature is more reminiscent of the Old Testament idea that human beings have been given "dominion over the beasts of the field and the fowl of the air" than it is of Aristotle's specific views about the Unmoved Mover, but whichever way one goes here, the idea of being maximally active seems itself to have dominated over our previous thinking. And everything I have been saying here about the importance of receptivity calls that basic Western view into question. Sheer or total activity or activeness *isn't* really a virtue because it is inconsistent with so much that we need and want in our lives: with intellectual openness, with love, with relationships, with caring, with moral thought, with . . . virtue and happiness.[2]

Now I am not saying that activeness or activity is a vice. We need to be active a great deal of the time and in many, many ways, and what I said in the last paragraph was merely that *sheer* or *total* activity is not the virtue or ideal state that it has been thought to be, that such an *exaggeration* of whatever is good in activity and being active is not a virtue. By the same token, then, sheer or total receptivity cannot be considered a virtue, and we in effect saw that point earlier when we were or at least I was so eager to distinguish between a receptive and a passive attitude toward nature. Passivity is receptivity without any admixture of or potential for activeness (or even reactiveness or responsiveness), and I don't think most of us want to regard or do regard passivity as any kind of virtue or ideal state.[3] All this means, however, that when we say receptivity is a virtue, we also need to acknowledge that there is virtue in being active, and in fact what we have just said shows us that it is impossible to make sense of or properly understand receptivity as a virtue unless we acknowledge the positive role that being active plays in our lives and our values. Older people are often told to keep active in their lives, and activity, or being active, has value at every stage of a normal human life; and think how active a child has to be to learn to walk, to whistle, or to tie shoelaces.

Similarly, our previous discussions of care ethics show us that receptivity can't be the whole story in or of morality, that it has to be counterbalanced or mingled with activity or activeness in the lives of morally decent or praiseworthy individuals. Empathically caring about others involves being open or receptive to their feelings, thoughts, and general point of view, but it also criterially requires action that grows out of that receptivity. In many circumstances where (through empathic receptivity) a caring person feels another's pain, he will be moved to act on behalf of that other, and someone who doesn't act can on constitutive grounds be criticized as not genuinely or deeply caring about the other. So being moral requires or involves both receptive and active elements.

Perhaps all of this means that we should think of activeness as a virtue alongside receptivity. But perhaps we needn't make that inference in order to regard receptivity as desirable and understand its nature as a virtue. After all, the fact that receptivity isn't the whole of virtue and that it is often best comingled with or limited by elements of activeness doesn't *necessarily* mean that activeness is a virtue. (The fact that the morally and rationally best receptivity is or remains open to the ideas of others, even while being partial to the opinions and attitudes of loved ones, also doesn't entail or suggest that activeness as such is a virtue.)[4] But what at this point *should be* clear is that, contrary to Faustian and Enlightenment theories or ideas about what is good or admirable in human life, receptivity plays a major role in some of the most important aspects or parts of our lives and is properly viewed as a virtue. Its role as a virtue may have to be understood in contrast with and even perhaps as requiring what is valuable about activity or being active, but a proper appreciation of that role also tells us that there are and have to be very substantial limits to the value we place on being active. By not recognizing or pointing to those limits, Faustian thought has given us a distorted ethical picture of human life, and my present aim is precisely to point out the distortions and show the way toward a more humanly adequate picture of human life and its values.

More strongly, I think receptivity actually functions as a kind of touchstone for other values. Activity/activeness and control over things or our lives are valuable, but only to the extent they allow us to accommodate receptivity and its values. And we may also better understand why we don't think of passivity as an important value in our lives once we recognize that it isn't at all necessary to receptivity and what receptivity makes possible for us (which is not to say that we don't often need to *rest*). Receptivity thus not only stands in contrast with both passivity and activity but helps us understand why passivity *isn't* a value and why or to what extent activity *is* one. And this stands in marked contrast with the way in which the traditional Western overvaluation of activity, control, and rationality pushes receptivity entirely out of the ethical picture.

Given what I am saying here, receptivity deserves or needs, rather, to be placed at the very center of things. We have seen that it helps define or determine the place of activity and passivity within our ethical scheme of things. But it helps us "place" a number of other ethical values as well. What I said in part I helps us to see how receptivity to other people's opinions and points of view grounds epistemic open-mindedness, fair-mindedness, and rationality in a way that Enlightenment-type thinking has never recognized. But we have also seen that receptivity of an epistemically nonrational and at least partly irrational kind is essential to valuable relationships and feelings toward others. We can and should be epistemically rational in most of our thinking about and dealings with the world and the people we come in contact with, but unless we are also *receptive* toward other people and their attitudes and opinions, we are going to miss out on much of what is most valuable in life. And the fact that we need receptivity to qualify, condition, or limit so many other ethical values/notions is my main reason for maintaining that receptivity is a touchstone for other values (some of which may even serve reciprocally to limit *it*). But let me now mention a very important *further* example of how receptivity functions as a touchstone for other ethical notions.

There is another major ethical notion that we haven't yet really focused on and that needs to be limited or qualified by considerations having to do with receptivity. That notion is autonomy: not the autonomy that features in Kantian metaphysics or in Kantian accounts of the foundations of moral thought and practice but the more ordinary kind that (simply) involves being willing and able to think and decide things for oneself. Kantian philosophy places great value on this ordinary notion of autonomy and, indeed, treats that value as some sort of support for its more general theoretical ideas about moral autonomy and political/legal *rights* of autonomy, but I don't propose to enter into any further debate with Kantian ethical thought at this point. I am assuming that we are all by now assuming care ethics as part of the background of our discussion, but a properly conceived care ethics will agree with Kantians about the importance of being able to think and decide things for oneself.

For example, in her groundbreaking *In a Different Voice*, Carol Gilligan points out that a patriarchal upbringing involves paying less attention to what little girls say and want than to what little boys say and want, and she claims (and I agree with her) that this can lead girls to become self-doubting and self-denying, unable or unwilling to think about things on their own or independently to decide what they want to have or do. This stilling of girls' and, as a result, women's voices constitutes, in my opinion, a failure to respect the nascent autonomy of young girls, an injustice that patriarchy perpetrates against women as a class or group. But my main point here is that a feminist who deplores the attitudes and effects of patriarchy can place great value on autonomously thinking and deciding things for oneself—and to that extent such a feminist will have a great deal in common with Kantians and, in fact, with most of the rest of us. After all, most of us do think there is at least some value and virtue in autonomous thought, desire, and action.

But how, then, are autonomy and receptivity related? They are clearly different, but are they consistent with each other? Am I saying that we have to reject or renounce the value of autonomy because it is incompatible with true and valuable receptivity? Clearly not. What I said just a moment ago about the evils or injustices of patriarchy should make it very clear that I think the ability and tendency to think and decide things for oneself is very desirable. However, those who emphasize that ability and tendency, those who place a great emphasis on the notion and value of autonomy, typically ignore or at least downplay the ways in which such autonomy needs to be and ideally *will* be less than absolute.

Yes, we need to be able and willing to think and make decisions about things on our own. Yes, it is totally undesirable and absolutely pathetic, if an adult either consciously or unconsciously submits to others or to some institution in regard to their thinking and their choices. But, as I argued earlier, it is also true, necessarily true, that someone who loves or is friends with another person is going to be more susceptible to their opinions and attitudes than a sheer "independent-minded" regard for scientific or empirical evidence would dictate or allow. So to the extent that we are fortunate enough to have friendly or loving relations with other people, we aren't and cannot be totally autonomous in our thinking and decision making. Life, ordinary life, thus necessarily attenuates the influence and value of autonomy in our lives, and this is something that Kantians and others who emphasize autonomy haven't, I think, realized.[5]

Now acknowledging this point constitutes a real challenge to care ethicists such as myself because it seems to be countenancing an openness to others' values that, in the case of patriarchy at least, can have disastrous individual and human consequences. If love dictates or implies a willingness to take in the loved one's opinions and attitudes, won't this mean that girls who took in their parents' (and not just their fathers') dismissive attitudes toward females were doing what it was entirely understandable and inevitable that they should do? And doesn't that undercut the critique of patriarchy and its influence on girls/women that a feminist care ethics would want to make?

I don't think so. It is certainly psychologically inevitable that girls who love (and don't resent?) their parents will tend to take in their parents' prejudices against women. But, according to care ethics, those prejudices and the parental actions they lead to will still be morally criticizable if they manifest a lack of empathic understanding and concern for what girls aspire to and want. A parent who tells his or her daughter "you don't want to be a doctor, dear; you would be much happier as a nurse" isn't taking the daughter's expressed desires or aspirations seriously, isn't seeing things from the daughter's actual standpoint, and that is obviously a failure of empathy and of concern. So we can criticize what happens under patriarchy even if we hold the general view that it is all right and even desirable for people to be open to the (subliminal) influence of those they love (or admire). But of course there is still the problem of how a morally bankrupt system like patriarchy can be overthrown and a more just state of things instituted. If girls who love their parents take in their prejudices, how is anyone ever going to recognize the injustice of what is going on and *do something about it*? This is a problem not just in relation to antifemale social arrangements but in relation to unjust social arrangements generally. If people are influenced or brainwashed by ideologies that serve the interests of some hegemonic group or class, how can justice ever be established?

This is not the place to try to answer these questions. But one thing is clear. Not everyone loves her dominating or patriarchal parents and not everyone is totally brainwashed by the ideology of their society or culture. And this is likely to occur, isn't it, precisely because those societies or cultures perpetrate or perpetuate injustices that it is possible to be sensitive to and react to. (Shades of the Cornell School!) The receptivity I am calling a virtue may be more receptive to the views and attitudes of loved ones or one's own society, but it also involves being open minded about or toward the opinions of those outside one's own group. If one isn't, then one's receptivity (like one's empathic concern) will be skewed and incomplete, and if we can educate people toward such a fuller receptivity/empathy/concern for others, then we can, I believe, overcome the injustices and disrespect that arise from or are constituted by less receptive/empathic/caring attitudes. (This is essentially what happened when feminists over several decades managed to raise the consciousness of other women and of the surrounding society concerning the injustices of patriarchy—though, of course, this process is still far from over.) But let us return to our main discussion, to considering how autonomy as a value relates to and affects the value of receptivity.

What I said above indicates that there are limits to the value and to what we might well consider to be the *virtue* of thinking and acting autonomously. Those limits exist precisely because there is virtue and value in being open and receptive to the opinions and attitudes of those we love and/or care about and more generally, so we can certainly at this point say that part of the value of receptivity lies in the value of the way it can and does limit the autonomy of thought, desire, and action. But something similar can, I think, be said about autonomy. We need to have autonomy limit the degree of our receptivity or else we end up or can end up with people who are totally under the influence of those they love, care about, or admire or who are totally under the influence of other people more generally, and who, as a result, never think or decide things for themselves.[6] Does this mean that, at least as regards the formation of belief and the initiation of action, receptivity and autonomy are coequal virtues?

Perhaps, in certain areas it does, but remember that the value we have placed on receptivity goes far beyond the issues I have just been talking about. If care ethics is correct, then receptivity plays a role in moral thought and practice and Kantian-type autonomy isn't the basis of our normative obligations or our thinking about such obligations. To be sure, care ethics emphasizes the importance of stepping back from one's actions and recognizing, for example, the harm that one has caused another human being or animal. Inductive discipline depends on such a capacity for self-conscious self-reflection, and that capacity is one well-known aspect of our human (capacity for) autonomy. But if we accept care ethics and, therefore, see moral values as grounded in how we (empathically) connect with others, then our separateness from others is morally *de-emphasized*, and autonomy by its very nature (care ethicists make a lot out of this) involves/highlights separateness from other people rather than connection to them. So I rather doubt that what I have been saying or can say about autonomy leaves it in a position of equal ethical importance with receptivity; and even if their importance did turn out to be roughly equal or comparable, that would still mean that receptivity was ethically significant and valuable in important ways that people haven't really ever suspected.[7] Receptivity turns out, in any event then, to be at or near the center of our values, but before bringing this discussion to a close, I want to say just a couple of more things by way of further describing what receptivity is.

We have seen that receptivity isn't the same thing as passivity, but I have frequently paired receptivity with something called openness, and at this point we might well want to consider, in a more precise way, whether those two ideas are the same or slightly different. I think, in fact, that they are slightly different, and it might help to bring in an example to illustrate that difference. Someone may be reluctant but still *willing* to make a minor or major change in his or her life, and this contrasts with cases where someone is *open* to making such a change. Openness suggests that one is *more than just willing* to consider making a relevant change, and that holds also for receptivity or receptiveness. If one is receptive to someone's suggestions for change, then one is more than willing to consider making such change(s). However, it also seems to me (check your own linguistic intuitions!) that being receptive to the idea or suggestion of change implies more *readiness* to change than mere talk of openness does. So I believe we have a spectrum of attitudes here running from unwillingness to reluctant willingness to openness to receptiveness and then finally, perhaps, to eagerness (and beyond?).

In that case, receptivity or receptiveness to anything is a rather *positive* attitude or predisposition, and that gives another sense in which it differs from passivity. And remember, too, how broadly the idea of receptivity paints its brushstrokes. We have seen that receptivity is involved in many various and important aspects of our life, and I think we can say, on the basis of what has previously been described and argued, that it pervades or percolates through our sense of values and of what is generally important in life. If its importance has previously been not only underappreciated but pretty much totally ignored, I can only hope that the present discussion can help to remedy this situation. In fact, it is my hope that receptivity will take its place alongside caring and empathy as a focal point for ethical theorizing and for intelligent general social discussion of what is valuable and important to us.

To be sure, receptivity isn't the whole or even the only important part of human moral and nonmoral virtue. One also needs to be autonomous and self-reliant to a substantial extent in one's thinking and one's actions, and a degree of epistemic rationality that goes beyond sheer open-mindedness is clearly necessary to being able to maneuver one's way through the world and through one's life. But, nonetheless, receptivity—the kind of virtuous receptivity that is generally open to other people's/groups' opinions even while it favors the opinions of those who are near and dear to one—looms over many other traits, goods, and virtues in the ways I have pointed out here (and perhaps in other ways as well); and that justifies us, I think, in according it—both philosophically and in a practical way—a central place in our lives.

NOTES

1. In *Caring* (p. 35), Nel Noddings says that "[t]he receptive mode is at the heart of human existence." And Noddings has certainly stressed receptivity in some of her work. But the emphasis has been on the role of receptivity in caring and, to a lesser degree, in aesthetic appreciation and human creativity; and the much more general idea that receptivity or stressing receptivity is an antidote to the errors/blinkers/distortions of Enlightenment thought and of Western Faustian thinking overall doesn't appear in her writings. Still, what I am saying here can be viewed as a *large-scale extrapolation* of what Noddings has said about receptivity—with one large *caveat*. Noddings has argued that the ethics of care should view caring as primarily a relationship and only secondarily a trait or virtue of individuals. And various care ethicists have followed her lead on this issue. But, receptivity is a trait or characteristic of individuals, so if, as Noddings and I both believe, it is essential to all caring relationships and lies "at the heart of human existence," care ethicists shouldn't perhaps think of relationships as ethically more important or foundational than individual character traits.

    And here is another reason why Noddings herself might have reason to question her longstanding insistence that good interpersonal relationships are prior to individual virtues. Noddings has said to me in private correspondence that if a mother or father has to paternalistically intervene to prevent an adult son, say, from riding his motorcycle without a helmet (he loves the wind in his hair and thinks it cowardly to worry about accidents), an ethics of care will recommend that the parent should intervene in this way even if it sours his or her relationship with the son. (They should, however, work hard after intervening in an effort to restore the relationship.) But if this is so, then the welfare of the son is taking precedence over the parent's relationship with the son—and empathic concern, a moral virtue, seems to that extent to be given greater weight than good relationship. How is that really compatible with deriving all virtue and value *from* good relationship(s)? I think this is another reason why Noddings and some other care ethicists should back off their insistence that interpersonal relationship is ethically prior to and of greater ethical importance than the virtue or virtues of individuals.

2. In his as yet unpublished "Rethinking Individualistic Conceptions of Care in Philosophy of Action," Seisuke Hayakawa has argued that what count as actions in the fullest sense always involve an element of receptivity and even uncontrollability. Meaningful actions involve caring about something or someone, and just as really caring about people involves a receptive empathic attitude toward their ideas and desires, so too, Hayakawa argues, does caring about a subject matter involve a receptive attitude toward what others have said about that subject matter. If Hayakawa is on the right track, then activity and receptivity/lack of control are more mingled together in what we do than most of us have ever thought, but this will/would only serve to underscore the importance of receptivity and the limits of rational control. If even activity requires receptivity, then it is perhaps even more important, even more central to our lives, than I have been suggesting in the main text.

   Note, too, that there are various forms of receptivity that are more mundane than anything we have described in the text. There is evidence, for example, that young women who live together tend to have their periods around the same time and also evidence that couples who live together long enough eventually come to resemble each other (more). But even though I don't propose to discuss these kinds of examples, they do constitute some evidence for Malebranche's general hypothesis that everything—abilities, habits, vices, postures, attitudes, beliefs—tends to propagate from any given person to other people. (See his *Search after Truth*, Cambridge, UK: Cambridge University Press, 1997, book V). But though he greatly influenced Hume, Malebranche was nonetheless a philosophical rationalist, and I doubt he would have countenanced our idea here that there are important receptive, emotional, sentimental elements in the epistemic/epistemological "search after truth." In general, I think I am putting more emphasis on receptivity than Malebranche would have felt comfortable doing.

3. As Otávio Bueno has pointed out to me, receptivity is compatible with responsiveness in a way that passivity is not. However, this may not be the only important difference between the two notions.

4. By the same token, we don't think activity or being active always means that someone is *lacking* in receptivity. But we do think this about someone who is closed off to the views of other groups and/or to caring about their well-being, through having imbibed the prejudices and antipathies of his or her own group. (Of course, such a person is also lacking in empathy.)

5. In the *Metaphysics of Morals* (*Doctrine of Virtue,* paragraph 39), Kant tells us that it is important to respect the opinions of others in our conversations

with them, but he never suggests that we should be open to their influence in an epistemically irrational way and never indicates that there is anything less than absolute value in being autonomous.

6. To be totally self-reliant in one's thinking, one might have to refer to other people's opinions in deciding what one has most reason to believe but be empathically uninfluenced by the fact or presence of such opinions; and, like Hume, I think no one or almost no one is like this. In any event, one is relatively self-reliant in one's thinking if one resists, or tries to keep at some distance, the opinions and attitudes of others in order to review things or think them through on one's own. That is a form of intellectual self-reliance, and there are similar forms of conative or desiderative self-reliance, but I would suggest that such strong self-reliance *isn't* a human virtue because those who have or practice it are necessarily less emotionally involved with others than it is desirable for anyone to be.

7. Note, too, though, that since thinking for oneself is fully consistent with being open minded and open-mindedness involves being receptive to the ideas of others, autonomy is at the very least compatible with a certain kind of intellectual/epistemic receptivity. Similarly, when I said above that autonomy involves or requires our separateness from others, that wasn't supposed to rule out receptivity to other people's opinions but only submission to or domination by the opinions of (certain) others.

Conclusion

What we have been saying in part II about the importance of receptivity and the misguidedness of Faustian notions/ideals of total control and activity also applies—and I have explicitly applied it—to the critique of Enlightenment thought I engaged in in part I.[1] That is because the Enlightenment insistence on rationalistic foundations and on the value of pervasive rationality in our lives seems to exemplify the Faustian impulse just as much as what I subsequently said, in part II, about living according to a life plan, about the liberal imperative to critically scrutinize every aspect of one's life, about controlling or dominating over nature, and about the quintessentially preferred rationalist notion of autonomy. And what I have said, therefore, in favor of receptivity favors a *positive picture of human life and its/our values* that incorporates the positive recommendations that flowed out of the earlier critique of Enlightenment thinking. Receptivity is a value, a virtue, whose acknowledgement as such can or should make us aware of how different life can be and how much more potentially valuable it is, if it isn't lived according to rationalist and/or Faustian strictures and blinders. Things can then *open up* and become *more interesting*, and it is about time they did. Many or most of us know or acknowledge that our contemporary situation is vastly more complex than what our ancestors faced, and philosophy might therefore need to get free of its own previous or traditional limitations and, in particular, its narrowing emphasis on always being rational, in order to better understand

and make appropriate and useful recommendations for individuals, for nations, and for international relations in present-day circumstances. (And the complexities aren't likely to go away in the future.)

An emphasis on receptivity involves and helps move us toward a greater regard for the emotions, for human feeling. It involves realizing that we don't have to be and shouldn't be rational or active or in control (of our lives) all or even most of the time, and to that extent it sets up a broader and more diverse ethical ideal that directly challenges and is clearly inconsistent with received rationalist views about the all-encompassing and foundational value of autonomy. Of course, being able to think and act for oneself is clearly a requirement of intelligent adult living, and that represents a somewhat substantial ideal of autonomy. And we can even say that such autonomy is a virtue, since there clearly is a good deal of virtue in being able and willing to think and act for oneself. A person who simply (or usually) submits to the opinions and recommendations/ orders of others is in an unenviable and, really, a pathetic condition, and I have said and would want to say nothing to deny that. So, as I argued in chapter 10, there is virtue, *substantial* virtue, in being autonomous, in habitually thinking and acting for oneself.

But as I also previously mentioned, those who think and act for themselves also need to be emotionally/empathically open and receptive to the ideas of others, and traditional rationalist thinking about autonomy either denies this in one way or another or ignores it. So what I have said about receptivity shows, I hope, the limitations of the rationalist ideal of autonomy and at the same time, by introducing a value or virtue that appropriately qualifies or conditions autonomy and its value, introduces a virtue that is at the very least as important as autonomy. And it is important in great part because it provides or represents an intellectual/ethical focus around which the values that a rejection of Enlightenment and Faustian thought enables us to appreciate can coalesce. The positive vision the present book offers is, at least in part, the vision of a more complexly understood world in which a sense of or the influence of the value of receptivity counterbalances the emphasis placed on autonomy. And the world positively envisioned in this way will also be one in which the ideals of domination, control, and activeness no longer dominate over our sense of values. Rather (as one might say, taking matters in risky fashion into the enemy camp), the ideals or realities of empathy, emotionality, personal connection/relationship, openness, and receptivity will themselves dominate the landscape of such a newly reconfigured and opened-out ethical universe. We will need to be receptive toward important aspects of our lives, toward nature, toward opinions and attitudes that differ from our own, toward those we know and love, and in many other ways that I have previously spoken of or that, for one reason or another—perhaps because they are less important, perhaps because I haven't managed to think of them—have not been mentioned in our discussion.[2]

But having just spoken of the importance of empathy, feeling/emotion, and receptivity as part of a new and better picture of our values, I think the reader should also remember that receptivity *goes beyond* empathy and emotion or feeling in important ways that the present book has pointed to and emphasized. In recent years, care ethicists and others have stressed feeling, emotion, and empathy—and the relationships or personal connection that depends on them—in new and important ways. But some of the most striking examples of receptivity we have discussed don't particularly involve these other factors. Thus receptivity toward what one's life has brought one or toward what it may bring one in the future is not, in any obvious way, a matter of being properly emotional or empathic, of having certain commonly identifiable feelings, and so the values articulated and defended in this book take us beyond the recent emphasis on feeling and emotion to a somewhat new intellectual/ethical terrain. Receptivity is involved in empathy and emotion, to be sure, but it also plays a role beyond anything having specifically to do with empathy and emotion/feeling, and to that extent what I have had to say here is a quite new development—though it can perhaps be seen as an *extrapolation* of what people have been so interestingly saying in recent decades about empathy, emotion, and feeling. As I said in the introduction, the notions of empathy and of caring have recently and in a very striking way become much more central to our ethical/social thinking, but the present book attempts to show that a new and larger notion, receptivity, also needs to be taken seriously by ethicists and our society as a whole. And the examples I gave that involve receptivity but don't particularly rely on empathy or on emotions/motivations/feelings/relationships, such as caring or love, demonstrate that need at the same time that they show the ethical limits or limitations of all the recent talk about caring, feeling, emotion, empathy, connection, and relationships.

However, what I have been saying leaves one very glaring but interesting loose end. The Enlightenment emphasis on rationality seen as independent of feeling and emotion can be criticized within a larger critique of Faustian values, and we have seen how this can work. But what about the Enlightenment belief that our ethical values can be harmonized/integrated and unified and thus allow for the possibility in principle of perfect happiness and perfect virtue or admirability? I criticized this aspect of Enlightenment thought in part I, but my critique had nothing to do with Enlightenment assumptions about the all-pervasive and foundational power of reason. Even some of the Romantics believed in human perfectibility (Rousseau, for example), and that belief clearly didn't rest on faith in reason. So although the reason-emphasizing side of Enlightenment thought can be subsumed under the longer-term Faustian history of our Western intellectual culture, it may not be possible to do this with its commitment to the possibility of perfection; and in that case, even if the critique of perfectibility offered in part I succeeds in its purpose, it falls or seems to fall outside the general critique of Faustian values and assumptions that has been the predominant focus overall of the discussion in this book.

Put it this way. I have been explaining how our critique of Enlightenment views about rationality in part I fits in with what has been said about Faustian values and receptivity in part II. But this leaves the critique of Enlightenment views about perfection that occurred in part I pretty much entirely off on its own, since it makes no reference to or use of ideas about the importance or nonimportance of rationality or reason and doesn't seem to turn on issues having to do with the value of receptivity. So at this point our book appears to have two independent foci of critical discussion, and the question then is: Can the two foci, the two parts, be brought together? In other words, does what I have said about receptivity and in critique of Faustian values (including the Enlightenment exaltation of reason) somehow relate to or even entail what part I said about the mistakenness of the Enlightenment belief in the possibility of perfection?

This is a question I have been wrestling with for some time now. We have separate arguments criticizing or overthrowing Faustian values and criticizing or overthrowing the assumption that perfection (either of happiness or of the virtues) is possible, and let us assume that both sets of arguments successfully make their points. We can then ask whether the points are really as separate as they initially seem. Can we, for example, fully acknowledge the value and virtue of receptivity without, at the same time, having a theoretical or philosophical reason to deny the possibility of perfection? Or, conversely, can we recognize the reasons for the impossibility of perfection without having at least the materials for defending receptivity against relevant Faustian and Enlightenment values?[3]

As I said, I have long wondered about this, but I believe I now see or am beginning to see a way in which the two sorts of issues are connected. I recently had a conversation in Beijing with a graduate student at Peking University named Yuan ("Ivy") Yuan who seemed to agree with my arguments for the impossibility of perfection but who then asked: Why, if perfection is impossible, should everyone have been so interested in the possibility of attaining it? Well, that is a good question, and in thinking about it subsequently, the following speculations—and they really are just speculations—have occurred to me.

Perhaps some of us are interested in the possibility of a perfection that turns out not to be realizable within any human life, because we are discontented with our general human situation or condition and are at least consoled by the thought that perfection is possible in principle. Soldiers who are in wartime denied decent food and are disgruntled about that often console themselves with fantasies about wonderful home-cooked meals, and perhaps the "fantasy" of perfection—and that is all perfection is, given the arguments of part I and, in greater depth and detail, of my *The Impossibility of Perfection* (New York: Oxford University Press, 2011)—represents for certain philosophers and others an imagined consolation for and possible refuge from what is regarded as the unsatisfactory nature of ordinary human lives. (This may not be the only basis on which philosophical/religious belief in perfection's possibility can occur, but if it is a major source of such belief, that will be enough for my purposes here.)

But why should we think or have thought that all ordinary lives are unsatisfactory or unacceptable? Well, that question effectively breaks down into two (potentially related) questions: Is ordinary human life basically and inevitably unsatisfactory? And if it *isn't*, why should so many philosophers, in particular, have thought that it is? The intellectual fossil record clearly shows that a lot of philosophers have expressed dismay or worse at the overall or underlying human condition and with human lives as they are ordinarily led. The Greek idea that the body is a prison (*soma sema*) is one example, as are Plotinus's similar view in the *Enneads* that virtue consists in ways of resisting and overcoming the ugliness of the body and Kant's claim in the *Groundwork* (second section) that we would all be better off without bodily/sensuous appetites or inclinations.[4] And Plato (e.g., *Republic* VI, S. 500) and various Asian religions agree with this Kantian view.

Similarly, the Stoic idea that there is no value in human emotion and feeling represents what we, from our present-day perspective, perhaps more wisely can recognize as a refusal to accept the realities of human life/living. The Stoic may *say* that he or she accepts our humanity but sees that the emotional side of that humanity is entirely suspect and without value; but we don't have to agree with this, and it makes sense, I think, to see the Stoic distaste for human feeling as a kind of distaste for life, for real human life, itself. The Stoics tell us, for example, that we have to learn to accept pain and to recognize that it has no genuine disvalue for us, but, turning the tables, we may want to insist that it is the Stoic who doesn't accept reality and ethical facts: most notably, the facts that it is not such a bad thing to have an emotional nature and that the emotions themselves can make an intrinsic contribution to what is valuable in human life or in intelligent life more generally. And also, of course, the fact that pain really is a bad thing in our lives.

Now I can't really explain why the Stoics or Plotinus or Kant or Plato or various Eastern philosophies found human life so inherently unsatisfactory and distasteful.[5] In fact, I don't think I am in any position even to *speculate* about that issue. But what seems somewhat less speculative and therefore somewhat plausible in its own right is the idea that those who are thoroughly discontented with all ordinary human life would want or be led to fantasize about what might not be unsatisfactory if human lives could or can be radically altered. And perfect virtue and happiness may therefore have been the understandable objects or foci of such fantasy.

But now the relation of the issue of perfection to the value of receptivity can perhaps begin to emerge. The Stoics seem not to have been willing to *accept* the emotional side of our human condition, and Kant's expressed wish for an existence free of "inclinations" constitutes, at the very least, an unwillingness to accept the physical or bodily aspect of that condition. But even if the Enlightenment insistence that we must always be rational doesn't touch directly, as far as I know, on issues of bodily desire and presence, it does seem to represent a discomfort with and an unwillingness to accept the emotional side of our lives. And since being rational has seemed to many philosophers to be a desirable way to exercise or exert the greatest possible control over one's life, we can also say that rationalism in both its ethical and its epistemological aspects/forms betrays a desire for more control over life or one's own life than human life itself allows for, a desire that expresses a rather futile unwillingness to accept the frequent satisfactoriness of human lives as they actually, basically, are.[6] To that extent, an insistence on the value of emotional receptivity constitutes a kind of acceptance of our human condition or its potential that may find a kind of parallel in an acceptance of or belief in the impossibility of perfection.

Similarly, and moving away from Enlightenment rationalism as such, we have seen that the virtue of receptivity in one of its aspects involves accepting the large amount of accidentality and unpredictability that characterize both normal and not-so-normal human lives. And the insistence on life planning and the (greater) control over one's life it is supposed to bring one therefore also constitutes an unwillingness or failure to see the potential or actual satisfactoriness of ordinary human lives as we typically lead them. Now I say potential here because I certainly wouldn't want to deny that war, poverty, oppression, hunger, disease, and natural disasters can render many human lives quite unsatisfactory and even tragic. My point, rather, is that in the relative absence of such evils, ordinary lives can be satisfactory or good in the absence of any overall life plan and that having a life plan really doesn't make sense as an overall basis for or means to living a good life. So the receptivity to life that doesn't feel a need to rely on life plans constitutes an acceptance of what is possible in and for ordinary human lives, an acceptance that at the very least runs parallel to and seems of a piece with the kind of acceptance that doesn't need to believe in the possibility of perfection as some kind of consolation for what is viewed as inevitably unsatisfactory or worse about being human.[7]

Thus given the value of and importance of accepting what is possible in and for ordinary human lives and assuming that both Faustianism and the belief in perfectibility can, in their slightly different ways, represent or express an unwillingness or inability to accept the potential value of such lives, there is, in the end, a common thread to *all* the arguments of the present book. At the most basic level, our deepest values call for an acceptance and positive ethical assessment of ordinary human lives as led in somewhat favorable circumstances; and the specific arguments that have been offered during the course of the present book thus constitute particular ways of giving intellectual and ethical expression to a deeper sense of the acceptability of what ordinary human beings are capable of.[8] I am not saying that the various arguments I have offered depend for their validity or plausibility on the connection I am now making to the value of accepting what is possible for us as ordinary humans. But I *am* saying that those arguments make more sense or are more deeply understandable in relation to that connection, and once we see *that*, we can also see that what was said in part I about the impossibility of perfection and what has been said about Faustian values and receptivity are more closely connected and more similarly motivated than at least initially appears. Moreover, even if, and in accordance with the impossibility of perfection, our values can't be thoroughly harmonized and often clash, our philosophical description or picture of this inharmonious ethical reality can be and seems to be a harmonious and intellectually integrated one. So philosophy may be able, in a sense, to do one better than life itself, but that is only possible if that fact about life itself isn't regarded as something unacceptable or irrecusably regrettable, but is seen, rather, as the source or basis of much of the richness and interest, for present times and into the future, of what life and ethics have to offer.

In effect, I am also saying that the question whether ordinary human lives can be satisfactory marks the or at least a major fault line for the field of ethics as a whole. If they can be satisfactory, then the many philosophers and others (think again of various Eastern religions) who have in their different ways at least implicitly denied that can be seen as having led people and the field/enterprise of ethics as a whole in the wrong direction; and a major question for ethics, then, is how to get things back on the right track, to the extent that still needs to be done. I am hardly the first person, for example, to point to the extreme implausibility of certain Stoic ideas (Kant himself did that), and Kant's ethical views in turn have been attacked as "anti-life" ever since they first appeared on the landscape of philosophy. So the present book can be viewed as offering some new ways of seeing or acknowledging the satisfactoriness of many, though hardly all or even most, human lives. Certain other philosophers have to some extent moved in this direction, and in recent times I think Bernard Williams, in several of his writings, is the philosopher whose work comes closest in flavor to what I am saying and suggesting here. But what I have said is more self-conscious and explicit about the need to see our ordinary human *potential* as satisfactory and about the dire consequences—intellectually, morally, and for our lives—of not doing so, than other philosophical approaches have been; and, in fact, I believe that psychologist Erik Erikson's well-known idea that as we near the end of life, it is best to have an "ego integrity" that takes in our past/previous life and deems it acceptable on the whole, provides more essential support for my argument than anything that has been said specifically by any philosopher.[9]

Note, too, that if we accept ordinary human lives as potentially and often, actually, satisfactory, then we in some sense have a receptive attitude to Life (with a big *L*) itself. I have spoken of receptive attitudes toward nature or toward our parents' attitudes and opinions, and I have even spoken of the ways in which we need to be receptive to one or another part or aspect of our lives. If we don't feel the need for a life plan, we manifest a more receptive attitude toward our future (life) than if we do feel that need, and if we don't feel the need to question every relationship we have inherited or been born into, then we are, in some sense, receptive to what life has given us in the past. But to accept life, actual and ordinary total human lives, as potentially satisfactory, as satisfactory when surrounding conditions are fairly favorable, is something larger, and I want to say it is or involves accepting not just certain ordinary human lives but, I really think, life itself. (It is easier to make this case if one isn't distracted by capital letters.) To be unhappy with all ordinary or normal human lives in the way the Stoics, Kant, and Plato were is a very deep and pervasive philosophical/psychological condition or attitude—and it seems no exaggeration (I repeat) to say it constitutes a kind of discontent with life itself. But if ordinary and familiar human life is, in fact and as I want to claim, potentially satisfactory for us, then such people, such philosophers, arguably show themselves to be unreceptive and even hostile to life itself. And to deeply accept what life actually has to offer can then, in turn, be characterized as a way of having a receptive attitude, of being receptive, to life itself.[10]

And let's consider, too, how what I have just been saying bears on the conclusions of chapter 5 and, in particular, on the thesis that perfect happiness is impossible. I have just claimed that ordinary human lives can be acceptable or satisfactory and that it is important, a form of virtue, to be receptive to and accepting of that fact. But what about the female executive raising a family who has to juggle career and family? Are the conditions and eventualities of such a life really satisfactory? Well, I have argued that such a life isn't *perfectly* happy or good, but I see no reason to argue that it isn't satisfactory or good simpliciter. To be sure, such a life will often be frustrating, and certain things about it will be unsatisfactory (having to choose between getting a report in on time and attending one's daughter's dance recital); but I don't think it follows, and I don't think the woman who leads such a life will normally want to say, that her life overall isn't a good one. If she is pretty successful in her work and pretty successful with her children (they resent her career involvement to some extent but see that she loves them and are grateful for that love and for all the help she has given them), then she can see her life as an overall good or satisfactory one, even if she can also readily recognize that it is or was far from perfect.

Nor am I assuming here that balancing career and family is the only way to have a life that is on the whole satisfactory. Someone who "specializes" in relationships can have, I think, an overall good or satisfactory life, even if that life is lacking in significant respects; and the same may be true of the lonely genius who misses out on relationships and feels that cost but also gains enormous satisfaction from all that s/he has accomplished. I am not entirely sure about these last points, but what does seem fairly clear to me is that it is part of a virtuous receptivity to life that one be able to accept life's imperfection(s) and at the same time be able to recognize the overall satisfactory character of the life that one is or may be fortunate enough to have led or to be leading.[11] In effect, then, I have argued that—in a certain sense and with respect to human lives—the best needn't always be the enemy of the good.

But now one final point that bears on the epigraph from Prichard with which this book began. Prichard noted how far discussions of moral philosophy seem from the actualities of human life, and if we confine ourselves to modern examples, I think I see his point.[12] Moral philosophers such as Kant, Rawls, Bentham, and Sidgwick (what I am saying applies less clearly to Mill) have made exceedingly important contributions to our understanding of social justice and individual morality, but those contributions, as one reads them, seem very remote from the complexities of human life, from the rich variety of values that our lives exemplify or that we ourselves seek to realize in our lives. Ancient Greek and Roman philosophy seems less remote and more geared to understanding human life as a whole and not just in what we would today call its moral aspects, but, of course and as I have been emphasizing, the philosophers of classical antiquity made many assumptions we no longer want to make, so we can't just take over their ideas if we seek a corrective to the narrow focus of modern discussions of moral philosophy proper (including discussions of what most of us take to be the moral notion of justice). We have to think for ourselves and (if I may say) ruthlessly discard or make use of ideas from the past as we see fit and can justify.

This is what I have been doing or attempting to do in this book. Its degree of success in offering a contemporary view of human values readers will have to judge for themselves, but in any event the present book *isn't* remote from actual and contemporary human life and history in the way classical modern discussions of moral and political philosophy typically strike one as being. I have had a good deal to say about morality, but overall I have tried to bring together and to some degree integrate a large number of ethical and epistemological values that aren't all specifically or exclusively moral. And the distinctive emphasis on receptivity has been my chief means to producing what I believe is a more plausible and richer picture of our values than our Western philosophical tradition has previously provided.

NOTES

1. In "The Virtue of Faith" (*Faith and Philosophy* 1, 1984, p. 18ff.), Robert M. Adams says that an inordinate desire or "lust" for control over our lives can prevent us from being virtuously trustful in God('s goodness). But he doesn't consider the relevance of issues of control to secular topics.

2. The Western emphasis on rational control can be seen as placing an almost exclusive value on yang rather than yin; but putting things in such terms seems less philosophically focused or specific (or literal?) than what I have been saying about the devaluation of receptivity in favor of rational control. As I mentioned earlier in the book, yin connotes both receptivity and passivity, and since I want to argue that passivity isn't a value, but receptivity broadly is, I need to make use of the latter notion rather than the more unfocused concept of yin.

3. In chapter 5 above, I spoke of adventure and adventurousness as (in some sense) limited or ambiguous values that illustrate the impossibility of perfection. But it is worth noting that the most important ancient ethical thinkers—Plato, Aristotle, and the Stoics—never speak of either adventure or adventurousness in any sort of positive way. In particular, the typical Stoic view that virtue is both entirely within each individual's power and also sufficient to ensure human happiness assumes that life is or can be made immune to ordinary risk and insecurity—and also assumes that this is desirable. But to admit the limited positive value of adventure and the limited disvalue of security and the impossibility, therefore, of perfect happiness is to be much more receptive to what life may bring our way than to assume, seek, and value a total and secure control over happiness in the manner of the Stoics. The implicit Stoic denial of the value of receptivity connects, therefore, with their inability or unwillingness to accept (certain arguments for) the impossibility of perfection, but I shall not dwell any further on this particular connection between receptivity and the recognition of or belief in the impossibility of perfect happiness.

4. Kant explicitly equates the inclinations he speaks of in the *Groundwork* with sensuous or bodily appetites, in his *Anthropology from a Pragmatic Point of View*, The Hague, Netherlands: Martinus Nijhoff, 1974. However, he softens

his earlier stand against the inclinations in the *Religion within the Boundaries of Mere Reason.*

5. Don't say they found human life unacceptable because they recognized that life is permeated by appetitive and other desires and saw all desire as essentially painful—and the pleasure of satisfying/relieving it as inherently valueless. We nowadays recognize that desire needn't be at all painful—when one looks forward to a great meal, one presumably has some sort of appetite for food (and wine?), but the total experience of such anticipation may be phenomenologically pleasant and even delicious, rather than unpleasant or painful. (On this point see, for example, Karl Duncker's "On Pleasure, Emotion, and Striving," *Philosophy and Phenomenological Research* 1, 1941, esp. pp. 420–25.) And of course the pleasure of eating in itself seems a positive good thing. The unwillingness or inability of most ancient Greek and Eastern philosophers to recognize these sorts of fairly obvious facts seems, therefore, to be more a symptom of their discontentment with ordinary life than its cause.

In *Sources of the Self: The Making of the Modern Identity* (Cambridge, MA: Harvard University Press, 1989, esp. p. 329), Charles Taylor points out that, unlike so many ancient Greek philosophers, many Enlightenment thinkers were willing to grant the value of appetitive pleasures. To that extent, they saw ordinary human lives as having value, but their distrust and devaluation of the emotions still represents, I think, a failure to see (what we conceive as) ordinary human lives as really satisfactory. (Taylor uses the term *ordinary life* himself, but gives it a rather specialized meaning.)

6. Remember that rationalism involves the belief that rationality in no way requires or inherently involves feeling or emotion, an assumption I questioned in chapter 1, above.

7. As has often been noted, it can take courage to face *unpleasant, unfortunate,* or *humbling* facts about ourselves and/or the world—such as that we have evolved from lower animals, that we face inner demons that are sometimes beyond our control, that there may well not be a God, that the good can suffer unjustly. But it can also take courage to accept our lack of control over many aspects of our lives, and if such acceptance is necessary to seeing human lives as potentially and frequently satisfactory, then, by contrast with the more familiar examples just mentioned, we here have a case where it takes a certain amount of courage to recognize what is potentially or often *good* or *fortunate* about our situation.

8. I am assuming here that the fact we are mortal doesn't automatically make ordinary human lives unsatisfactory, and in this I have been influenced to a considerable extent by the view of death's place in good lives that Erik Erikson offers so movingly in *Childhood and Society* (New York: W. W. Norton, 1950, ch. 7—"Eight Ages of Man"). In later work (see E. Erikson, J. Erikson, and H.

Kivnick, *Vital Involvement in Old* Age, New York: Norton, 1986, chapter II), Erikson moves toward the view that death *does* negatively affect the overall satisfactoriness of human lives; but if mortality is the only thing that makes someone's life unsatisfactory, that is a far cry from the sorts of philosophical criticisms of or objections to basic human existence that we have considered and rejected above. So even if our mortality is a deeply unsatisfactory fact about the human condition and about all our lives, I think the above arguments will still be on the right track and will only require certain qualifications in order to succeed in their purposes.

9. See Erikson, op. cit. and in several other works. In the light of what I am claiming in this concluding chapter, Erikson's (earlier) views about ego integrity at the end of life—about the capacity for seeing one's whole previous life as fundamentally acceptable—reverberate back through what he says about earlier stages or periods of human life. For example, and most significantly, Erikson argues that the development, early on, of a "basic trust" in things is essential to living a good full life; but an undue desire for control over our lives and a concomitant lack of receptivity toward what life has brought or will bring us constitutes a lack of basic trust (a mistrust of life) and, as per our whole discussion, also therefore embodies a failure to recognize how satisfactory ordinary human lives can be.

To that extent, then, what I have been saying in this book fits in well with certain aspects of Erikson's social-psychological account/theory of human life (but not, I trust, with the gender biases that Carol Gilligan so incisively pointed out in her *In a Different Voice*, Cambridge: Harvard, 1982, pp. 11–13). However, we have also been operating at a far more general and philosophical level than anything to be found in Erikson. Erikson never mentions the deep pervasive opposition between trustful receptivity and the untrusting desire for control and the philosophical issues that that opposition raises and/or illustrates, and doing all this is precisely, in my opinion, the business of philosophy and not of psychology. (Even those Eastern or green philosophies that have criticized Western attitudes for their emphasis on domination, control, and activeness haven't generalized their critique to the wide variety of philosophical issues we have focused on here.) In any event, and for what it is worth, almost any clinical psychologist, psychiatrist, or psychoanalyst will tell you that seeing human life as invariably unsatisfactory and being basically mistrustful about life are both signs of psychological problems. This is Erikson's view, but one can find it in many other places: for example, in D. Barlow, ed., *Clinical Handbook of Psychological Disorders*, New York: Guilford Press, 2008, pp. 167, 231. Of course, there is a difference—though it can take courage or perceptiveness to recognize it—between the potential satisfactoriness of human lives and the satisfactoriness or nonsatisfactoriness *of one's own life*; and, finally, it is also worth noting that the claim that life can be satisfactory is somewhat weaker than the claim that life can be good and is more like claiming that human life is *good enough*. (On this latter concept, see my *Beyond Optimizing*: Cambridge, MA: Harvard University Press, 1989, esp. chapters 1–3.)

10. Ancient Greek and Roman virtue ethicists accepted the eudaimonistic idea that one needs virtue in order to lead a good human life, but what I have been suggesting here is (what might be called) the *metaeudaimonistic* thesis that we need to (implicitly or philosophically) recognize or appreciate the virtue of receptivity in order to (implicitly or philosophically) recognize or appreciate that ordinary human life can be good, satisfactory, or acceptable. However, I have also been arguing here that a balance between receptivity and autonomy is ethically most virtuous, and one might then want to say that such a balance is necessary to living the happiest kind of human life. I don't at this point have any arguments to offer in favor of such a contemporary form of eudaimonism, but if we could defend such a view, it would certainly run counter to the "antireceptive" spirit of *ancient* forms of eudaimonism. The defenders of eudaimonistic ancient views about human good/happiness often claim it as an advantage of such views that they emphasize human activity and deemphasize the kind of passive experience that modern-day hedonism (about human good) seems to value most highly. But if the present book is on the right track, then each of these other approaches is one sided, and that really does suggest that the best human lives may involve a balance between receptive and active elements.

11. What I have just been saying about career vs. family also applies to the other issues discussed in chapter 5. A life that lacks adventure really *is* lacking to some extent, but I see no reason to think that such a life can't be satisfactory as a life even if it isn't perfect. And a life of surmounted dangers involves a lot of fear and insecurity and seems less than perfect(ly happy), but why shouldn't such a life nonetheless be a good or satisfactory one overall?

12. See H. A. Prichard, "Does Moral Philosophy Rest on a Mistake?" in his *Moral Obligation*, Oxford, UK: Clarendon Press, 1949.

INDEX